I'VE LIVED LIKE A LORD

Also by Edward Ward

NUMBER ONE BOY

Edward Ward

I'VE LIVED LIKE A LORD

LONDON
MICHAEL JOSEPH

First published in Great Britain by
MICHAEL JOSEPH LTD
52 *Bedford Square*
London, W.C.1
1970

7181 0779 9

Set and printed in Great Britain by Tonbridge Printers Ltd, Peach Hall Works, Tonbridge, Kent, in Garamond eleven on thirteen point, on paper supplied by P. F. Bingham Ltd, and bound by James Burn, Royal Mills, Esher, Surrey

List of Illustrations

Chapter One

When the war was over and there was no more excitement I felt like a pricked balloon. Back in London I had almost been in tears begging the girl in movements control in the War Office to get me a seat on an RAF plane to Belfast. She pulled a lot of strings on my behalf and in twenty-four hours I was on my way.

I went by myself. My marriage with Maisie had broken up after I had returned from Finland. It had been all my fault. My father and mother met me at the airport. I told them I didn't want to see anyone; I just wanted to rest. I think my mother realized that I was very near some kind of a breakdown. I had never known her to be so completely understanding. We drove home and for a week I just pottered about and had breakfast in bed and did nothing. After that week I felt a different person. Sailing with my father, fishing in the evenings after dinner, I began seriously to think that Castle Ward was the life for me. I believe with any encouragement I would have given up my BBC work and gone and taken a course in estate management.

But after another couple of weeks I was already finding the time passing slowly. I got out my typewriter and began to write a book about my time as a prisoner of war. At first I only wrote for a couple of hours in the mornings. Then I wrote for four hours. After a few weeks I was writing all day long and I finished the book in just over a month.

I had written most of it already in Germany and had my manuscript censored as I went along by the German camp authorities. So most of the work I did at Castle Ward was writing an account of the six weeks I spent in Germany after my release.

Then, in July, about a fortnight before the atomic bomb was dropped on Hiroshima, I had a telephone call from the BBC. They wanted me to go to Ceylon and cover Mountbatten's projected 'pincer' landings in Malaya. I was overjoyed at the proposal and without giving the matter a moment's consideration, I agreed. Even later, when on thinking it all over I had decided that the 'pincer' landings would be a suicidal operation, I was longing to be on the move again. And then the bombs on Hiroshima and Nagasaki ended the war in the Far East. Fortunately the BBC still wanted me to go out East to cover the Japanese surrender in Hong Kong. So in the beginning of August I was in a noisy old York transport plane on my way to Ceylon.

Lord Mountbatten had established his headquarters in a kind of Douanier Rousseau setting in the Botanical Gardens at Kandy, where the nights were cool and where we lived in huts made of plaited palm leaves called basha bungalows. I had to wait for the best part of a week for the ship that was taking General Festing, who was to be Military Governor and GOC British troops in South China, and his staff; Civil Affairs experts, whose task it was to put Hong Kong on its feet again and several units of commandos, who were to garrison the colony.

At last the ship was due to sail and I drove in a convoy of cars and trucks to Trincomalee.

'Welcome aboard the hellship *Llanstephan Castle*,' a commando shouted down from the deck as we approached the one-time passenger liner in a tender. It wasn't long before it became very clear to all of us that his greeting was no exaggeration. It was a terrible trip. Veterans of many journeys on troopships said they had never been on a worse one. The officers' accommodation was bad enough. The troops' was beyond description. The food was almost uneatable. Steaming through tropical heat there wasn't even enough water to drink, let alone to wash in. Everybody's clothes were filthy. All we were able to do was to soak them in a salt water bath or trail them over the side at the end of a long line.

We dropped anchor opposite the Hong Kong and Shanghai Bank. A man came aboard with a sheaf of Hong Kong papers – the *South China Morning Post* and the *China Mail.*

'What's this?' asked the Civil Affairs experts on board who had come to get things going again in Hong Kong. 'Newspapers?' I bought a couple and took them to Victor Sassoon, who was supposed to be producing a rudimentary broadsheet and at the same time starting a radio service of some kind. He had been asking my advice about this during the journey.

'Looks like you're going to have an easy time, Victor,' I said. 'You haven't got to worry about the radio either. Look at the programmes here.' The electric light was working, the water was turned on, the police force was organized. There was nothing for the experts to do. All their planning had been a waste of time. They looked bleakly at each other and asked themselves why on earth they had come to Hong Kong and why somebody hadn't known about all this before they started.

We had all come with the idea in our minds that the civilian population, fresh from prison camps, would practically have to be spoon-fed. It was quite an anti-climax to read in the papers that there had been a meeting of the golf club to elect a new president; that the cinemas were showing full programmes including the latest newsreels; that the Café Lido offered its patrons a fine cuisine and excellent wines; the Siberian Fur Store a wide selection of sables, ermine and silver fox; that a Chinese grocer was celebrating victory by a great sale of provisions, wines and spirits. And, in the gossip column, that 'the problem now will be to avoid looking too fat when "they" arrive'.

Hong Kong was undamaged in the centre of the city but like London at that time it was shabby looking. Unlike London at that time there was every imaginable luxury in the shops – at a price. Pat Henry, the Army PRO, and I got a large room in Hong Kong's best hotel, the Gloucester. It was on the seventh floor and the lift didn't work but we were very comfortable and well looked after.

The taking over of Hong Kong had been a fantastic muddle right from the start. General Festing had come to assume the duties of Military Governor and GOC British troops in South China. He found Admiral Harcourt installed in Government House. It might all have been very awkward if it hadn't been for the tact and diplomacy shown by the two chief figures concerned. Admiral Harcourt stayed on at Government House as Governor and General Festing went to live at Flagstaff House and looked after the military administration of the colony. I had met Frankie Festing just before the convoy sailed. He was a correspondent's dream of what a general should be.

'Come along and see me any time you like and ask any questions you want. If I know the answers I'll tell you,' he said when I first met him. As soon as we were settled in in Hong Kong I called at his office and saw his ADC, Captain Peter Boddy.

'The general's a bit busy at the moment,' Boddy said. 'Come round for a drink at Flagstaff House about seven this evening. It'll be much easier like that and a lot pleasanter, too.' After that first evening I was a regular visitor to Flagstaff House. Frankie Festing knew more than anyone in Hong Kong what was going on and he got along with the Chinese wonderfully well. I learned more sitting talking in the cool of the evening over drinks on the terrace than I ever would have in formal interviews.

Everyone was waiting for the Japanese surrender ceremony. When Admiral Sir Bruce Fraser (as he was then) arrived in the *Duke of York* it seemed imminent. It was. It took place the following day. The BBC was well represented. Stanley Maxted who had been with the British Pacific Fleet arrived and Captain Anthony Kimmins who had done so many good naval broadcasts had been in Hong Kong since Admiral Harcourt's arrival.

'I'll tell you what, Eddy,' he had said to me, 'there's no use duplicating over this ceremony. Now, this is what I suggest. These Japanese will be coming across from the mainland and there are sure to be Chinese demonstrations. Heaven knows what may not happen. Now, you as an experienced journalist, know very well that *that's* the real story. The ceremony in Government House will just be routine stuff. Nothing to it. I suggest I cover that and you do the real colour story of them bringing the Japanese over.' I looked at him with admiration. Nobody had ever before made such a charming attempt to sabotage me.

'Of course you're quite right, Tony,' I said, 'but somehow I don't think the BBC will see it quite like that. They've gone to a certain amount of expense sending me all the way out here to cover this ceremony and I can't help feeling they'll expect me to be in Government House.' The merest shadow of disappointment flitted across Tony Kimmins' face.

'You really think so? Yes, I suppose you're right. Pity, though. I'm sure the trip over is the real story.'

'Why don't you do it then, Tony?' But he was with me in Government House when the surrender took place. The two Japanese came into the main hall. They signed the 'instrument of surrender', bowed stiffly from the waist and marched out. It was very restrained, very correct and rather boring. However I would not have done well to have taken Captain Kimmins' advice because there were no Chinese demonstrations and the whole journey of the Japanese from the mainland to the island went very quietly.

I teamed up with Reg Harris, the *Sydney Daily Telegraph* correspondent. We interviewed the commandant of the Stanley prison camp, Colonel Tokunaga, who was accused of withholding thousands of Red Cross parcels from the prisoners when they were desperately short of food. He must have been a strange character. He was a keen bridge player and because he wasn't able to make up a four from his own officers, he often used to invite prisoners to play with him. A former internee told me the prisoners used to enjoy these invitations because Tokunaga always entertained them extremely well when they went to his house. We interviewed the notorious Captain Saito, the medical officer of the prison camps who refused to issue serum when a diphtheria epidemic was raging. We interviewed a terrible man called Sergeant Matsuda, whom the Chinese called 'The Tiger' because he used to ride in front of Colonel Noma, the chief of the secret police, and slash with his sabre at anyone who got in the way.

Reg and I as well as several other correspondents were honorary members of a naval mess. One evening we made a lot of noise, which annoyed some senior naval officers and we were told we could no longer belong to the mess. I didn't care one way or the other, but Reg Harris took it as a personal affront to him as an Australian. I had become very friendly with No. 1 Commando and was entertained at their mess so well and so often that I asked if I could become an honorary member so that I could buy drinks and return a little of the hospitality I had had. After a certain amount of argument it was agreed. One day, shortly after our eviction from the naval mess, I said to Reg:

'Come round and have a drink at No. 1 Commando mess this evening, Reg.'

'No. I don't want to have anything more to do with a lot of Pommie bastards. You go, but you don't catch me coming.'

'Don't be such a bloody fool, Reg. They're a hell of a nice lot.' At last he agreed to come and I arranged to meet him at the mess at 7 o'clock. I got there ahead of that time and explained the situation to the officers in the mess and asked them to be particularly nice to Reg, who, I explained, was a very good fellow. The evening was an enormous success. On our way back Reg said:

'You know, Eddy, they're nice fellows. I enjoyed the evening.'

'I told you you would,' I said. Not long after, I left Hong Kong for a month. When I returned I found Reg had become the second honorary member of the mess. He had made all the arrangements for an officer to go to Australia and buy sports equipment for the troops. He had taught them surfing in 'Big Wave Bay'. No. 1 Commando were no longer Pommie bastards.

* * *

From General Festing I learned that the Chinese Communist guerrillas had their advanced headquarters in the village of Shatoukok, right on the border of the Hong Kong New Territories and China. Half the village is in one and half in the other. Pat Henry, the PR officer, and I went to see them. We took a lot of cigarettes to give as presents and we also took an interpreter with us, a keen Chinese scoutmaster, who insisted on wearing full scout's uniform.

Shatoukok was a large and prosperous village, as Chinese villages go. We asked an old man where the Communists' HQ was and he directed us to the old Customs House. We drove as far as we could and then had to continue on foot because the street had become too narrow. Going hastily past Shatoukok's public lavatory, we reached the back of a long building that had been the Customs House before the war. A man wearing black, shiny 'coolie cloth' and with an obvious bulge on his left hip was standing at the back door. Our interpreter explained who we were and he opened the door. We filed through a narrow passage into a courtyard where a group of Chinese, all wearing the same shiny black clothes were lounging on a verandah. Our interpreter walked across to the verandah and said a few words in Cantonese. One of the guerrillas got up.

'You are very welcome,' he said in accentless English. Seeing my look of surprise he added: 'I suppose you didn't expect any of us here to speak English. Well, you see I'm a graduate of Hong Kong University. I'm afraid I haven't spoken English for some time so I'm a bit rusty.' He took us over to present us to his chief, a tall, lanky man, who carried a long-barrelled Mauser and a Browning automatic stuck in his belt. All the other guerrillas were armed. We all sat down and tea and cakes were brought. We began exchanging the inevitable compliments. A small boy with two hand grenades hanging from his belt stood behind me listening.

'He's one of what we call our little devils,' the University graduate told me. He's twelve and he's been with us for four years. Actually it's the Japanese who first called them the 'little devils'. We had a lot of them. They used to go out at night and give the Japanese plenty of trouble. They'd pitch a couple of grenades into an officers' mess, or blow up an ammunition dump, or set fire to a store. They were very useful getting information about troop movements and so on. This kid, as it happens, saved an American airman's life. His plane was hit over Kaitak aerodrome. We saw the pilot baling out and we sent the boy to find him. He got him all right and brought him back to us and we were able to smuggle him through to Chungking.'

'Things are in a strange way now,' the chief guerrilla said. 'When the Japanese surrendered we thought the end of the fighting had come. But that doesn't seem to be the way the Central Government sees it. They are employing Japanese against us now. And they prefer to have towns and villages garrisoned by Japanese than by us. You ought to go and see Shamchun; it's only a few miles from here. We could have taken it if the Japanese had had orders to surrender their arms to us. On the contrary the Central Government has told them to keep their arms and defend Shamchun against us until they bring up their own troops. Is this what we have been fighting the Japanese for all these years?' he asked bitterly. I asked him about his administration of the area that was under his control. Was he doing anything like introducing collective farming. He looked surprised.

'You mean taking the land away from the farmers? Oh no we're not introducing any Marxist measures at all. We'll revise land taxes later but at present we are simply here to help the local population in every way we can. We have some Japanese prisoners we send to help with work in the fields. We've re-opened the schools; we distribute our newspaper free. We take absolutely nothing in taxes from the people,' he said proudly, 'we are as poor now as on the day we arrived.' I was frankly much impressed by the Communist guerrillas.

It was early October and China's great national festival the 'Double Tenth', takes place on October 10th, the date of the overthrow of the Manchu dynasty. This year it would be the first

'Double Tenth' held in peacetime since 1937, so it would have a special significance. I decided to go to Chungking with Carl Carlyon, the BBC engineer, to report the celebrations. Daniel Lee, the Chinese war correspondent for China's most important newspaper, the *Ta Kung Pao*, arrived in Hong Kong from Japan at this time and said he'd like to come too. But first he had some business to attend to in Canton and he suggested I come with him. We could both stay with his family, who lived just outside the city, he said. The best way was to go by train from Shamchun, which had now been taken over by Central Government troops.

So Danny, Carl and I set off in a jeep for Shamchun, where we met the garrison commander Major Hou Chen-wen, a small, slightly-built Southerner and a typical modern Chinese officer with an extremely attractive personality. Major Hou had been having talks with the Japanese colonel, whom he had supplanted as garrison commander.

'It's a long and tedious business,' he said. 'He doesn't speak Chinese and I don't speak Japanese so we sit opposite each other and I write what I want done in Chinese characters. The Japanese use the same characters in their own written language of course. He reads what I have written and then writes his reply. One of our talks covered eight closely-written pages!'

There was no train leaving for Canton until the following day at the earliest. The next morning we were taken on a tour of Shamchun.

We saw all the captured Japanese arms and at the end of the day we were taken to a little temple. I had noticed a Japanese soldier carrying a long object wrapped in blue silk. At the entrance to the temple he handed it to his colonel, who slowly opened the package and took from it a short Japanese Samurai sword of beautiful workmanship. He turned to face Major Hou.

'This is my personal sword,' he said as he solemnly handed it to the Chinese officer. 'It has been handed down to me from my ancestors. I value it as much as my life and it is the last weapon I possess. I present it to you now as a symbol of peace. And I hope when you look at it in the days to come, you will remember this occasion and the spirit in which this sword was given.'

That was all. Superficially, at any rate, it was a highly civilized little ceremony. Major Hou had told me the day before that I could see for myself whether the Japanese were sincere in their humility. All I could see was that the Chinese and Japanese, being both orientals, understood each other far better than we of the western races could ever hope to understand either the one or the other of them. When I said later to Major Hou that I found it hard to understand the forgiving attitude of the Chinese after all they had suffered at the hands of the Japanese, he smiled indulgently.

'When the fighting is over we cannot keep up bitterness and hatred. It simply is not part of the Chinese nature,' he said.

Danny Lee caught the train to Canton that afternoon but Carl Carlyon and I decided to return to Hong Kong for fear of being delayed and missing our trip to Chungking.

Chapter Two

The Dakota rose steeply to clear the hills at the end of the hopelessly inadequate runway at Kaitak airport. It bumped badly as it struck the air eddies over the peak of Hong Kong and then we swung westwards over crumpled, brown mountains, following the line of the West River, flying over Wuchow, Liuchow and at last reaching Kunming. When we landed I asked at once if there were any RAF planes going on to Chungking that same afternoon. Nobody knew. The RAF only occupied a tiny corner of Kunming's gigantic American airfield. At the RAF mess a wing commander said there would probably be a plane the following day.

We spent the night at the excellent RAF mess. The next morning Carl and I drove into Kunming. On the way in we jostled past American trucks, past jeeps, jeeps and more jeeps. Even in Germany I had never seen so many jeeps. The Chinese were stealing them at the rate of thirty a day. We squeezed past the local pony-drawn buses, which took eight passengers; past sweating coolies staggering under immense burdens slung from bamboo poles; and at last we reached the outskirts of Kunming. It looked like a Chinese version of a Western frontier town, but infinitely more crowded and filthy. American soldiers drove in jeeps or sauntered along the muddy pavements with slick, pretty Chinese girls, dressed in American military clothing. Rickshaw coolies shouted obscenities as they bumped into each other. Chinese policemen stood on pedestals under concrete umbrellas and tried frantically to direct the crazy mix-up of traffic.

We stopped at a gold shop to change Indian rupees into Chinese national dollars. Under the counter were shining gold bars, gold coins and ornaments. I got three hundred dollars for a rupee. I discovered I had missed getting in on a great currency racket. Rupees were in great demand in Kunming, which was the terminus of the Burmah Road. In Hong Kong nobody had any great use for rupees. The Hong Kong dollar and the Indian rupee were roughly worth the same. So you bought rupees with Hong Kong dollars. You took say, 1,000 rupees to Kunming and turned them into 300,000 Chinese national dollars. You took these back to Hong Kong. They were much needed there for trading with China. You were given 12 Hong Kong dollars for 1,000 Chinese national dollars. You ended up with 3,600 Hong Kong dollars, having started off with 1,000. To make real money, of course, you did this on a far larger scale and you went on doing it – provided of course, that you had any way or any excuse to travel back and forth between Hong Kong and Kunming by air. Quite a lot of people had.

There was no RAF plane to Chungking. American Air Transport Command had a plane going later. But I had to get official orders to fly. And I had to pay. Since the end of Lease Lend all foreigners flying by ATC were charged. The British consul advanced the money. The American consul signed papers giving Carl and me priority to fly. We left the British consulate with two great bricks of Chinese banknotes.

'It'll be a terrible rate of exchange,' the British consul said, 'but if you want to get to Chungking, there's nothing else you can do – and don't blame those fellows up at the airfield. They're a nice lot. They're just obeying orders.'

It seemed ridiculous to be handed one little American 100 dollar bill a few minutes later in exchange for this mountain of money.

I argued our way aboard a special plane that was leaving at ten. We climbed aboard a C-47 – same as a Dakota – it was mountains all the way and we all had parachutes. Two and a half hours flying and there was a dirty ribbon of water below us – the Yangtse. And then Chungking straggling and sprawling along its banks.

Outside the airfield building I saw a jeep with a Union Jack painted on it. There was room for one. I left Carl with the recording machines and left to make what arrangements for the broadcast I could. There were a few triumphal arches and streamers across the streets and flags hung out of most windows (put there by Government order I learned later) but no sign of any celebrations. Not even a single firework. Most un-Chinese. I'd already written my piece in my head and it wasn't working out the way I had expected at all. I didn't see what Carl and I were going to record.

At the Ministry of Information I met Stanley Smith, the information officer, a dynamic Australian. I had cabled him from Kunming asking him to alert the BBC and make the necessary arrangement with Chungking Radio.

'I don't know what the hell you're going to find to say,' Stanley said, 'because nothing whatever's happening. Anyway there's plenty of time and the "Gissimo" and Madame Chiang are giving a reception at four o'clock. You'd better come along.'

The reception was in Government House, an ugly modern building in which Chinese and Western architecture, had been unsuccessfully blended. It was decorated for the occasion. Chiang Kai-shek made a short speech in Chinese, which was translated into English. He said all the things everyone expected him to say. A momentous 'Double Tenth' because it really did celebrate China's independence . . . Nevertheless grave tasks lay ahead . . . I left at six o'clock. It was pitch dark, but still no celebrations. Carl was at the Ministry of Information when I returned. He and Stanley went to look for local colour, while I worked at a script for which I had next to no material. The only thing to do was to say why there were *no* celebrations. Chungking had been a relatively unimportant river port. When it was chosen as a wartime capital its population swelled to over a million. What most of the people living in Chungking wanted to do was to get out of the place as soon as they possibly could. They had nothing to celebrate. Chungking is a horrible place. It has the worst climate in China – hot and muggy in summer, enveloped in cold dank mists for most of the winter. No wonder all the people from Nanking and Shanghai wanted to get out and go home as soon as they could. They didn't want to waste money on fireworks. And the original inhabitants of Chungking? They had seen their city rise to artificial importance; seen industries start up which they knew were uneconomic and were only wartime necessities. They knew their city would sink back into its former comparative obscurity. They didn't feel like celebrating either.

So I did a broadcast very different from the one I had had in mind when I left Hong Kong. I hadn't any real confidence that it was even being picked up. But there my pessimism was not justified.

I spent my days in Chungking writing scripts which I intended later to record; and my evenings going to a succession of parties. At one evening party at the Australian Legation I met Dr T. F. Tsiang, the head of CNNRA, the Chinese distributing end of UNNRA, who had once been Chinese ambassador in Moscow. This meeting changed my whole plans. At the dinner party I had begun an extremely interesting conversation with Dr Tsiang and he asked me to lunch at his house the following day.

He lived in a suburb of Chungking called Chiaoting Village in a house perched high up on the steep bank of the Yangtse.

'I hope you like Szechwanese food,' Dr Tsiang said, 'you may find it a little highly seasoned. They are very fond of the little hot chillie peppers in the province of Szechwan – and so am I.' It was a delicious meal. Afterwards we sat in the drawing-room and the conversation turned from the particular problems of Chungking to the more general problems of China as a whole. We discussed the question of the rehabilitation of the refugees. Dr Tsiang mentioned off-hand that a shipload of them was going down river to Nanking and Shanghai in a couple of days.

'I didn't even know the Yangtse was open again to navigation,'

I said, 'now that's a trip I'd give anything to make.' Dr Tsiang laughed.

'I'm quite serious,' I said, 'I really would give anything to do it.'

'Well, if you really mean it we shall have to see what can be done. It would certainly give you a fine opportunity of seeing a great deal of China and her problems for yourself; and any publicity we can get about that would be most welcome.' Dr Tsiang looked at me and smiled. 'I think somehow that a note from my department would secure you good accommodation,' he said. I explained that I would need accommodation for my engineer as well and that if this were not possible we should have to return to Hong Kong on the plane leaving the following day. Two hours later a double cabin had been booked for us on a ship called the *Ming Lien*. I was to go down to the Water Transportation Department the following morning where I would be given all the necessary details. It was very quick work and for China little short of miraculous.

The cost of the trip was a staggering sum in Chinese National dollars but it worked out at £40 a head – a lot in those days for a ten-day trip. But what a trip! The Yangtse Gorges; the first through run from Chungking to Shanghai since the war; and, apart from a few missionaries, we should be the first foreigners to travel the Yangtse for many years.

I borrowed £100 worth of Chinese national dollars from the British Embassy and took a large bag of bank notes to the WTD. We had to be aboard by eight o'clock that evening, which just gave me time to attend Chiang Kai-shek's first post-war press conference. All we really learned from it was that the capital of China would be moved from Chungking to Nanking – and not Peking – which we already had a pretty good idea would be the case.

Stanley Smith was bustling round getting things together for us to take on our journey, when I returned to the British Information Office. He had a bottle of Chungking gin, several hundred cigarettes and a large tin of powerful insecticide, which he said would be invaluable. That afternoon I had changed my sterling into American dollars and everyone had said I must change these into Chinese national dollars because the rate was far better in Chungking than in Shanghai – for this reason fortunes were being made by people able to fly between the two cities. I had had no time to change my American dollars.

'No problem,' Stanley said. 'Fong will do it for you.' Fong was his No. 1 boy.

'It's rather a lot,' I said. 'I mean I have nearly 200 dollars.'

'Oh that'll be a fleabite to Fong,' Stanley said. 'He's got millions of CNC tucked away in the kitchen – and gold bars, too. Fong's a very successful speculator.' Fong took my American dollar bills and disappeared into the kitchen. In a few minutes he returned with two large bricks of banknotes.

Stanley sent Fong with us to the ferry – the *Ming Lien* was moored on the far side of the Yangtse. We stopped the car at the top of a steep flight of steps leading down to the water's edge. In the pitch dark Fong found coolies to carry our heavy recording machines and we climbed down the stairway. After long negotiation he got hold of a sampan to take us across the river. I had thought it would simply be a question of poling the sampan across. But in Chungking the current courses by at about six knots. When we had gone at least a mile upstream, the helmsman boldly swung the boat out into the raging current and the boatmen rowed frantically with three outsize oars. The crossing of a 500-yard-wide river had taken over an hour. The cost was several thousand dollars but the men had worked so desperately hard that for once there was no argument over the price.

The *Ming Lien* (which inappropriately means 'Bright Face') looked like a sort of down-at-heel Mississippi showboat. When we pushed our way through dense crowds of Chinese and at last reached the gangway, a soldier examined our tickets and waved us aboard. The ship was a seething mass of humanity all carrying the gigantic bundles of bedding and clothing which seem to be inseparable from Chinese when they are travelling. Passengers were strewn all over the decks trying to sleep and shouting furiously when people stepped on them. The invaluable Fong found our cabin which, judging by general standards, was remarkably good. It had two beds and a wash basin and everything seemed to be reasonably clean. We dumped our baggage and inquired about dinner. There would be no meals until after the ship sailed the following morning. We were starving. Fong found us a filthy restaurant on the slopes above the river where the food was exquisite – and considerably more expensive than a meal for two was to cost us ten days later in the luxury Cathay Hotel in Shanghai.

The *Ming Lien* was as crowded as ever, when we found our way back there. The noise was past belief. Men, women and children covered every square foot of deck space. We tripped over them and at last found our cabin. We had to awaken the sleepers before we could squeeze in. There seemed to be no bed bugs and insect life was represented only by a few cockroaches. Most of them were very small, though there was one giant the size of a mouse. As a reprisal for our having woken them up, the Chinese outside our cabin talked and played the 'finger game' at the tops of their voices until after two in the morning. The Chinese finger game is unbelievably noisy. Two players each put up their hands with none up to four fingers and a thumb extended. Simultaneously they guess at the tops of their voices how many the combined number of fingers will total. So for hours we listened to shouts of: 'San ko! Liu ko! Wu ko! Pa ko!' – Three, six, five, eight fingers and so on.

Chapter Three

At eight o'clock the next morning the *Ming Lien* started dead on schedule. The noise became worse than ever. The Chinese camping outside our door started singing 'Auld Lang Syne' in their own language for no apparent reason and then our steward knocked on our door and mumbled mournfully: *'Chih fan.'* Food. Breakfast was ready. Carl and I found we had been put at a table with the other foreigners aboard: the head of the Methodist Missions in China, an American missionary called Dr Roberts, a young Welshman called Glyn Hughes, who was working with the Quakers' Friends' Ambulance Unit, a Chinese American in the United States Army and an old Russian attached to the Chinese Army, and his wife.

It was a disgusting breakfast. Rice congee – rice pudding made with water, greasy pork and onions and an uneatable dish of vegetable pickles. No sooner were we back in our cabin than the Chinese students outside opened up with *'Hark the Herald Angels Sing'*, which they sang in Chinese for a solid half hour. Lunch was another example of how bad Chinese food can be. In the afternoon Carl and I went to the bridge to pay our respects to the captain.

Captain Hanish was half Scots and half Chinese. He had never been out of China in his life. He had sailed the Yangtse for thirty-four years and knew every rock and every shoal. He was a short, thickset man, with smiling Chinese eyes, an aquiline nose inherited from his Scottish father and a close-cut toothbrush moustache. He always wore a macintosh and a dark blue beret. His Chinese wife, who had never missed a trip with him, was aboard and so was a horde of children and grandchildren.

After welcoming us and telling us to come along to the bridge whenever we felt inclined, he began talking about the Yangtse.

'The charts don't mean much,' he said, 'because the old river changes so. You've got to be able to read the water.' Suddenly the helmsman took the ship on a wild swing towards the far bank. 'White water there,' Hanish said, 'that means a shoal.' Hanish was a charming old fellow and knew all the folklore and legends of the Yangtse. He pointed to a long, narrow sand-spit.

'That's called the Sparrow Rock,' he said. 'When the floods cut a channel through it, the junkmen say it's good *joss* for their vessels.' At intervals we passed little signal stations perched on the banks. A triangle hoisted on a cross-pole with its apex pointed downwards meant that a vessel was going downstream. An arrow fixed on the same flagstaff also pointed downwards. That meant the water was falling.

'It's got another twenty feet or so to drop,' Captain Hanish said. 'It'll be at its lowest by February and then a ship of this size couldn't make the upper reaches. In the Gorges the difference between low and high water is as much as 190 feet.' We approached a village where there was a fine old temple.

'That's where the pilgrims used to go to buy passes to let them into Heaven,' Hanish said. 'They used to pay as high as a dollar for them and that was a lot of money in those days.'

Navigating the Upper Yangtse is a very hazardous affair. Although Captain Hanish knew the river as well as anyone, we carried a pilot. The Upper River pilot takes the ship from Chungking to Ichang. The Middle River pilot carries on to Hankow and the Lower River pilot for the rest of the journey to Shanghai. The Upper River pilot's is by far the most responsible job. Ours was paid the equivalent of £25 for the four day's trip – but other companies were charged ten times as much. Our pilot had a gnarled, lined, mahogany-coloured face and always wore a black cloth cap with a long peak. He stood just ahead of the helmsman, his beady eyes fixed on the river with the utmost concentration. He never looked round and never said a word. He held his right hand out a little from his body and gave all his signals with his thumb.

We anchored for the first night at the small Yangtse port of Chungchow but didn't go ashore as it was already dark. During the following morning we called at the port of Wanhsien. Carl and I went ashore and laid in a large store of oranges, tangerines, walnuts and biscuits – we had struck at breakfast that morning and demanded fried eggs and pancakes. An American missionary and his wife, Mr and Mrs Parker, came aboard at Wanhsien, where they had been all through the war. They both came from Pittsburgh and belonged to the American Evangelical Mission. Wanhsien had never been occupied by the Japanese but although Mr Parker continued to get money from his mission he was scandalously 'squeezed' by the Chinese.

Mr Parker told me a story which showed how much the Nationalist Chinese war effort had been worth. A Chinese recruiting officer came to his village. He collected all the criminals, mentally defective and diseased people for the army. Parker remonstrated with him. But the official explained that what he was doing was perfectly logical:

'You see,' he said, 'if we put all our best men into the army and they go into the line and get killed, we shall only have this riffraff left. Better put them in first – they're no use anyway – and let them get killed. Then China will have a chance after the war.'

'Of course,' Parker said, 'there wasn't any real argument against this. It was a typical piece of Chinese reasoning. As a result of this policy students were able to go on with their studies and the standard of education in China now is higher than it has ever been before, because parents hastened to send their children to the schools and universities to save them from a call-up.'

All this was a typical example of Chinese logic – and an

example, too, of China's war effort against Japan. Most Americans were disgusted with this kind of thing. They had believed the 'China's gallant stand' propaganda stories. When they arrived in China they had found the country riddled with graft. They had found the troops of the Central Government underpaid – if paid at all – underfed and ill armed. They found that no serious fighting had taken place since the early days and they realized that the Central Government's policy was to conserve its troops as much as possible in order to maintain political power after the war. When the collapse of Japan came they found the Chinese 'we won the war' attitude intolerable. This, of course, was not official American opinion but it was the opinion of every individual American I met in China at that time.

I spent hours talking to old Hanish.

'I reckon I can call myself "Old Man River",' he said to me one afternoon. 'I'm now the senior skipper on the river. I've skippered sixteen ships during the 34 years I've been navigating the Yangtse and I made five hundred trips in just one of them. I suppose I must have been up and down the river a good few thousand times.' He did some gallant work early on in the war when he was constantly being attacked by Japanese planes. 'I used to take cover under the shelving banks in the Gorges, so that they couldn't get at me,' he said. 'But in the end they caught me out in the open. I swerved and zigzagged to try and escape them but they hit the ship at last and sank her. I was slightly wounded but nothing serious.

'Oh yes,' the old skipper went on, 'we've had all sorts of hazards on the Yangtse. In the old days it was the Chinese bandits. They were very well organized. They divided the river up into stages. At the first stage they stopped the ship and demanded their 'squeeze'. It might be the equivalent of £10 or £20. If this was paid without any argument the bandits put a representative aboard to take the ship safely to the next stage. There the same thing happened again. Altogether it cost maybe £60 or £100 to take a ship up or down river.

'But of course,' Hanish explained, 'we were carrying valuable cargoes then and the shipping companies were making plenty of money. So it was far better to pay the bandits' "squeeze" than risk losing your ship. As long as you played ball with them they treated you very well. And I will say I've been very well entertained when I went to their camps to negotiate with them.'

It was early on the second morning of the journey that we entered the first of the famous Yangtse Gorges, called the 'Windbox'. We coursed down the swiftly running river with eddies and whirlpools swirling round us. Ahead rose the towering black cliffs that stood at the entry to the Gorge. The river narrowed abruptly from five hundred to a little over one hundred yards in width with cliffs rising almost vertically on both sides, terminating in three-thousand-foot peaks. The speed of the current increased alarmingly. It was a scene of magnificent and dramatic grandeur. The pilot's face became more tense and Captain Hanish stood by the telegraph continuously, giving orders for increased speed from time to time to carry us over the dangerous stretches. For if once a ship lost way and the terrific current gained control, it would be the end of it.

'False' gorges led into the 'Windbox' from time to time and you had a brief glimpse of the wild, mountainous country behind. It took us an hour to get through the 'Windbox' and I have often since grieved that I didn't have a modern tape recorder with me. What a recording I could have made with the Volga Boatmen-like song of the junk coolies hauling the heavy junks upstream, themselves trudging precariously along the narrow razor-sharp rocky edges of the gorge; the roar of the waters and the echo and re-echo of Captain Hanish's siren. The record Carl and I did make on our antiquated machine at least had the distinction of being the first ever made in the Yangtse Gorges.

Some slightly flatter country followed and then we entered the 'Wushan' Gorge and the old *Ming Lien* shivered and shook as she ploughed through the rapids. Alarming rocks reared out of the foaming water, sometimes in midstream. At least when the water was low, which it nearly was at this time, you could see them, at high water a pilot must have uncanny knowledge of the river to be able to pick his way.

The Yangtse quietened down and fishermen on the banks lowered and raised large square nets stretched on wooden frames. Soon we arrived at the port of Ichang. Dr Tsiang had told me that Ichang was one of the most heavily damaged cities in China but at first glance there was little evidence of it. The big buildings along the 'Bund' looked unscathed and among them I saw the office and *godown* of Jardine Matheson and Company. In Chungking one of their directors, John Keswick, had given me letters and money to give to all the Company's offices down the river. I found the *godown* swarming with Chinese troops and at last managed to locate Mr Li, Jardine's manager. He told me that a missionary called Dr Tucker was waiting out in the street to see me. I found a charming old Scotsman who had lived in and around Ichang for forty years. He had escaped the Japanese occupation and had only returned the evening before. Apart from him and an American missionary, Father Morse, whom we met later, we were the first foreigners to visit Ichang since the Japanese occupation.

Behind the solid waterfront buildings, Ichang was in a sad state. The Japanese had bombed the city before they took it and the Americans after. Dr Tucker said that well as he knew Ichang he had great trouble in finding his way about. We walked a long way through shattered and devastated streets until we came upon a *pailo* – a kind of triumphal arch – decorated with faded evergreens. An inscription in Chinese characters ran along the top of it. A little way beyond the arch was a tomb with a number of faded wreaths piled against it. The tomb was in the form of a circle of brickwork and it marked the communal grave of six American airmen. The inscription on the *pailo* said that the Chinese did honour to six brave American flyers, who had died in the service of China. Their bomber had crashed right in front of a nearby temple and had almost totally destroyed it.

On returning to the Jardine office we discovered that Mr Li

had arranged a banquet – I can call it nothing less. There were a dozen delicious dishes and there was excellent 'hsiao-hsin' the delicate, yellow Chinese rice wine, which tastes like sherry and is served hot in little teapots. And as at all Chinese dinners there was a lot of toast drinking and 'kan pei-ing'. Kan pei literally means 'dry cup'. When someone raises his wine cup to you and calls 'kan pei', you have to drink yours down and turn the empty cup towards him as a proof that you have. None of the missionaries drank except Father Morse who, although not Roman Catholic was a member of some very High Church American mission. He kan-pei-ed with the rest of us. It was a superlatively good dinner and even Carl, whose faith in Chinese cooking was being sorely tried by the fare aboard the *Ming Lien*, agreed that it was one of the best meals he had ever eaten. I only hoped that it was Messrs. Jardine Matheson and not Mr Li who paid for it. Ichang had the reputation of being the most expensive city in China at that time.

The *Ming Lien* had been several hours under way by the time I got on deck the next morning. We seemed to be in a different country. Gone were all the mountains. We were passing through dead flat country and the river was at least half a mile wide and sometimes a mile. It gave one an idea of the immensity of the Yangtse – we were still over a thousand miles from its mouth. When we stopped at the port of Shasi, Carl and I once again laid in a supply of stores. At a little street kitchen we bought some freshly fried doughnuts and some meat pies that looked like Cornish pasties and tasted far better and they cost the equivalent of less than a penny each. The old lady in the shop wrapped them up in a large lotus leaf and I stuffed them into the haversack which I always had to carry round to hold my huge wads of bank-notes. Included in the cargo carried by the *Ming Lien,* incidentally, were twenty *tons* of thousand-dollar notes. Heaven knows how many milliard dollars that came to!

Although we never saw any of the riverside fishermen catch a fish, somebody must have because in Shasi market were enormous fish weighing up to 100 lb. each and looking like outsize grey mullet. The ship bought a supply but by the time the galley had done its work on them they were scarcely recognizable as fish at all. By this time Carl and I had decided to leave the dining saloon alone except for our eggs for breakfast and rely for our food on what we could buy in the little street kitchens, which was always excellent.

The river followed a snake-like course as the high buildings of Hankow's Bund came into view. I was now coming to a city which I had known well before the war and I wondered what I should find. As we drew close to the Bund I could see the terrible results of the heavy American raids of the previous year. We went ashore and walked along the water front on our way to find American Headquarters which was in the old Russian Concession. I passed the British Consulate-General which I had known well. It was a blackened shell. I found it very hard to find my way about. At American Headquarters a naval captain said they were having a tough time protecting foreign and particularly British property.

'Why don't you British send somebody up here to look after your own property here?' he asked. 'We're doing what we can but it's tough work – these Chinese are supposed to be our allies – and boy what a mess their troops made of your Asiatic Petroleum building.' I had a letter to the Chinese manager of Jardines and also a parcel containing a quarter of a million dollars. If I couldn't find him I was to hand it over to the Swiss consul, Mr Schoch.

Mr Schoch was delighted to take the quarter of a million dollars.

'It's just about what Jardine's manager owes me,' he said. And he, too, complained about British apathy over their property. Britain, in spite of her immense interests in China had been caught napping by the sudden collapse of Japan. There simply wasn't anybody to send to places like Hankow.

The next evening we reached Kiukiang. I had been there before the war in high summer, when the temperature was over a hundred in the shade and the humidity very high. They told a story about an old British Kiukiang resident who had lived a bad life and deservedly went to hell when he died. After a day there he sent up for blankets. Now in the wonderful Central Chinese autumn weather, Kiukiang was very pleasant.

General Wang, a director of the Ming Seng Company, invited Carl and me to a special dinner that was being given aboard. We accepted with great misgivings, which fortunately were not entirely justified. The General was a collector of antiques. After dinner we wandered through the streets of Kiukiang. An antique dealer from whom we bought a few things said that if we could wait in Kiukiang a couple of days he could get some wonderful antiques to show us. It was a great pity it was not possible; fantastic bargains could have been picked up in Kiukiang at this time. It was completely cut off from the rest of China.

At Nanking we forced our way through the seething crowd that had come to meet the ship.

After lunch and a shopping expedition, when I bought some beautiful silks and brocades to bring back to England, General Wang, who had been showing us round Nanking, suggested we go and see the famous Sun Yat-sen Mausoleum, so we went for a long drive outside the city walls. We drove through beautiful park land, planted with fine trees and we came to the mausoleum, built up the slopes of Nanking's Purple Mountain. The setting is splendid and although some people think the Mausoleum itself is banal, I admired it. It is carried out on a grand scale: marble triumphal arches, flights of steps, tree-lined avenues and finally the blue-tiled main pavilion where Sun Yat-sen is buried. Looking round the Mausoleum we met some of the other richer Chinese passengers and they invited us all to dinner that evening.

The streets of Nanking were all lit up with neon lights and everything looked very bright and gay. We walked to the restaurant, which was right in the centre of the old part of the city. The dinner was being given by a Mr Chao, the manager of the Taiping Insurance Company, and why Carl and I were invited to it, and even more why we were treated as guests of honour I shall never know. It was an old fashioned restaurant and, as in all such places, we ate in a private room. There were about a dozen of us altogether and Carl and I were the only foreigners. Since both of us agreed afterwards that it was beyond question the best meal we had ever eaten in our lives, judged by any standards of cooking (and in over twenty years since I have never known another meal like it) I propose to give the menu of this banquet, which consisted of some sixteen courses.

We began with an hors d'oeuvres consisting of smoked ham, duck livers, sliced breast of chicken, fillet of pork and various vegetable dishes, all cold. The main meal opened with 'Chicken Velvet' a famous Chinese dish in which the chicken is pounded into a paste. Next came a dish of freshwater shrimps, a great local delicacy. Then roast chicken, followed by bamboo shoots cooked in cream. Awabi, a shellfish, and another great delicacy, cooked in cream, followed and then candied pork. Then came Nanking Duck, which is stewed, and Peking Duck, which is roast and which was specially ordered for my benefit because I had said I liked it. Shark's fin soup came next on the menu, followed by candied sweet potatoes and then fried crab's meat – a superb dish. A huge Mandarin Fish – a kind of carp – was then brought in whole and we ended up with chicken soup with a whole chicken stewed in it. With this memorable meal we drank beer and a wonderful twenty-year-old yellow rice wine.

It was a very gay party. One of the guests was an agreeably drunken old Chinese poet, who insisted on 'kan pei-ing' with full glasses of beer, which somewhat taxed one's capacity after the first four or five. Toasts followed in the rice wine and it ssemed a crime to toss back cup after cup of anything so good in one go. The party grew pleasantly hilarious and we noisily played the finger game, in which the loser had to drink a cup of wine.

There are two excellent things about a Chinese dinner. First, although you eat a stupendous amount, the dishes are so well balanced that you never feel crammed. And secondly, when you are invited to dinner, you are invited to eat. As soon as the meal is over you are expected to say good night to your host, thank him and go. It is quite in order to look in at one dinner for a couple of courses, then make your excuses and go on to another dinner somewhere else.

So we thanked our host profusely for his magnificent entertainment and went out into the street. General Wang wanted to add to his jade collection, so we made our way to a nearby street where there were several curio shops. I bought a Sung Dynasty bowl of doubtful authenticity and Carl found some jade bracelets. We picked up General Wang's car again and drove back to the *Ming Lien.*

About noon the next day we left the Yangtse and swung into the Whangpoo. It was a great contrast. We had become used to the spaciousness of the open river and now we were threading our way through a mass of shipping – mostly American. All morning the crew had been busy rigging firecrackers on long poles, because this was an occasion to celebrate. We were the first ship to come down to Shanghai from Chungking for eight years.

Then suddenly we rounded a bend in the river and I saw the tall buildings lining Shanghai's famous Bund, which I had last seen ten years before. We tied up almost opposite the Cathay Hotel and then all hell was let loose. I knew the fireworks would make a good deal of noise, but I was not prepared for the roar of artillery, the bursts of machine-gun fire which started up and went on for over a quarter of an hour without pause. Carl and I tried to record this appalling noise from the bridge but the gunpowder smoke became so thick that we had to abandon the attempt. Thousands of people came down to the landing stage to meet the ship and see the fun. It made a fine ending to a great journey that had taken just eleven days.

Chapter Four

Superficially, Shanghai looked much the same as it had ten years before. But there were no lines of parked cars along the Bund. Instead the streets were packed with American military vehicles. Shanghai had become an American garrison town. The American dollar was to all intents and purposes the local currency. The American forces occupied almost all the big hotels and blocks of flats. It was almost impossible for a civilian to get any accommodation. Fortunately, as a war correspondent, I was all right. The Press was established on two floors of one of the most modern blocks of luxury flats, Broadway Mansions.

Although I was not yet accredited to the American Forces in China, their PR officer fixed me up in the transit room with three others. One was John Ridley, in China for the *Daily Telegraph*, and it was not long before we managed to get a room and bath to ourselves. We lived in a degree of comfort that I don't think I have ever before experienced. The two 'boys' who looked after John and me were paragons. Never have I had such superlative service. For the privilege of staying in Broadway Mansions – and it was, indeed, a privilege – we were charged the nominal sum of 50 American cents a day to cover the cost of the 'boys'. 'GI' meals cost 25 cents. They were good, if a bit monotonous. If you didn't feel like GI food you could, for the modest sum of one dollar, order a first class meal from the 'Aero Club', an excellent night club and restaurant that had been opened in the basement of the 17-storey building for the benefit of the American Air Force.

* * *

My first afternoon in Shanghai I took Carl on a tour of the city. The Chinese were making a fortune out of the Americans. All troops are suckers and the Americans were bigger suckers than any others because they had more money. They were buying every kind of junk as souvenirs: Japanese-made Parker pens, Chinese-made Japanese Samurai swords, hideous embroideries and kimonos, so-called Mandarin coats sprawled over with gigantic gold dragons, – it was a frightening thought to speculate on what their womenfolk would look like in a few months' time.

The currency situation had become chaotic. I had made a sad mistake in changing my American dollars in Chungking at the rate of 850 CN dollars. The rate when I arrived in Shanghai was over 1,000. A week later it was over 2,000. The exchange speculators who had been selling American dollars in Chungking and buying them back in Shanghai, simply reversed the process.

If the Chinese were fleecing the Americans, they were closely followed by Shanghai's large White Russian population. These émigrés had always more or less controlled the night life of Shanghai. Since the Russian Revolution practically all the taxi-dancers in the night clubs and dance halls for which Shanghai had always been famous had always been Russians. If the girls I had known ten or twelve years before had maybe faded from the picture, their daughters or younger sisters had grown up in the meantime and maintained the tradition of beauty and an ability to get things out of men.

But the White Russians, though they were making a lot of money, found themselves in a difficult position. Most of them had no passports. The Chinese authorities gave them the unattractive choice of becoming Chinese or Soviet citizens. The Soviet Consulate in Shanghai put out a great deal of propaganda about the advantages of becoming Soviet citizens in the daily Russian language newspaper which they sponsored, *Novosti Dnya* – the Daily News. As a result many White Russians applied for Soviet papers. One day I was calling at a photographer's to pick up some prints and I found the shop filled with White Russians having passport photographs taken. I believe they seriously thought they would be allowed to stay in Shanghai indefinitely, running bars and night clubs. One Russian I talked to had other ideas. I asked him if he were taking out Soviet papers.

'Yes,' he said, 'they are practically ready.'

'Have you ever been in the Soviet Union?'

'No, I was born in Manchuria and I have since lived in China.'

'Well, now that you are taking out Russian papers I suppose you'll be going to live in the Soviet Union?' The man looked at me as if I were mad.

'Live in the Soviet Union? Do you think I'm out of my mind? I can imagine nothing more ghastly!'

'Well, what are you taking out Soviet papers for, then?' The Russian grinned.

'So that with a Soviet passport I can go to the United States, where I intend to take out American papers,' he said.

The White Russian women had another and far more attractive alternative. If they could marry an American or an Englishman their problem was solved. In some ways it was better to marry an Englishman because an Englishman's wife becomes a British subject the moment she is married, while an American's foreign-born wife has to live in the United States for some time before she can become an American citizen. Many of them succeeded in doing this. Graham Barrow, of Reuters, whom I had known in Hankow before the war, had lived in China for many years, spoke Russian very well and had lots of Russian friends. A girl he had known well for a long time came up to him one day.

'We are old friends, GB,' she said, 'I want you to do something for me.'

'Well, of course, if I can. What do you want me to do?'

'I want you to marry me.'

'You want me to *what*?'

'To marry me. No, don't misunderstand me. It's going to be a purely business arrangement. It'll only be for about three months and then we shall arrange a divorce. You see I am engaged to an American boy and the trouble is he is still married. He has to go home to get his divorce and he won't be able to return to China. I can't go to the United States because I have no passport. If you will do this for me I can get a British passport and then with it I can go to America. You will, won't you? It isn't really asking much of you.' GB thought it was asking a very great deal!

My first night in Shanghai I went out with Bill Turner, whom I had met a fortnight before in Chungking.

'I'll show you Shanghai's night life,' he said – he had been in Shanghai for a week so he knew all about it. 'We'll have an early dinner because with the curfew everything closes down at 11.30,' he proposed. 'Then we'll go round to one of the bars. There we'll pick up some Russian or Chinese girls – whichever you like – and take them on to a nightclub. We'll have to buy them out, of course, because they more or less belong to the bar. But it'll only cost two or three thousand dollars. And there's no use going to a night club or a dance hall on your own because you'll never find a free girl there.'

'Whatever you say, Bill. Sounds a good plan.' We spent too long over dinner. It was too late to go to a bar to buy out girls. We went straight to a dance hall called the Paramount, miles from the centre of Shanghai. We travelled in 'pedicabs'. The pedicab, a Japanese invention, had nearly put the old-fashioned rickshaw off the streets in Shanghai. It was a kind of tricycle with two seats over the back wheels and the driver pedalling in front. There was another kind where the driver pedalled from behind but they weren't so good because if there was a crash the passenger got the worst of it.

The Paramount was a fascinating spectacle. The enormous dance floor was packed with a vast crowd – the men nearly all American troops. A long bar was crowded eight deep for its entire length. Bill was most concerned because we had no partners. I was too fascinated watching what was going on to care much. The large orchestra on its raised platform under huge American and Chinese flags, blared out the tunes of the day. GIs and willowy little Chinese girls, sailors and pretty, hard-faced, blonde Russians, whirled round, locked together: or sat at tables talking earnestly: or drifted out of the hall and on into the street. A constant stream of people was coming in or going out. Graham Barrow came in and sat down at our table. I hadn't seen him for a dozen years but he greeted me as if we had met the day before. We drank vodka and ginko (a kind of Chinese Coca Cola) and then as curfew hour was getting close we left with the idea of looking in at another place before it was too late. But when we got there it had already closed and somehow or other Graham Barrow and I lost the rest of the party.

'Let's go round some of the Russian dives,' GB suggested. 'They don't bother about the curfew. It's only for the American troops. Pity you're in uniform, they may think you're an MP. But they all know me and I'll vouch for you.' He took me first to a tiny little bar called the Crimea, on Avenue Joffre, the main street in the old French Concession. It was like getting into a speakeasy. A man opened a little grille in the door and after satisfying himself that we weren't going to cause any trouble, furtively let us in. I saw a new side of Shanghai's night life. There were no Americans here. They'd all had to go home because of the curfew. But the place was packed with Russians and now they were being themselves. Since GB and I both spoke Russian we were accepted as one of them. We went to half a dozen of these little bars. There was Russian music and plenty of vodka and the prices plummeted once the Americans weren't there. It was all a lot of fun and we didn't get home until dawn in spite of the curfew.

John Ridley had got to know the Princess Sumair, the sister of the Maharajah of Patiala, who for some reason had been living in Shanghai for several years during the Japanese occupation. She had a lovely house with a swimming pool just outside the city at Hungjao, where there was a floating population of guests. One fixture was a Polish Baroness Budzhinska, with whom I became very friendly – but this was strictly a case of 'just good friends' because Budzhinska was not in the least interested in me or any other man in any other way. John and I used to go out to Sumair's house quite a lot, and one day Budzhinska said:

'Eddy, they say that in Soochow is the most beautiful wimmins in all China. Let us go to Soochow and have orgy (she pronounced the "g" hard).'

'That's a fine idea, Budzhinska, let us do just that,' I said. We found the easiest way was to go by train. On the way Budzhinska told me about her life and adventures in Poland and all over Europe before the war. Among her other accomplishments she had been Poland's champion woman motor-cycle rider and had won a lot of races. Walking from the station to the centre of Soochow we passed a police post, where one of the policemen had a bright red 'Indian' motor-cycle. Without saying a word Budzhinska seized it, kick-started the machine and went roaring down the street in a cloud of dust. The Chinese police were so surprised they scarcely knew what to do. Within a few minutes she came roaring back, braked the motor-cycle sharply, stopped, jumped off and handed it back to its owner. The Chinese police were lost in admiration of the yellow-haired foreign woman who rode a motor-cycle with such *panache* and applauded to a man. Budzhinska acknowledged their ovation with a bow, thanked them in English, turned to me and said:

'And now, Eddy, we have orgy. But first we have lunch.' We had an excellent lunch, but unfortunately the myth that Soochow had the most beautiful women in China dated, I think, back to the Sung Dynasty, nearly a thousand years ago, when Soochow, for a time was the capital of China. The contemporary women of Soochow were not at all alluring.

I had been in Shanghai for nearly a fortnight. Carl had already left as the BBC wanted him to go to Australia, and I felt it was time I was on the move again. One soon became sickened by the artificial, money-grubbing atmosphere; by the feeling that everybody was on the make. That didn't only go for the local population. In their own idiom it was monotonously true of the American troops themselves. With all the luxury and fine hotels and beautiful women and good food and comfortable living nothing had any real meaning. Shanghai was just a huge, shallow, cosmopolitan city living off its own fat. And when there wasn't any more fat, what then? And what, anyway, of the millions who weren't getting any fat? The hundreds of thousands of miserable unemployed? the beggars who lined the streets? the wretched Chinese covered with newspapers, who crouched shivering in doorways at night? the unfortunate Central European refugees, who were concentrated in an out-of-the-way part of the city where they wouldn't be noticed and where they eked out a miserable existence? I saw them there and I pitied them. They were mostly German and Austrian Jews or political refugees. They had no money and no influence. And China is no country to find yourself in if you have neither of these. But the Nazis, who had amassed vast fortunes during the war, were strutting round Shanghai as free as the air and were living in comfortable houses, many of which were the property of British or Americans. Even if they were sent back to Germany – which was most unlikely because in China if you had money you could do pretty well what you liked – it wouldn't really have mattered. They had large fortunes salted down with Chinese friends and they could always have returned to China in a year or two when things had settled down. The Chinese authorities were making far more fuss about repatriating the poor refugees. Poor people were an embarrassment. Rich people, on the other hand, could always be 'squeezed'. So Nazis and notorious collaborators could be seen in all the best hotels in Shanghai, doing just what they liked. I used to go to the lounge of the Palace Hotel around noon every day. I always had a window table from which I could see friends walking up the Nanking Road or out of the Cathay Hotel opposite. At noon, sharp, every day the former German consul general strolled into the hotel, walked the whole length of the lounge, peering about him through his monocle, and then strolled out again. We used to say he was looking for Hitler. When he did his rounds twice in the same morning we started a rumour that Hitler was beyond doubt in Shanghai. The Führer couldn't have found a better place to hide out in if it came to that.

From a business standpoint, Shanghai was in a shocking state. In the course of my work I called on the heads of many large

British firms and they were to a man pessimistic about the future. The graft and squeeze that went on as former Japanese property was taken over by the Chinese was immense. CNNRA was shipping in large quantities of materials to help in the rehabilitation of the country. The Chinese were cynical enough to advertise these shipments as for sale in the local press. I asked a Chinese official of CNNRA at a press conference one day how much he reckoned it cost to distribute one dollar's worth of CNNRA goods. He thought for a moment and said, quite calmly:

'I would say ninety cents.'

Chapter Five

Thanks to the captain of HMS *Belfast* and the efficiency of his radio technicians, I was able to record my impressions of the trip down the Yangtse and airmail them back to the BBC. There was a British plane flying to Hong Kong via Kunming – a somewhat circuitous route. I decided to take it. An old friend of mine, Erik Watts, whom I had known in Tientsin before the war and who had been Press Attaché at the British Embassy in Chungking, travelled with me. Perhaps as a result of my reports when I had first arrived in Shanghai, so did a party of British representatives, who were heading for Hankow. Erik and I agreed that they didn't look likely to do much for British prestige.

After two stops we reached Kunming in the late afternoon. The British part of the airport was cluttered up with unserviceable Halifaxes and Dakotas. There was nobody to service them. The Americans had helped out in the past but now they were in the middle of pulling out of Kunming and handing over to the Chinese. The following morning I found that the plane I had come in was also unserviceable. I called in at the British Military Mission, where I found another friend, Sam White, today the almost legendary Paris correspondent of the *Evening Standard,* who in those days worked for the *Sydney Daily Telegraph.* Sam had been pottering round Kunming for some days and was in the middle of collecting a fascinating story. A missionary had just arrived who, with his wife and two children, had been living for the past ten years among strange tribesmen near the Burmese frontier. We went straight away to meet him at the house of the British Press Attaché.

Mr Andrews was a burly, capable-looking American of about fifty. His wife was a bird-like little woman and exactly one's idea of a missionary's wife. The daughter was an attractive girl of about thirteen with a shock of red hair. And the ten year old boy was so much the typical American schoolboy that it was almost impossible to believe that he had spent his entire life in the little town of Likiang, in extreme south-Western Yunnan, twenty days' mule journey from Kunming, which was the biggest town he had ever seen.

Mr Andrews had made a profound study of a people about whom practically nothing is known to the outside world. They had an ingenious pictorial writing of their own. Mr Andrews had a powerful transmitting and receiving radio set with which he kept in touch with world events. He ran a news service for the tribesmen and certain things had particularly appealed to them. One was the Atlantic Charter. A group of the more learned of the tribesmen decided to set it down in their own hieroglyphics. Mr Andrews had a copy of it, beautifully painted on a long scroll, which he was taking back to the British Museum.

He had some curious stories to tell about magic. He had a number of photographs taken by himself showing the marks made by heavy stones on the doors of the upper storey of his house, stones which he had established beyond doubt could not have been thrown by a man. He had gone carefully into angles to prove this to his own satisfaction. A Chinese general who had been staying with him had been understandably sceptical when, as they were sitting on the upper verandah, he had told him about this occult stone throwing. The general said it was a lot of nonsense. No sooner were the words out of his mouth than a stone as large as a big potato, coming from nowhere, struck him on the side of the head and put him out for an hour. The general was convinced.

At certain seasons of the year these tribesmen held devil dances in the course of which Mr Andrews had seen them take steel swords and tie the almost rigid blades into knots – a feat which is physically impossible.

Mr Andrews was not only a good doctor, he was a first class mechanic and engineer. His station was high up in the mountains and directly on the line of flight of the allied planes which made the hazardous 'Hump' run between Calcutta and Kunming. Mr Andrews thought that an emergency landing field could well come in useful for any plane in trouble. So entirely on his own he supervised the construction of one on a fairly level plateau. He told the authorities what he had done by radio, and his field was quite often used.

Sam White and I were taken one day to a research institute ten miles outside Kunming where, among other things, they manufactured penicillin. We followed the new Burma road the whole way. Running alongside it was the old flagstoned caravan road that had been used for centuries. Vast parks of vehicles lined the ten miles we covered almost solidly. I saw literally thousands of trucks, jeeps, bulldozers and every other imaginable vehicle on four wheels or more. They had all come into China by the Burma Road and had never got any further than the terminus of the road – Kunming. Most of them were brand new – or as new as a trip over the Burma Road leaves anything. Now they were all being handed over to the Central Government. How or when all this material was going to be paid for was another matter. Most individual Americans were very bitter about it and up at the airport they were burning immense quantities of stores rather than hand them over to the Chinese. I saw beautiful flying jackets that had never been worn going up in flames.

I had only been back in Hong Kong for a few days when I had a cable from the BBC ordering me to go to North China to cover the 'war' between the Central Government and the Communists. The cable ended: 'assignment should not last over a fortnight.' It made me laugh. I knew it would take over a fortnight even to get to North China.

I was delighted at being ordered North. I was going to have suggested it myself anyway. I cabled back that I was on my way, but had to get to Shanghai for a start. There were many alternative methods but I hadn't the right priorities for any of them. Then by great luck I met a British officer who also wanted to get to Shanghai. He told me that the minelayer, HMS *Apollo* was leaving Hong Kong for Shanghai the next day and the captain agreed to take me.

In Shanghai I found that John Ridley was also headed North. So was Dixie Tighe, correspondent for the *New York Post* and one of the most fabulous women I have ever met though on first acquaintance she was a rather formidable person. I never believed at this early stage that the three of us would make such a successful partnership or what a good friend and ideal companion Dixie would be. Dixie was, I suppose, in her middle forties. She must have been staggeringly beautiful when she was younger. As a girl she had been a newspaper correspondent in Hollywood.

'I tried them all,' she told me once, 'all those glamour boys. And were they useless!' Dixie then looked remarkably like Mae West in her hey-day and was just as funny.

She and John were both accredited to the American forces in China, which meant they could travel free in American planes among other advantages. I was not, which meant that I had to pay for air transport. Before leaving we bought all the Shanghai newspapers. 'Gunfire could be heard all over Peking,' we read, 'and trigger-happy US Marines were patrolling the streets of the old capital by night.' And much more in the same vein.

After a four hours flight Peking lay below us, the superb imperial yellow roofs of the Forbidden City sparkling in the clear midday sunshine. We banked steeply over the Summer Palace and landed on the West Airfield, a mile from it. I listened for gunfire as I stepped from the plane. Not a sound. It was all very peaceful. Farmers were digging up their cabbages and piling them into clamps for the winter. Trains of camels padded along the sides of the road, carrying heavy sacks of coal from the Mentoukou mines. Children were playing outside the houses. We reached the West Gate of Peking, towering above the massive walls and looking like a gigantic dovecote, with its tiers of loopholes. Inside the gate Peking looked just the same as when I had last seen it. At the Wagon-Lits Hotel, where we got rooms, nobody had heard of any fighting. Neither had the United States Information Service, whose offices were in a Chinese courtyard across the way. I asked some marines about these tense trigger-happy patrols they were supposed to be making. They laughed and said they were chiefly occupied in eating Peking duck and buying souvenirs to send home.

The BBC had wanted as much advance information about the fighting as possible. I had been able to find out nothing in Hong Kong, nothing in Shanghai and in Peking, which was getting near the scene of activity, there was no information either. But I'd be sure to hear something in Tientsin, I was told. All that talk in Shanghai about gunfire in Peking was nonsense, but I'd find plenty of it in Tientsin. So after only one night in Peking we took the early morning train to Tientsin.

As we pulled into Tientsin station my mind went back over ten years to the time when Maisie and I had made our midnight dash to Europe, with only Rupert to see us off. But I had to think of the present and of the war-torn city that we had come to. There was no trouble near the station and when we reached Victoria Road the only activity to be seen was provided by large numbers of Chinese hawkers selling every conceivable kind of rubbish to the American marines. Tientsin was as quiet and peaceful as Peking.

The American Public Relations officer told us that the nearest fighting was going on in the region of the Great Wall of China, near the port of Chinwangtao. We decided to go there. We were discussing ways and means in the lounge of the Astor House Hotel, when a tall, cadaverous man came to our table.

'I overheard what you were saying,' he said. 'I, too, want to go to Chinwangtao. The railway is impossible. The Communists are tearing up stretches of the track and blowing bridges all the time. But – there's a Chinese Customs launch going there in a couple of days and I think you should be able to get a passage. The KMA, who have chartered the vessel, will give you all the details and then you'll have to go down to the Chinese Customs and get their okay. But I don't think there should be any trouble.'

At the offices of the Kailan Mining Administration everyone was out to lunch, but I got the address of Allan Murray, whom I had known in the old days in Tientsin. My chief contribution to our team of three was the fact that wherever we went I always seemed to know somebody who came in useful. There was also my sketchy knowledge of the Chinese language and a certain flair for dealing with the intricacies of exchange rates. Dixie had the job of getting more than we were entitled to out of the American authorities; more food and drink from the PX, priorities on planes, accommodation in hotels when none was apparently available. Dixie could wheedle anything out of her compatriots.

Allan Murray arrived at his house about the same time as we did. His wife Betsy came to join us. I had known her well when she was a girl of eighteen before the war. Now she had two children. All four of them had spent over three years in the Japanese civilian internment camp at Weihsien, in Shantung Province. Allan confirmed that the launch was leaving for Chinwangtao, probably the following day but they were waiting for a telegram from there and the boat couldn't leave until it arrived.

John and I went to the Customs House and saw the Commissioner, who authorized our passage. Going down the stairs later an English official pointed out of the window at a vessel tied up alongside the Bund. It looked like a small tug.

'There she is,' he said. 'That's the Customs launch. D'you see the name? *"T'ien Hsiang"*. It's a good name. D'you know what it means?'

'I know what it *could* mean,' I said. 'It could mean *"Heavenly Elephant"*.' The man laughed.

'Ah, so you speak the language, do you? Well that's exactly what it does mean. *"Heavenly Elephant"*.' As it happens the Customs official, like me, was no Chinese scholar. The word '*hsiang*' can mean elephant. But this wasn't the 'elephant' character. This '*hsiang*' meant 'fragrance', but we didn't know that then. We were enchanted with the name and rushed off to tell Dixie. Later on we all refused to listen to any explanations from sinologues that the second character was not the 'elephant' 'hsiang'. To us she was always the '*Heavenly Elephant*'. We used it to dateline our stories with – 'Aboard the Heavenly Elephant . . .'.

The telegram from Chinwangtao took four days to come. We meanwhile went to see the Chinese general commanding the Tientsin area but he could give us no information about what was happening near the Great Wall. He said the town of Shanhaikwan, where the Wall runs down into the sea, was in Nationlist hands, so we sent cables saying so. The next day a French captain returned from Chinwangtao and reported that Shanhaikwan was definitely in Communist hands, so we sent another cable contradicting the first. Nobody seemed to know anything.

We sampled Tientsin's night life and found it far cheaper and pleasanter than Shanghai's. We found yet another kind of Chinese dollar in the north – a puppet currency issued by the Japanese 'Federal Reserve Bank'. These dollars were called FRB. The Central Reserve Bank dollars used in Shanghai were called CRB and the official Central-Government-issued Chinese National currency were called CNC. The Chinese complicated matters even further by calling 'CNC' in their own language 'Fa-Bee', which, of course, sounded exactly like FRB. For a long time we kept thinking we were getting tremendous bargains in the shops, only to find when the bill was added up that we were paying five times as much as we thought – the FRB dollar was five to one Fa-Bee. This crazy currency situation completely defeated Dixie. When she had to pay for anything she used to push over an enormous bag stuffed with bricks of banknotes – she never carried less than half or three quarters of a million 'CNC' all mixed up with wads of 'FRB', which she persisted in calling 'FDR', and say weakly:

'Pay him, Eddy, for God's sake. Give him a hundred thousand; give him a million! Give him anything!' – and sheaves of notes would tumble out on to the table and the floor, mixed up with lipsticks, combs and handkerchiefs.

* * *

While we were waiting for the *Heavenly Elephant* to sail we got to know the captain quite well. He was a large, fat, amiable Chinese in his late thirties or early forties and his name was Captain Wang. At last the necessary telegram from Chinwangtao arrived and he said we must be aboard at 11.30 the next morning as he was sailing at noon. Dixie had already stockpiled a vast quantity of provisions she had wheedled out of the PX and we also took with us a great many bottles of vodka to keep the cold out. A lot of our Tientsin friends came to see us off and we decided to throw a farewell party. We made excellent cocktails with vodka and grapefruit and pineapple juice from the PX and Dixie had also bought plenty of biscuits and sandwich spread and peanuts. The little saloon had been neat and tidy when we arrived. Within a few minutes the table was covered with bottles of vodka, tins of fruit juice, biscuits, peanuts, glasses and teacups.

'It didn't take us long to get a nice homey atmosphere, did it?' Dixie said as she tried to persuade Captain Wang to have another glass of vodka. But after one small glass he refused to have any more.

'Make my face go red,' he said. Chinese often do go red in the face when they drink much and Captain Wang wasn't going to let that happen to him. The other passengers thought we were mad but joined the party in self defence. At last Captain Wang said he was very sorry but the visitors must go ashore. He had delayed sailing for an hour and half because we were all enjoying ourselves so much, but now we had to leave. We sailed down the Hai Ho and reached Tangku at the mouth of the river, the same evening. The following evening we reached Chinwangtao and immediately set about making arrangements for moving into Manchuria. We had learned that General Tu Li-ming, the commander of the Nationalist armies, had pushed on about eighty miles beyond the Great Wall.

The Chinese liaison officer with the American Marines at Chinwangtao, General Tung, promised to inform General Tu

Li-ming that we were coming to visit him. General Tu would certainly send a special train for us, he said. We thought this wildly unlikely but we waited. There wasn't much else we could do. But that same evening we were told that a special train had arrived. Surprised and delighted we went to Chinwangtao station and there it was: a locomotive and one first class carriage. A Chinese captain and a guard of half a dozen were aboard as an escort. The captain said he thought a night trip would be dangerous and it would be better to wait until the following morning. We would have none of this – particularly Dixie. We had already wasted an hour waiting. We must move at once. Half an hour later we left. The train crawled the fifteen miles to Shanhaikwan and then stopped. The captain said the train would have to wait a little while in the station and we would be more comfortable and warm in the waiting room. There were more arguments in favour of waiting until morning but by sheer obstinacy combined with threats that we would make an unfavourable report to General Tu, we wore down the opposition.

There were no lights for security reasons and no heating for inefficiency reasons. Dixie and John sat huddled together to one seat. I climbed into my feather sleeping bag to keep warm. At 3 a.m. the train stopped at the town of Lienshan where the captain said General Tu had established his headquarters. He went to wake up the guards, who had been sleeping soundly since we had left Shanhaikwan. Carrying our baggage we stumbled over railway lines until we reached another train. Here we were handed over to a Chinese major, who spoke a little English. We hadn't been expected so soon and no accommodation had been prepared for us. General Tu had his headquarters on this train, the major told us and we, too, should be staying on it. He took us to the dining car and in a surprisingly short time an excellent Chinese meal was served. We were well ready for it. We had to doss down as best we could in the dining car which, unfortunately, was also used as an 'Operations Room'. All through the night staff officers came in, studied maps and held telephone conversations at the top of their voices.

When we got up we were taken to a drawing room car which

was shared by two generals. They were in process of dressing in civilian clothes as we entered. They were both political advisers on Tu Li-ming's staff. Their names were Chiao and Chang. General Chiao was a tall, extremely cultured, westernised Chinese who had spent many years in England and spoke English almost without any accent. General Chang looked exactly like the average westerner's idea of a sinister oriental. He was small and thin, with a parchment-like face, very slanting, slitty eyes and a thin-lipped, cruel mouth. Years before he had been Russian adviser to the 'Old Marshal' Chang Tso-lin, in Manchuria. He didn't speak a word of English, but he spoke Russian like a Russian.

We cleaned ourselves up and then General Chiao took us to the dining car for breakfast. Because we were foreigners we were each given three fried eggs. There was no bread because the Chinese don't eat bread. The only other dish was fried peanuts. There were no knives or forks and eating softly fried eggs with chopsticks takes some doing. When we had finished this difficult meal General Chiao took us to see the Supreme Commander, Tu Li-ming.

It was a strange setting in which to find a commander-in-chief. The observation car, which was his headquarters, was decorated with a profusion of potted ferns, which gave it a curiously seaside boarding-house appearance, an effect heightened by the dark red tablecloth with a tasselled fringe, which covered a round table in the middle of the car. In contrast to this decoration scheme, the walls were covered with large-scale strategic maps, which gave the room its only military touch.

Sitting in an armchair on the far side of the table, and scarcely visible when we first came in, was a slight, boyish figure wearing an American sailor's jacket with 'US Navy' stencilled on it, a pair of plain khaki GI's slacks and Chinese cloth slippers. Tu Li-ming wore no decorations and the only clue to his identity were two brass stars on his collar which in the Chinese army meant he was a lieutenant-general. General Tu looked to be in his middle twenties at the most, though later I learned he was forty-two. He was one of the few Chinese I have ever met who was not afraid to give a direct answer without hesitation even to the most embarrassing question. He was obviously a man of great quality and, I felt, completely ruthless. As we talked he kept dipping into a box of American candy, which was lying on the table in front of him, and munching toffee. Staff officers came in from time to time with papers for the general to sign, or to get orders from him. Tu seemed to have all the details of the situation at his fingertips.

Tu Li-ming was making an official visit to the small seaport of Hulutao and said we could accompany him. We drove at a furious pace in a jeep through hilly, moorland country that might have been Cumberland, passing long columns of Chinese infantry, trudging along the side of the road carrying immense bundles on their backs. Hulutao, like Lienshan, was a modern town built by the Japanese. Its discouraged-looking inhabitants turned out to give Tu Li-ming a welcome by waving Kuomintang flags in an apathetic way. But when they saw Dixie, with her blonde hair, they cheered and shouted and waved their flags madly. They had seen Chinese generals before but a foreign woman with yellow hair – and dressed up like a soldier, too – that was something really worth turning out for.

That evening on the train Tu Li-ming outlined his plan for taking over Manchuria. It sounded so good that we confidently expected to return in a fortnight in time to enter Mukden. Tu said that the only place where the Communists had put up any resistance had been at Shanhaikwan but even there the casualties had been negligible. After that his tactics had been to advance on a town from several directions at once, leaving the Communists an easy way of escape. Then he sent word to them that he intended to take the town on a certain date at a certain time. Invariably the Communists had moved out several hours in advance and the town had fallen without a shot being fired. They had captured a few thousand stragglers but most of them had been farmers who had been forced into the Communist Army. They had simply been sent back to their farms. Genuine *'Pa-lu's'* – *'Pa Lu'* in Chinese means literally 'Eight Road' and was the name given to the Communist Eighth Route Army – were concentrated down the line at a town called Suichung, where they were given 'political education'. We saw some 'political education' when we left the following day. It was bitterly cold with the temperature around zero. All down the main street of Lienshan were men, with their hands behind them, tied round the telegraph poles. They were wearing only singlets and cotton trousers.

We saw no point in waiting for Tu Li-ming's unopposed entry into Chinchow so we asked the general if we could return in a fortnight. He said he would be glad to see us again and promised to let us have a jeep to drive back to Chinwangtao the next morning. I spent the rest of the evening drinking vodka and talking Russian to General Chang. He said my vodka was poor stuff and that if I would bring along an empty bottle before we left the next morning he would give me something with a bit more kick in it.

The next morning I took some photographs of Tu Li-ming, who had dressed for the occasion in a smart uniform with all his medals and with both the Chinese and American Air Forces' wings, one worn on either side of his tunic. General Chang filled my bottle with a colourless liquid and we set off in a jeep at 8.30 a.m. A truck followed with twenty armed soldiers. Tu insisted against our protests that he was responsible for us. It was a brilliant, clear, bitterly cold day and I was glad of the padded cotton Chinese peasant's coat that I had bought in Tientsin. Just after midday we approached a chain of mountains and there, winding like a ribbon, was the Great Wall of China, twining and twisting its way over the hilltops away into the distant west. In Shanhaikwan we invited the guard commander to lunch and asked him to accept a few thousand dollars to give to the guard so that they could buy themselves something to eat. He refused to take the money. I fell back on the trump card that always wins:

'If you do not take the money, I lose face,' I said. It worked like a charm.

Chapter Six

We had been in a hurry to get back to Chinwangtao because we didn't want to miss the *Heavenly Elephant.* Captain Wang was in no hurry whatever. The morning after our return the weather was perfect but Captain Wang had a dinner invitation. The next day it was blowing half a gale and he refused to sail. By the afternoon of the following day the wind had dropped and we persuaded the captain to leave. We were towing a lighter loaded with 500 tons of coal, which was far more than the *Heavenly Elephant* was capable of dealing with safely. As soon as we got outside the harbour the ship started behaving erratically. We continued on our way for an hour. I was up on the bridge when a flock of wild duck flew past, heading out to sea. Suddenly they turned back towards the land again.

'That settles it,' Captain Wang said. 'If the ducks don't like the look of the weather, then neither do I. The ducks know.' With that he turned the *Heavenly Elephant* back to port.

I went to the railway station the next day but there was no hope of travelling by train. I returned to the dock and was hailed by Captain Wang, who said he was sailing at any minute. We left three hours later. The sea had calmed, fortunately we saw no ducks and by nightfall we were well on our way.

In the middle of the night I awoke to find the *Heavenly Elephant* behaving in the most alarming manner. She was heaving and plunging to such an extent that I became very frightened and was convinced that she was going to founder. John woke up, too, and we both lay jittering for several hours. We wondered how Dixie was getting on in her cabin down below the waterline. Before we had started from Tientsin she had said that the slightest movement of a ship prostrated her. She had survived the outward trip but it had been calm. This was enough to upset the most hardened sailor. About eight o'clock I got up, dressed with some difficulty and staggered out on deck. None of the crew seemed to be about. The galley was empty and its fire out. I climbed down to Dixie's cabin to see how she was, expecting to find her half dead. I was greeted with:

'I thought none of my boys was ever coming down. When do we get breakfast?'

'Dixie, if we want breakfast we get it for ourselves. The galley staff are "out" and I don't think they'll be any good today. The galley fire's out, too.'

'You and John try and get that going and I'll be right up to fix the breakfast,' Dixie said. The *Heavenly Elephant* was leaping about like a bucking steer as I climbed the stairway leading up from Dixie's cabin. John was up and dressed. We went to the crew's quarters and found the galley staff lying on the deck groaning. In the galley was a pile of coal but no kindling wood.

'I've got an idea,' I said. We had tried General Chang's 'vodka' the night before and had found that it wasn't vodka at all but a liquor as near to 100 degrees as it is possible for alcohol to be, distilled from millet, which the northern Chinese call *pai-kaerh.* Its only virtue was its phenomenal strength. It tasted awful. I fetched the bottle and we stuffed some old dusters and dishcloths into the stove together with some broken up pieces of broom handles and a few scraps of wood we found. Then I poured half the contents of the bottle over it all, stood well back and threw a lighted match at it. It went off like a bomb. A sheet of blue flame shot out of the top of the stove. We banked it down quickly with coal, put back the circular iron top and soon had a good fire going. Dixie arrived with a handkerchief tied round her head. It was blowing a full gale outside and the *Heavenly Elephant* was behaving worse than ever.

'Well, what've we got?' Dixie wanted to know. John found a bucket full of eggs which had miraculously survived. There was nothing to fry them in but Dixie found a lump of greasy fat pork on a shelf and set to work to render it down in a large frying pan. We put in a couple of extra eggs for Captain Wang, but when I went up to the bridge to tell him breakfast was ready, I discovered that he too had succumbed and was lying, green-faced, on his bed. Fried eggs had no appeal for him. Dixie, John and I settled down to a large breakfast. We had no sooner finished it then we realized that if we wanted lunch we had better start preparing it right away. I was given the key of the larder by the semi-conscious cook, who was so far gone that he didn't even care that he was losing face by not doing the cooking. In the larder we found a large quantity of very fat pork, cabbages and potatoes. A live chicken was tied up outside. Another had found the storm too much for him and was lying dead. We didn't feel like executing the chicken, so it had to be the fat pork – hardly an ideal dish in the circumstances. We set to work cutting it up into large dice, chopping up the cabbage and peeling the potatoes. Three of our fellow passengers helped us. None of the others had made an appearance. We prepared just enough for ourselves.

I shall always remember the spectacle of Dixie – whom the slightest movement of a ship prostrated, – balancing herself in that tiny galley, while the ship heaved and plunged about in the angry sea, frying fat lumps of pork. It was a heroic performance. Just as she had finished the cooking a fluttery little woman passenger came up and trilled:

'Oh, Miss Tighe, we are all up now so there will be four extra for lunch. That will make eleven altogether. Do let me know if there is anything I can do to help, won't you?' Dixie looked at her malevolently.

'Thank you,' she said. 'I have just finished cooking lunch – for seven. The galley is all yours.'

By the time we reached Taku Bar, outside the mouth of the Hai Ho, the weather had improved and the *Heavenly Elephant* was only lurching spasmodically. The galley staff came to life again rather sheepishly and we didn't have to cook the evening meal. Back in Tientsin the following morning Captain Wang was most apologetic about Dixie having had to cook the meal the day before and didn't want to accept any money for our food. He confessed he had felt very nervous during the storm and swore he would never go to sea again in the *Heavenly Elephant.*

John and Dixie flew back to Shanghai. I stayed on in Tientsin for a few days. I had many friends there and I decided to take a short holiday. At first it annoyed me only to be able to go to the Tientsin Country Club, of which I had been a member for years, as the guest of an American marine, but I became used to it. Back in Shanghai I was greeted by John with the news that the fall of Mukden to Tu Li-ming was imminent. We rushed north again. To our great sorrow Dixie couldn't come with us. Her paper had ordered her to stay in Shanghai.

In Tientsin we found the railway was running reasonably well again – that is to say a train only took two days to cover the hundred and fifty miles from Tientsin to Chinwangtao. It didn't run at night and the journey had to be broken at the mining town of Tangshan.

At Tientsin railway station a fighting, shouting mob of Chinese was trying to get in and out of the doors of the train simultaneously. The only way to enter was through the windows. Fortunately the battle for the doors was about equally matched, so we were able to secure seats, which otherwise would have been out of the question. To my surprise the train started on time. Feeling exhausted by the struggle I took a bottle of whisky out of my bag, which I had meant to reserve against the cold of Manchuria, and poured myself a drink. An American marine sergeant was sitting next to me, so I offered him one too. He also was on his way to Chinwangtao.

A little later the sergeant got up, took a suitcase from the luggage rack and opened it. It was a well stacked travelling bar. There was whisky, brandy, gin, rum and plenty of bottles of Coca-Cola.

'I sure do wish I still had some of our Okinawa whisky,' he said to me. 'We sank the last of it only last night; and it was real old stuff – over three months old. You know when we were on Okinawa we collected all the canned fruit, raisins, prunes and sugar we could get a hold of. We made a "mash" and added some yeast and we rigged up a still and we were making about twenty bottles of "whisky" a day. Trouble was we didn't get a very big issue of the raw materials. Not like the God-damned army, who got all they could use. So what did we do? I'll tell you. We sold the whisky to the army at twelve bucks a bottle and we only had to use a small bit of that to buy enough stuff at the Army PX to make another lot. So we were drinking free on the army and boy did that make us feel good!' There wasn't so much a spirit of rivalry between the US Marines and the US Army as a feeling of real hatred. I had bought a pair of those dove-grey army officer's slacks in the PX in Shanghai. When I appeared wearing them in Tientsin a Marine friend of mine took me straight to their clothing store and issued me with a pair of dark olive green Marine slacks. 'You're not walking around Tientsin wearing those goddamn army pants,' he told me.

General Tu Li-ming's new headquarters were in Chinchow, an important railway junction in Southern Manchuria. We were met by a Colonel Li and taken to the 'Press Camp', a Japanese villa built in English suburban style, but inside split up into the usual Japanese box-like compartments. The next morning, on our way to see Tu Li-ming, we met General Chiao, who said if we had come with the idea of going on to Mukden, we were in for a disappointment.

'We could move in tomorrow,' he said, 'but this has become a political war between Chungking and Moscow. The Soviets are back in Mukden. They let the Communists take the city and all the military equipment the Japanese left behind. Then they pushed the Communists a few miles outside Mukden and established themselves there again. As long as they stay there we can't move in.'

Tu confirmed what his chief of staff had said. He was disgusted with the whole situation and made no attempt to disguise his feelings about the Russians. Horrific stories of pillage and rape by the Russians were coming in every day from Mukden and Changchun. In Chinchow, when they were there, no girl went out into the street if she could possibly help it; and if she did she would carry a bundle looking like a baby on her back, which gave a certain degree of immunity. We called to see a doctor in Chinchow and while we were talking his little six-year-old daughter came into the room, saw John and me and ran screaming out. Her father called her back, explaining that we were 'good' foreigners.

Although the Russians had behaved very badly to the civilian population – and the older men and women remembered the Russian soldiers in the Russo-Japanese war almost with affection – most people agreed that the Chinese Communists had behaved extremely well, particularly to the poorer people.

One thing that pleased me in Chinchow was finding a Sung Dynasty bowl – that could have been genuine – in an antique shop and offering American dollars in payment. The shopkeeper refused to take this money. He wanted Japanese yen. I told him American dollars were the best money in the world and everybody wanted them. Maybe, he said, but he didn't; he wanted Japanese yen; and so I couldn't buy the bowl. But it was gratifying in a way to find at least one person who had no use for the mighty dollar.

John and I flew back to Shanghai as there seemed no prospect of being able to go to Mukden. Three weeks later the news came through that Tu Li-ming's troops would definitely enter the city on January 15th. By this time I had succeeded in becoming accredited to the American forces so I could fly anywhere I wanted, free. Back to Peking we flew. The hotels were full and fortunately I found another pre-war friend, Neville McBain, who had a house in the British Embassy compound. He at once asked John and me to stay.

We stayed in Peking several days. One morning we were drinking our usual vodka and Chinese Coca Cola in the Peking Club, when a man addressed us in an exaggerated stage-English voice.

'I say you fellows,' he said, 'why don't you join me and have a real drink?' John and I moved over to his table. He pulled a bottle of blended American whisky out of his pocket and poured three glasses. 'Well, what do you think of that?' he asked, as if he had offered us some priceless liqueur whisky. Neither of us liked it much but it was a change from vodka and ginko. It was a well known brand of American whisky which I shall call Sheldon. 'Yes, it's great stuff,' he said, without waiting for any comment from us. I'm the sole agent for it in the Philippines and China. It's selling magnificently over here.' By way of making conversation I said:

'Did you meet Peter Colville of Caldbeck MacGregor's in Shanghai?' – Caldbeck MacGregor's were the biggest wine merchants in China.

'Old Peter? Good Heavens, yes! Saw a lot of him – and did some very good business, I may add.' John and I made our escape as soon as we could. A few weeks later in Shanghai I asked Peter if he had met the Sheldon agent.

'Did I meet that awful chap? I'll say I did. He tried to sell me that rotgut, but of course we don't stock that kind of thing. Still, he was in the same trade in a way, so I asked him to a party I happened to be giving in the Cathay. D'you know he did nothing but plug that stuff of his to all the guests. Well one of them was a middle-aged US Marine colonel, who had been knocking it back quietly all evening without saying a word. At last he spoke up.

' "You know," he said, "we were there at the storming of Okinawa, and, boy, that was a rugged business. There we were, down on the beaches, the Japanese giving us no rest – mortars, machine-guns – our boys lying wounded and bleeding – no comforts – no anything. And then – we saw a wooden case floating in. There was something written on it – it came closer – it was a case of whisky! Two of our boys waded out and dragged it in – and those poor, wounded, bleeding boys thought that they had received something from heaven. And then they read the label on the case. And they cried:

' "Sheldon! Take it away! We'd sooner die!" '

'Well, that was the end of the party as far as the Sheldon agent was concerned,' Peter said. 'He got very red in the face and walked out. The old Marine colonel talked quite a lot after that. He saved the evening for us.'

This time John and I flew to Chinchow and it only took two hours. We found half a dozen war correspondents at the Press Camp. Why weren't they in Mukden? we wanted to know.

'The Russians,' one of them said. 'So long as a single Red Army soldier is in Mukden no American or British correspondents can go in. The Russians say they can't guarantee our safety.'

'Nobody asks them to,' said Reynolds Packard, who had flown in with us. 'Nobody ever has guaranteed war correspondents' safety. If it's okay for Chinese troops to go in, it's okay for us.' But it wasn't. Those were the Russian orders – so the Chinese said. Later the Russians said it was nothing to do with them, it was a Chinese order. I was so disgusted I said I was going to fly straight back to Peking. In the end all the other correspondents followed suit and Tu Li-ming's headquarters was evacuated *en masse* by the foreign press.

In Peking pacification teams consisting of one nationalist, one communist and one American were being sent out by air to trouble spots to bring about a ceasefire. John and I went down to the office of Bill Brittain, the American PRO and put down our names for a flight to Ta t'ung in Shansi Province. It wouldn't be leaving for several days, so we settled down to enjoy life in Peking for a while.

John Ridley, perversely, professed not to care about Peking. I have never before or since met anyone who subscribed to such rank heresy. To me Peking was – and it is sad to have to use the past tense – one of the really great cities of the world, one in which I would have been prepared happily to end my days, growing slightly madder year by year as I learned more and more Chinese characters and became increasingly affected by the electrically dry, sparkling atmosphere. To me the cloudless skies, the unbelievably lovely buildings in their even lovelier settings the fascinating shops, the fairs, the markets, the restaurants, the easy, pleasant manners of its inhabitants, all combined to make Peking an enchanting city. John persisted in looking upon it as a museum piece – something lovely but lifeless. So Neville McBain, who had lived most of his life in Peking, and I made use of those few free days to take John round and really show him something of the city. We drove out to the Temple of Heaven with its dazzling, deep-blue, three-tiered roof – like everything else in Peking lovingly restored by the Japanese during their occupation. We stood at the 'Centre of the Universe' on the Altar of Heaven, where the Chinese Emperors used to sacrifice at the New Year. We wandered through the Forbidden City, with its massive Venetian-red walls topped with Imperial yellow tiles and its exquisite pavilions and gardens and we wondered how the present-day Chinese could have had such villainous taste as to stick a great poster of Chiang Kai-shek, like an outsize circus billboard over the majestic entrance. We climbed up the famous White Dagoba above the Winter Palace and watched the people of Peking, like the figures in a Breughel painting, skating on the North Lake far below us. We drove out to the old Empress Dowager's Summer Palace, which she had built instead of building a navy, which contributed to China's ignominious defeat by the Japanese in 1898. We bargained and bought curios in the shops outside the Ch'ien Mên. We discovered a little market tucked away in the Tartar City, where you could buy marvellous porcelain and old pottery, most of which was cleverly faked. We ate every kind of Chinese food. We went to two of the Thursday afternoon receptions given by a celebrated Peking character, Jacques Bardac, where we met 'everybody' in Peking. We visited Dr Burchardt, the greatest living authority on ancient Chinese ceramics and bronzes. We kept up to date by giving parties at Neville McBain's house to which we invited people like the exquisite Madame K'ung P'ang, at that time the secretary of Chou En-lai and we asked her why she didn't use a little make-up and make herself even more beautiful than she already was. We had a wonderful time and at the end of it John was converted. Then one morning Bill Brittain the press officer telephoned and said we must go out to the West Airfield straight away. We were to have a better trip than we had expected; we were to go first to Chining, in Inner Mongolia and then on to Ta t'ung.

Chining was held by the Chinese Communists and we were excited at the prospect of seeing part of the famous Eighth Route Army. The moment we landed, a jeep came out to meet us. It had been brought in the plane that had gone ahead of us with the pacification team. Out of it jumped Colonel Craig, the American representative, Colonel Li, the Nationalist, and General Sun, the Communist. They all climbed into the plane for a conference with Colonel Hudgins, the American intelligence officer, who had brought the latest instructions from Executive Headquarters.

A large crowd appeared from nowhere and stood in a line fifty yards from the plane. They wanted to crowd in on it but Eighth Route Army troops kept them back with fixed bayonets. They looked much the same as other Chinese soldiers except that they were far more heavily and spectacularly armed. Apart from their rifles nearly all of them carried three or four hand-made grenades slung on their belts as well as a Mauser pistol with a piece of bright red cloth wrapped round the stock. It was bitterly cold because Chining is over five thousand feet up and all the troops and the local inhabitants wore enormous fur hats, made of wolf skin, red fox and hare or rabbit. There were some wonderful types among the crowd, tall, flat-faced Mongolians, high-cheek-boned Tartars, Turkomans with big, hooked Semitic noses. Some *'Palu'* cavalry galloped up on their shaggy little Mongolian ponies that looked as if they had never been groomed in their lives and probably hadn't. The cavalrymen wore enormous, dirty sheepskin coats.

The conference ended and Colonel Hudgins said we were to spend the night in Chining instead of going on to Ta t'ung the same day.

General Tu Li-ming,
Commander of Nationalist
forces in Manchuria,
on his train at Lienshan,
January 1946

The Bishop Rock
Lighthouse – three weeks'
imprisonment

Father Giulietti and one of the 'Piccoli Mutilati'

Marjorie and little Vittorio – blinded in the fighting in Italy

Colonel Craig, a very charming Southerner, invited us into his room at the headquarters of the pacification team, which was in a compound of long mud huts with latticework windows, which had once been a Japanese barracks. He was optimistic over the outcome of the cease-fire order and said he was getting every possible co-operation from the Communist authorities. The colonel took us to our quarters, a hut with a large Chinese *k'ang*, a bed built of brickwork, which ran the length of the wall. On top of the *k'ang* were thick straw mats which didn't look very clean. The *k'ang* is an excellent kind of bed for a cold country. It is hollow and a fire is lit inside it, so that you sleep on what is really a slow oven. A *Palu* interpreter, who had learned English at Tientsin University came in and apologised for the the discomfort of the room and also for his poor English which he hadn't spoken for over eight years. He was a delightful and, as it turned out, extremely efficient man.

General Sun invited us to an excellent Chinese dinner, punctuated by many toasts drunk in the powerful *pai kaerh*. After dinner we had a long talk with the general, who was the Communist political director of Inner Mongolia and Shansi Provinces, which between them cover a vast area. He spoke a little English, which he had learnt at school in Peking, but we relied mostly on the interpreter. General Sun had been a school teacher but soon after the Japanese attack in 1937 he joined the Eighth Route Army and organized bands of saboteurs in Hopei and the other North China provinces. He spoke very bitterly against the Central Government.

'We were supposed to be fighting together against a common enemy,' he said. 'We did our part but we never got any help from Chungking. We never got any arms from them. Not directly, anyway' – the general chuckled – 'we got quite a lot of the weapons their troops threw away in their retreats from the Japanese. And we got no help from Soviet Russia either. But we continued to fight the Japanese all the time. And now that the war is over, we and the Central Government are fighting again. It was inevitable. We won't stand for a one party government in China. We don't have one ourselves. Only a proportion of the Yenan Government is permitted to belong to the Chinese Communist Party. We believe a one party government is completely undemocratic.' I am sure that General Sun was talking quite honestly. I believe he really did think in this way at the time. 'The Chinese people are terribly backward politically,' he went on, 'and the first thing we shall have to do is to hold nation-wide political meetings to explain the forthcoming programmes to the people. When at last it comes to voting there must be a secret ballot and an absolutely free vote for everyone – just like you have in your country.

'Certainly anything like a Communist or even a Socialist Government is quite unsuitable for China for a long time to come. The nation is far too conservatively minded for anything like that and it must be allowed to evolve politically in very gradual stages.' The general looked at me.

'You seem surprised,' he said, 'but if you imagine we are going to have anything like the Russian revolution in our country you are greatly mistaken. No, our party concentrates on five main points' – and he began reeling them off on the fingers of one hand. One – national independence. We've got that. Two – a true democracy with a continuance of capitalism but with some control on profits. Three – a general increase in wages to improve the standard of living of the masses and to increase their spending power. Four – a lowering of land rents which would benefit the small farmers who represent eighty per cent of the population. And five – a decrease in taxes on essential products. Increased production should compensate for the loss of revenue caused by this.'

'But General Sun,' I said, 'this isn't Communism. It isn't even Socialism. It's a kind of mild radicalism. You call yourselves Communists but you don't seem to follow any Marxist principles.'

'But we're not Marxists,' he said. 'We believe in ultimate Communism in China, but it will be a Communism of a peculiarly Chinese kind and it will take a long, long time to develop. Nobody alive now will see it. We have a long period of evolution to go through first.' I have often thought since of that conversation with General Sun Chih-yuan and wondered at what stage he came to change those firmly-held convictions of his. For things could hardly have worked out more differently from what he had so confidently predicted. But then General Sun really believed that no Government could survive unless it represented the free will of the people. He had been shocked when I had said that, given a strong man at the top, power distributed among a sufficient number of carefully chosen and well controlled key men, an efficient secret police and a faithful army, the free will of the people was of no consequence whatever.

The next morning General Sun decided to come with us to Ta t'ung. He wanted to go on to Peking to confer with the Communist Commissioner there. It wasn't until we were aboard and the pilot was warming up his engines that the general confided to me that this was his first flight.

'How did you get to Chining, then?'

'I rode there on a pony. A hundred and fifty miles, and mostly across mountains.'

Chining had no airfield. We had landed on a flat piece of semi desert. The pilot put the C-47's nose into the wind and we took off like a fighter, after an incredibly short run. The general took his first flight (which was bumpy) very well and looked out of the window fascinatedly, particularly when we were flying over the Great Wall. Soon after this we could see below us the large walled city of Ta t'ung. We circled round and round because the airfield was tiny. When we did touch down we hit the ground so hard that we bounced thirty or forty feet up into the air again. This happened three times before we at last stayed on the ground. A large crowd gathered, mostly soldiers. Some of them were boys who couldn't have been more than thirteen years old. I took a photograph of Colonel Hudgins with them. He was over six feet tall and looked like Gulliver with the Lilliputians.

After a long wait a car came to meet us. A Chinese colonel jumped out. He didn't speak a word of English and neither did his driver. I had to become the interpreter with my very indifferent Chinese. I was able to tell the colonel who we were and where we wanted to go. I was also able to explain to General

Sun that we would only be away for a couple of hours and to suggest that, all things considered, it might be better if he stayed in the plane and did not accompany us. We weren't sure how it would work out if we brought a Communist general into a Nationalist camp and we didn't feel like taking any chances.

We skirted the massive forty-foot wall and entered Ta t'ung through one of its splendid gateways. It must have been a fine city at one time but it was sinking into the state of decay caused by neglect which seems to be the fate of all Chinese cities. Grass was sprouting between lovely glazed roof tiles. Paint peeled off great brass-studded doors.

After driving for several miles through narrow, crowded streets we stopped outside a large building. A bustling, smiling little Chinese came out to greet us. He was wearing a uniform with the badge of rank of a major-general. His name was Ch'u. When he discovered that I spoke a little of his language he slapped me on the back and burst into a torrent of speech, three quarters of which I didn't understand. Then he led us to the headquarters of the Pacification team. Colonel Hudgins met his opposite number and we arranged to meet again after lunch.

A Belgian missionary came out of the building and we got into conversation. Could I take any mail back to Peking for him? He would be very grateful. What could he do for us? Could he recommend a restaurant where we could have lunch? we asked.

'That's easy,' he said. 'Come to the Catholic Church with me and take pot luck in the refectory.' While we were talking General Ch'u asked if he could have a word with me.

'I wonder if you would do me a great favour,' he said. 'I am very anxious for my wife to go to Peking. Would it be possible for her to travel in your plane?' I knew there was a strict rule that all passengers must have parachutes flying over mountainous country in China and I knew we had no spare parachutes. But I thought I could persuade Colonel Hudgins to stretch a point and I told the general I was confident it could be arranged. I took the opportunity of asking if I could borrow one of his staff cars to take us to lunch. The general arranged this personally.

We were taken into a sitting-room in one of the buildings in the church compound and introduced to another Belgian *père*. Cigarettes were produced and also an enormous bottle of *pai-kaerh*. I don't much like this Chinese vodka made of millet, but when the glasses were poured it turned out to be a powerful but delicious liqueur.

'The base is, of course, *pai-kaerh*,' one of our hosts explained. 'Then we make an infusion of various herbs and add a little sugar and the result is, I think, not bad.' We agreed. We drank three glasses before going into the refectory for a simple but excellent meal. They were wonderful people, the Catholic missionaries in China. They understood the art of living and they really understood and got on with the Chinese. I remembered before the war going to a small town on the borders of Inner Mongolia. It was a walled town and the Catholic priest looked after the defence of the place when it was attacked by minor rival warlords. He explained how he had organized a team who brought up buckets of boiling water and threw them from the battlements on to the attackers. Rupert Bibby said:

'I always thought boiling oil was much better.'

'So it is,' the missionary replied. 'So it is – but, of course, far too expensive.' There are none of these missionaries left now in China and I feel sure they are greatly missed by very many Chinese.

Colonel Hudgins agreed to take General Ch'u's wife back to Peking. A complication arose when the general insisted upon going down to the airfield to see her off, because General Sun was sitting in the plane. There was nothing we could do about it. As we approached the plane, to our horror General Sun stepped out of it, and the two generals stood face to face. They stared at each other and we wondered what was going to happen – they had been fighting on opposite sides up to a few days before. And then they rushed forward to meet each other, embraced, slapped each other on the back, drew back to look again, slapped each other on the back again and burst into tears. It turned out that they were old school friends and hadn't seen each other for fifteen years. It was a most touching reunion. General Ch'u introduced his wife to General Sun and everyone was happy –

not least Colonel Hudgins who had been very apprehensive about this meeting.

As the plane took off I saw the rapidly decreasing figure of General Ch'u waving goodbye from the airfield. His wife carried on an animated conversation with General Sun all the way back to Peking.

As soon as I got back to Peking I decided to return to England. There didn't seem to be any point in staying on in China. There was obviously going to be a succession of cease-fire orders, which at best would be truces. I remembered what a shrewd English businessman had said to me two months before in Shanghai.

'It is the greatest mistake to suppose,' he had said, 'as many people do, that the war has unified China. All it has done is to interrupt the process of her revolution. Now that the war is over that revolution will continue on its natural course.' Perhaps even he, at the time, didn't realize the colossal truth of what he said.

I also had personal reasons for returning to England. I had met a girl whom I had known and been very fond of before the war in Tientsin. She had been in a Japanese internment camp all through the war and now she and her fellow ex-prisoners were being repatriated. I met her in Shanghai and managed to get accommodation on the same ship at least as far as Hong Kong. When I reached Shanghai I found a telegram from the BBC waiting for me. It contained orders to go to Java to cover the fighting that was going on there. A brisk exchange of telegrams followed. I replied that my original assignment in the Far East was only supposed to be for two or three months. I had been in China for six and wanted to come home. They sent a second telegram saying it was essential I go to Java. I replied that I wished to return to England even if it meant handing in my resignation. The BBC's next telegram said that in that case it did. And that was that. I was thrown off the evacuation ship in Hong Kong by a fussy commanding officer who said – I suppose with some reason – that I had no business on a repatriation ship. I flew to Saigon and from there to Singapore, where I was just in time to book a passage in the *Andes*, a former luxury cruise ship, transformed into a troopship. I had to see the purser in order to book my passage. I had been told that he was a keen collector of Chinese porcelain. I showed him two of the bowls I had bought months before in Nanking and he admired them enormously. I said I had plenty more and would be very happy if he would accept them as a slight expression of my appreciation. He had, after all, secured me accommodation at the last minute in a very crowded ship. This turned out to be an astute move on my part. I was given a large four-berth cabin to myself, while lieutenant colonels were sleeping four to a cabin. I kept very quiet about my good fortune.

Chapter Seven

The *Andes* beat the repatriation ship to Southampton by over a week. I drove down to meet it. Unfortunately, so did my girl-friend's mother. That was the first nail in the coffin of our romance. We were together constantly in London, but there was the problem of divorces – on both sides – and of the Roman Catholic religion, on one side. Our love for each other did not survive the strain.

John Ridley returned to London. He was about to set out for Spain for the *Daily Telegraph* and asked me to join him. I said I would meet him in Madrid in about ten days time. Alex Clifford had asked me to stay for a few days in his house in Paris, where Alan and Lucy Moorehead were also staying. Except briefly in Germany I hadn't seen any of them since the war days in Cairo and the Western Desert, so I accepted the invitation with delight. They gave a party one evening and one of the guests was Leila Heaton, who worked at the British Embassy. We dined at a restaurant in the Place du Tertre in Montmartre and when the party ended I took Leila back to the small flat opposite the British Embassy, where she was staying. Inexplicably, I proposed to her that first night and couldn't understand the coolness of the congratulations from my friends the next morning. A few days later I left alone for Spain, promising to return to Paris in a few weeks time to collect Leila – who was going to give notice to the Embassy – and take her back to Spain again with me.

John and I stayed in Madrid in a boarding house in a street just off the Gran Via, which was very comfortable and ridiculously cheap. We stayed there for a fortnight and then travelled north to San Sebastian with Tony Olascuaga, of the Spanish Press Department, with whom we had made great friends. Spain is a country of anomalies. With a semi-Fascist Government in power, you find sometimes examples of a democratic way of life that could not exist anywhere else in the world. The Gaztelupe Club in San Sebastian was one. Tony Olascuaga met a member one day who invited us all to dine there. There were no servants in the club. The members took turns to wait and cook and dispense wine from the '*Bibliòteca*'. And the members ranged from grandees and deputies from the Cortès to fishermen and taxi drivers. The first night we went there the kitchen was in the hands of a marquès and a fisherman. We were waited on by a rich businessman and a shoeshine; a member of parliament poured out our drinks. No money changed hands; the members signed chits and put them in a box and accounts were settled monthly.

One day John, Tony and I lunched in a good restaurant in the old part of San Sebastian. While we were having coffee the sound of singing came from a room down the corridor.

'That's Lola Flores,' Tony said. 'Manolo Caracol is sure to be there, too. Let's go and join them.' At that time Lola Flores and Manolo Caracol were the top flamenco singers in Madrid. When we went into the private room where they had been lunching we found with them Manolete, probably the finest bullfighter of all time, his girl-friend and his doctor, who accompanied him everywhere. We all sat down and Manolete ordered brandy. And then Lola Flores started to sing and Caracol, who wore very heavy rings on all his fingers, accompanied her by rolling his hands on the table to the rhythm of the song and in the end joined in it himself. Manolete said very little and seemed sunk in gloom. He must have known that if he went on fighting, a bull would get him in the long run. He was paid such enormous fees for his appearances and the prices of seats in the rings when he was fighting became so expensive that the crowd increasingly demanded the impossible from him. In fact he only had less than a year to live before he was killed, tragically, by a bull that threw up its head as it died.

John and I travelled through the Asturias and Galicia for a couple of weeks and then I took the train back to Paris from Irun. I spent a week there with Leila and then we took the train to Madrid. In Paris Randolph Churchill, whom I had known well in Cairo during the war, asked me to drive back a Hillman Minx he had left in Madrid a couple of months before.

Leila's sister, Maggie, had a job with the British Embassy in Madrid and we stayed in her flat. I had no international driving licence and to obtain one in Madrid meant not only passing a driving test but also quite a complicated mechanical test – in Spanish. I decided to take a chance with the Spanish police and drive to Gibraltar, where getting a driving licence was simpler. John, Leila and I set out to drive to Gibraltar by a most roundabout route. We made our way leisurely to Cordoba and spent a couple of days there. Then we drove on to Seville and on to Jerez, where the autumn *feria* was just about to begin. John and I had seen a good deal of Stani Domecq in Madrid and he was in Jerez when we arrived, staying with his brother Josè-Ignacio, the managing director of the famous sherry firm of Pedro Domecq. In the fairground the Domecq family kept open house in a large pavilion and members of the family and their friends rode up on splendid horses or arrived in open carriages drawn by four magnificent mules. We went to the bullfights every day – except Leila who couldn't bear them – and never got to bed before five or six o'clock in the morning. At last we drove on to Gibraltar, where I got my driving licence and the very day we left Gibraltar I was stopped by a *guardia civil* and asked to produce it.

We really got our money's worth out of Randolph Churchill's car and drove back to Madrid by way of Malaga and Granada. I was running out of foreign currency and we returned to London and took a flat in Beauchamp Place, where we settled down to wait until I could get my divorce from Maisie.

Just before Christmas I met Laurence Gilliam, head of the BBC Features Department, in the 'Stag', a pub opposite Rothwell

House, the headquarters of the Features and Drama Departments of Sound Radio. I had known Laurence since before the war.

'How would you like to spend Christmas Day on a lighthouse?' he asked me.

'Don't be ridiculous, Laurence,' I said.

'No, I mean it,' he said. 'It's part of the Christmas Programme – we're concentrating on people leading lonely lives – a shepherd up in the Shetlands – that kind of thing. Anyway you wouldn't have to go there until Christmas Eve and you'd be off by Boxing Day at the latest – and the fee is fifty guineas.' Laurence Gilliam's Christmas Day Programme was one of the great annual events in Radio. It was all done 'live', as most broadcasting was in those days and apart from anything else was always something of a technical triumph. Laurence loved it. He was at his best when he was seizing a telephone and demanding Sydney or Vancouver or Hong Kong. I agreed to do the lighthouse story. It was to be the Bishop Rock, just off the Scillies.

'I think, Laurence,' I said, 'it would be a nice idea if I could take a turkey and some other Christmas fare, including a number of bottles.'

'Leave it to me,' Laurence said, 'I'll get it all laid on. It's a very good idea.'

The day before Christmas Eve I took the train to Penzance where I caught the boat for St Mary's in the Scillies. There I was joined by an engineer from Plymouth called Charlie Coombs. On Christmas Eve a launch took us to the Bishop Rock. The weather was perfect with hardly a ripple on the water and we landed very easily on the little jetty cut into the rock. I felt like a kind of Lord Bountiful arriving with all my Christmas 'goodies' and the three lighthouse keepers were delighted at the idea of having an extra good Christmas. There had been a little contretemps about taking alcohol to the lighthouse because lighthouse keepers are supposed to be strictly teetotal on duty, but the Elder Brethren of Trinity House agreed to make an exception. At any rate there was no reason why *I* should be 'dry'.

Between us we hauled the heavy transmitting gear up the

narrow spiral stone stairway and when we reached the radio room, where the lighthouse crew get in touch with St Mary's and other lighthouses every morning, Charlie Coombs started to set it up, ready for the broadcast the following day. I was taken up into the lantern by the head keeper and he gave me all the information I needed to write a script for the broadcast. We also agreed upon some short interviews with him and his staff. Charlie and I were given quite a comfortable cabin-sized room and that night we turned in early.

The broadcast on Christmas Day went off quite well and when it was over we all celebrated with gin and then settled down to the turkey, which one of the lighthouse crew had cooked. The plan was that we should leave the following day. That same evening there was a gale warning. On Boxing Day morning the sea was very rough and the wind was strong. There wasn't a hope of getting off the rock. Day after day it was the same. All the gin and whisky went. The turkey, plum pudding and mince pies became dim memories. The lighthouse keepers shared with us the food they had brought with them increasingly – and understandably – grudgingly.

I was never able to understand what could possibly persuade anyone to become a lighthouse keeper. The pay – in those days at any rate – was miserable. They were not even fed. All that the authorities provided was flour and 'iron rations' to be used only in an emergency. The keepers brought big jars of potted meat – big cubes of meat, stewed and sealed on the top with fat. They brought vegetables and biscuits and chocolate. All that went, too. We ended up on iron rations: bread, hard biscuit and small portions of bully beef.

I had always imagined that lighthouse keepers were industrious folk, spending their time laboriously putting ships into bottles and carving scrimshaw objects of one kind and another. On the Bishop Rock, the head keeper made rope soles which he sewed on to canvas uppers which his wife made in St Mary's. They sold the finished product to the tourists in the summer. The other two keepers did absolutely nothing. They listened almost incessantly to the radio; they played cards in a desultory way and one or two games like ludo and 'L'attaque'. Of course there were the official duties, the trimming of the lamp wicks, keeping the oil supplies up to the mark; and there was the daily baking of bread and cooking and washing up. But what a life!

Every morning I went into the radio room and joined in the conversations with the Wolf Rock and the other lighthouses and with people in St Mary's, including the lifeboat chief. Although I had never seen any of these people, after a week or two I felt I knew them quite well. One morning after we had been marooned for just three weeks, the lifeboat man said to me:

'The wind seems to have gone down quite a bit and we haven't had the boat in the water for weeks. I thought we might get her out tomorrow and have a go at getting you chaps off. I'm not promising anything because the sea is still pretty rough, but if you're game we'll see what we can do.'

'If you can get me aboard that lifeboat alive, that's all I ask,' I said. Charlie Coombs had been listening to the conversation.

'Here, I don't know that I like this idea,' he said. 'What about all my gear?'

'I should have thought that could wait until later,' I said. 'But if you don't feel like coming, you can always let me go first and then we can say the wind and the sea made it impossible to get you off. Maybe it will, at that.'

The 'prisoners on the lighthouse' had already achieved considerable fame. Helicopters had been buzzing round the Bishop Rock daily. I had done a special broadcast for an American network, which had gone on the air from coast to coast. We had even made Time Magazine. The following morning preparations were made to get us off. The seas were still so high that we would have to be lowered by a winch operating on the lantern gallery, instead of one far lower down the tower, which from the top to sea level was well over 150 feet.

At last the lifeboat arrived. Fortunately it was a very large one. But it was bobbing up and down alarmingly in the heavy swell. I stood in a doorway about two thirds way down the tower. From a hundred feet above they lowered a rope. A big loop had been tied in it and through this I stuck one leg. Then I hung on desperately to the rope and from far above me they started lowering the winch. It occurred to me that it would be very difficult to judge vertical distance with any accuracy from so far above, and the fact that the boat was rising and falling at least ten feet in the swell didn't help things. I became acutely aware of a sharp anchor fluke on the deck which seemed to be directly below me. I had uncomfortable premonitions of descending with a jolt just as the boat rose swiftly to meet me and landing on that anchor fluke. Fortunately it didn't work out like that. I landed gently on the deck just as the boat was at the bottom of the swell and I could have had a pocketful of eggs and wouldn't have broken one. Charlie Coombs came down safely a few minutes later. Celebrations in the hotel at St Mary's. Plenty of publicity on the radio and in the newspapers. Back in London I wrote an article for *Picture Post* and was invited to lunch with the Elder Brethren of Trinity House – though I fear that anything I broadcast or wrote could scarcely have stimulated recruitment of lighthouse-keepers.

One thing the ordeal of the Bishop Rock did for me was to get me back into broadcasting again. It also was the beginning of my long association with my great patron in the BBC and even greater friend, Laurence Gilliam. It was Laurence who decided later in that year, 1947, that I should go to Spain to do a feature programme on Holy Week in Seville – including a commentary on a bullfight.

I was on a short visit to Castle Ward when the engineer who was to accompany me – this was some years before correspondents took small tape recorders with them and made their own recordings – it was before the BBC used tape recorders at all – telephoned me one evening.

'Don't you think it might be a good idea,' he said, 'if you had a secretary with you on this trip. I think it would save you a lot of donkeywork and I happen to know the very girl. She did secretarial work at the Nuremberg Trials and understands this kind of thing very well.' I did some quick thinking. I knew the engineer had been at Nuremberg for some months. Obviously the girl was his girlfriend. I didn't want a secretary at all. But on the other hand I didn't want a disgruntled and un-cooperative engineer. I said 'All right'.

We reached Madrid a few days before Holy Week. It was packed. I was fixed up. I was staying with John Marks, who later married Leila's sister, Maggie. We tried all the large and small hotels, all the *pensiòns* for the engineer and his girlfriend. Everything was booked up. Then Maggie said why didn't they stay at her flat – she was in a nursing home at the time. It seemed the obvious solution. There was a room with a large double bed. Unfortunately it appeared that the relationship between the engineer and his girl was strictly platonic. While I was pondering upon this curious situation the telephone rang. One of the *pensiòns* we had telephoned earlier and asked to ring back if they had any cancellations, came through to say that they had two small rooms. Maybe it was the fact that this *pensiòn* had the rather inauspicious name of 'La Concepciòn' that persuaded the couple to opt for Maggie's double bed. (I understood later that even this did not in any way change the nature of the relationship.)

At least we had booked rooms in advance at the Hotel Madrid in Seville. We made some remarkable recordings of the *Semana Santa*, largely through the help of the curator of the museum in Seville, Juan Lafita, who smoothed out all obstacles – of which there were many. We recorded some wonderful *saetas*, those flamenco outbursts of religious fervour which some individual standing on a balcony feels impelled to deliver as a procession goes past. The images from the different churches of Seville, dressed in magnificent robes, adorned with necklaces and rings of fabulous value, lent for the occasion by the rich women of the city, were carried on huge, heavy, canopied 'floats' by the *cofradias*, the members of the religious fraternities. And the *cofradias* followed, often barefoot, wearing long robes and sinister, tall, conical cowls, with slits for them to see through, like members of the Spanish Inquisition or Ku Klux Klansmen.

We recorded splendid Holy Week music in Seville Cathedral and one day, to give us a rest from the processions that went on uninterruptedly day and night, Juan Lafita took us out to lunch in an attractive village just outside Seville. While we were lunching some boys broke into the recording van and stole a few relatively unimportant objects. Lafita was outraged. He stood on the steps of the van and delivered an impassioned oration to a large crowd that had gathered.

'This is a disgraceful and appalling thing for this village to have done to foreign visitors to our country!' he thundered. 'It is even more unforgivable because they come from England, a country I once visited, where the milkmen leave full bottles of milk on the doorsteps of peoples' houses and nobody dreams of touching them.' This had evidently enormously impressed Juan Lafita. His impassioned oratory resulted in the return of the small small coils of wire and batteries that had been taken.

On Easter Saturday we went out to a roadhouse a few miles outside Seville where, traditionally, the bulls which will be fought the following day, can be seen. It was here that I met the great *torero* Juan Belmonte, one of the most celebrated bullfighters of all time. His brother was the director of the Seville bullring and I asked him to use his influence for me to get permission to take my recording machinery into the *callejòn*, the corridor that runs between the front spectator seats and the barrier round the bullring itself. This was granted without any trouble.

At the time that Belmonte was beginning to become famous, the greatest matador in Spain was Joselito. As a young man, Belmonte had something of a triumph in the Seville ring and his supporters carried him on their shoulders over the Guadalquivir to the suburb of Triana, burst into the church of San Jacinto, dragged out the 'float' which in Holy Week carries one of Seville's most celebrated and revered 'Virgins', La Macarena, put Belmonte on it and started to drag him in triumph through Triana. They had scarcely got out of the door when an outraged priest rushed up to the procession.

'What appalling blasphemy is this?' he shouted. 'To take the carriage that bears our most sacred image to carry a common bullfighter!' He paused, out of breath. 'Mind you,' he muttered, 'if it had been Joselito it would have been quite a different matter.'

We arrived at the Seville *Plaza de Toros* a good three quarters of an hour before the *corrida* was due to begin. We installed the heavy disc recording machine in the *callejòn* and were just beginning some level tests when a man came up in a great state of excitement.

'Take all these things out of the *callejòn*,' he said, 'I can't have the place cluttered up with all that machinery!'

'Oh no,' I said, 'I have permission from Señor Belmonte to bring this recording apparatus into the *callejòn*. I am doing a special broadcast for the British Radio on the Easter Sunday *corrida*.' The man relented a little.

'Well, *you* can stay in the *callejòn*,' he said, 'but you'll have to get all that machinery outside, through that gate there—'

'But Señor Belmonte—'

'Señor Belmonte may be the Director of the Seville *Plaza de Toros*, but *I* am the manager on the spot and it is *I* who make the final decisions. I am not going to be responsible for the safety of that doubtless valuable machinery. Suppose a bull jumps out of the ring into the *callejòn*? What then?'

'I hope we're not going to have bulls like that,' I said, 'or I'm not going to have much to broadcast about.'

'I hope so too, but you never know.' So the engineer set up the recording gear just through a gate under the front seats and I held the microphone on the end of a long lead.

Out of the six bulls no less than three jumped out of the ring into the corridor. Each time I hurriedly put down the microphone and like everyone else jumped quickly into the ring, until they swung a gate across the corridor which made an opening into the ring. The bull returned through this and we all hastily jumped back into the *callejòn*. Out of the lot only one bull was fairly good and without too much exaggeration I was able to make it all sound dramatic and exciting. (The broadcast caused a storm of protest from cruelty to animals and anti-blood-sports organizations later.)

Chapter Eight

My next job for Laurence Gilliam was a much more important one. I don't know why I was chosen to be one of the team of reporters to cover the handover of power in India and Pakistan. My previous knowledge of the Indian sub-continent was confined to a landing in the middle of the night at Karachi airport two years before and another a few hours later at Delhi. But maybe this was enough to justify my being selected as one of the team. My colleagues were Louis MacNeice, Francis Dillon, Wynford Vaughan Thomas, Richard Sharpe and a young man who looked like a youthful edition of the late Sir Stafford Cripps.

I started off in New Delhi, where I met Bob Stimson, the BBC correspondent in India, and Richard Sharpe. We were all invited to tea by the Mountbattens at the Viceregal Lodge. We sat down to a typical English country house tea round a large circular table. When we had finished and the tea things had been cleared away, Lord Mountbatten talked to us for about three quarters of an hour. I swear if I could have had a hidden microphone and a tape recorder and I had later played back that discourse, that anyone listening would have been convinced that Lord Mountbatten had been reading from a carefully prepared script and that he really knew how to read a script so that it sounded as if he were adlibbing. But there wasn't any script and Lord Mountbatten *was* adlibbing, rattling off the names of dozens of Indian States one after another, saying how they would react – everyone was going to toe the line, there might be a little superficial trouble in Hyderabad and Kashmir, but that was all. If only it had all worked out like that how nice it would have been. But within a few days of that confident talk one of the great mass migrations of history was in progress and some of the bloodiest massacres.

I was assigned to Karachi, where I waited for weeks for something to happen and nothing ever did. Wynford Vaughan Thomas was reporting hideous atrocities in Amritsar and Lahore and I took the train to the Punjab to see if there were any stories I could get. But things had quietened down by then and in any case it was Wynford's territory. On the way back to Karachi I shared an air-conditioned compartment with a Sikh officer. He was a nice fellow but throughout the journey I wished I were sharing a compartment with *any*one else. The Sikhs had been responsible for some particularly horrible massacres of Muslims in Amritsar and were anathema to all Pakistanis. Every time the train stopped at a station I expected an enraged mob to storm into the compartment and kill the Sikh – and me too, as literally a fellow-traveller.

Back in Karachi I teamed up with Freddie Palmer, whom I had known during the war in the Western Desert, when he was a War Office cameraman. We did a few trips in Sind Province and Freddie, who was now working for the *Weekly Illustrated of India*, took pictures and I wrote a series of articles for the paper. I had been trying for some time to get an interview with Mr Jinnah. Pakistan had only been in existence for a few weeks and, as its first Governor General, Mr Jinnah was naturally a very busy man. But at last I was told to be at Government House at nine o'clock the following morning.

Just as I was leaving the Palace Hotel, Freddie Palmer came running up.

'D'you mind if I come along with you, Eddy? I might get a few good pics.' I wasn't overjoyed at the idea.

'All right Freddie, so long as you understand that I do my piece first.'

'Of course, cock. Naturally. After you've done your piece I'll get a few shots of the old *Qaid-i-Azam – Zindabad*!'

'Okay, Freddie, just so long as you remember that I do my interview first.'

At Government House we went to the office of Jinnah's ADC.

'If you wouldn't mind waiting a few minutes,' this young Pakistani said, 'Mr Jinnah and his sister are just finishing breakfast.'

'Of course—'

'Just the thing!' Freddie shouted. 'Excuse me—' and before anyone could stop him he darted out of the room with his camera and ran up the stairs. That was the last I saw of him for over an hour. I didn't see Mr Jinnah for an hour either. When I finally did see him I found him remarkably amenable. It was a most satisfactory interview. Of course I didn't know at the time the kind of softening-up process he had undergone at the hands of Freddie Palmer. I knew nothing about that until I got back to the hotel. Freddie was waiting on the verandah.

'Nice work, Freddie,' I said. 'I hope you got all you wanted. The fact that I might have missed my interview didn't worry you too badly, I hope?'

'But you got it all right, didn't you, Eddy? Of course you did! Sorry but you know I simply couldn't miss the chance. I got it. I got the lot. "A day in the life of the old *Qaid-i-Azam*" – super it was. You know when I went up the stairs—'

'I certainly do—'

'Well, I bust into the room at the top and there 'e was, with Miss Fatima sitting opposite 'im, eating 'is breakfast. Bananas they were eating – would you believe it! Well, I got that one quick before 'e could even screw 'is eyeglass into 'is eye. Caught 'im right off balance. Then I followed up with a quick one.

' "I noticed on the way upstairs, Mr Jinnah, that there was a billiards room. Are you partial to a game of billiards, Mr Jinnah?" He'd got 'is eyeglass in 'is eye by this time.'

' "Well, I, ah—" 'e started off. I didn't let 'im get any further.

' "Now if I could just have a shot of you knocking the balls about," I said to 'im, "it'd be just the thing." 'E was like a lamb. Finished 'is banana and went right down to the billard room with me. Oh, I got a beautiful shot of 'im sighting down the cue just going to bring off a nice natural angle. Lovely! Well, then we went down to 'is office. 'E wasn't feeling any pain any more now. I got a couple of beautiful shots of 'im with the ADC bringing in the morning mail—'

'Oh, that's where the ADC got to while I was—'

'Yes, sorry, Eddy, but it made a smashing sequence. Well, then we went into the drawing-room and Miss Fatima was there. I don't know if you went into the drawing-room, Eddy? You did? Well you'll 'ave noticed the pictures of the King and Queen. Couldn't miss that. I got a lovely shot of the old *Qaid-i-Azam* standing under the picture of the Queen and Miss Fatima under the King. Beautiful. Then we went out into the garden. Lovely flowers there. I said to 'im:

' "D'you like flowers, Mr Jinnah?"

' "Well, I, ah," 'e started off again.

' "Now, if I could just 'ave Miss Fatima picking some flowers and maybe handing you one for a buttonhole – like that. Yes, that's the ticket. Hold it one moment. That's it. Got it. Lovely. Now, Mr Jinnah," I said, "I noticed that you and Miss Fatima 'ave two lovely little dogs – what kind of dogs are they if I might ask?"

' "They're Australian dogs called Sydney Silkies," old Jinnah said.

' "Oh yes, of course," I said – never 'eard of breed, naturally – "now if I could just 'ave one last pic of you and Miss Fatima playing with the little dogs?" but 'e wouldn't buy that one.

' "Mister Palmer" 'e said, "I don't think you can say I 'aven't been co-operative this morning. But 'ere I must draw the line. I am 'ead of a Muslim state and dogs are not well looked upon by people of the Muslim religion. My sister and I are perhaps more broadminded in these matters, but I am afraid that it would not do at all to 'ave a picture published showing us playing with dogs." 'E wouldn't 'ave it at any price.' Freddie sighed. 'Well, you can't 'ave everything, I suppose.'

'No, not everything,' I said. You really had to hand it to Freddie Palmer. He really got away with murder over this sequence of pictures of Jinnah. And how it paid off! Very shortly afterwards Jinnah died and Freddie's pictures were used – and paid for – all over the world.

It became evident that nothing was going to happen in Karachi beyond overcrowding by the hordes of refugees that streamed into the capital. I decided to go south, to Hyderabad. Hyderabad and Kashmir both had the same problem – in inverse ratio. Kashmir had a Hindu Maharajah and aristocracy and a predominantly Muslim population. In Hyderabad it was the other way round. The Nizam and the aristocracy were Muslim and the population almost entirely Hindu.

Freddie Palmer came with me and so did the BBC engineer, Jimmy Caldwell. We all travelled in the BBC recording van. The Nizam of Hyderabad, who lived in an exaggeratedly frugal way himself, had a guest house for visitors like ourselves, which was like a free Ritz. The rooms were magnificent and the food and wines marvellous. A Swiss maître d'hotel looked after us wonderfully and if we wanted to make an expedition in the country we always took with us a hamper containing a superb picnic lunch and a couple of bottles of champagne. Staying at the guest house was the *Times* correspondent, Ian Morrison, a man of enormous charm and the best foreign correspondent I ever met and I have known almost all the good ones of my generation. What a tragedy it was that he with two other friends of mine, Uni Nayer, the Indian journalist and Christopher Buckley of the *Daily Telegraph*, should have been so uselessly and unnecessarily killed in Korea, when their jeep ran over a mine miles behind the front.

In Hyderabad at the time were Sir Walter and Lady Monckton. Sir Walter was and had been for years the constitutional adviser to the Nizam and spent three months every year in Hyderabad. He lived in a magnificent house with a large garden where all the trees were lit up by fairy lights. He entertained on a lavish scale. For luncheon he kept open house and Ian Morrison and I were told to turn up whenever we liked. We took this invitation seriously and often lunched at the Moncktons. Walter Monckton told me once:

'I really make very little out of being constitutional adviser to the Nizam, although I am paid a stupendous fee. But I am making a great deal at the Bar just now and by the time surtax has been busy there is really very little left out of it. But – one thing I do insist upon is that during these three months I spend in Hyderabad every year, I live like a maharajah.' And he did. He lived on a far more princely scale than his employer. I once asked Walter Monckton if all the stories about the Nizam's frugality were true. Among other things they said he drove about in an old T-model Ford.

'Oh no, the T-model Ford story is nonsense,' Walter Monckton said, 'but he does have a very modest car. I think it's a Studebaker or something. I know his son, the Prince of Berar keeps his Rolls-Royce well hidden. But he really is an extraordinary man,' Sir Walter went on. 'Do you know, in all the years I have worked for him I have never been invited to his house for a private, informal meeting or dinner or anything. I have, of course, been to the Palace for official functions, but that's all. I talk business with him in his office – and you should see his office! It's a long room with a lot of clerks and secretaries typing away at cheap deal desks. There's a wood and glass partition at the far end and behind this is the Nizam's office. You can hear the clatter of the typewriters all the time. He will discuss State secrets with me in English at the top of his voice, fondly imagining that none of his clerks understand the language – and I know that nearly all of them speak it fluently. And then, while we are talking, tea will be brought in. Lipton's tea in chipped, white canteen cups and – well you certainly wouldn't think he's one of the richest men in the world, if not the richest.'

With Ian Morrison I drove down to Golconda and one of the things I shall remember all my life is watching the flocks of peacocks flying in at dusk to roost on the battlements of the ancient fort. And we travelled, too, far to the north – Hyderabad is about as large as France – to the Ajanta and Ellora Caves. When we were asked to pay for our railway tickets and for our hotels rooms in Aurangabad, we indignantly refused. We had been the guests of the Nizam for some time and we had become accustomed to everything being free. We got away with it.

We marvelled at the Ajanta and Ellora Caves and spent several days looking at the wonderful temples and sculptures, carved out of the solid rock. And, at Ajanta we admired the superb paintings.

I liked southern India and decided to travel further south, to Bangalore in the state of Mysore. Freddie Palmer and Jimmy Caldwell stayed on in Hyderabad. In the hotel in Bangalore I met the correspondent of the *Madras Mail*, a Brahmin called Subramanion. We used to eat together in the hotel quite often – he keeping to a strict vegetarian diet. Subramanion had spent some time in London at one period of his life and had worked for a London estate agent. I have never met anyone with such an encyclopaedic knowledge of London. He was better than any taxi driver. He told me it was his hobby, in his free time, to walk miles and miles through every part of the city.

We had long talks about the caste system. Once I asked him if he would accept an invitation to a meal from Sir Ramaswami Mudaliar, the Dewan of Mysore State. I knew he wasn't particularly high caste.

'Certainly not,' replied the little Brahmin correspondent of the *Madras Mail*. 'It would be quite out of the question. It would be all right for him to come and eat at my house – provided, of course, that my wife wasn't present.' In Bangalore I saw a good deal of a great Indian personality, Sir Mirza Ismael. Sir Mirza had once been Dewan of Hyderabad but he spent so much money beautifying the city by pulling down the walls that hid some of the loveliest buildings, that the parsimonious Nizam sacked him. He then became Dewan of Mysore and built some fabulous water gardens in Mysore city on which he spent countless *lakhs* of rupees. Everybody said that Sir Mirza had really overdone it this time but the gardens turned out to be an enormous commercial success. An entrance fee was charged and thousands of people came from all over India to see them.

One day Subramanion asked me if I would like to make a

day trip to Mysore. He had to go there to get material for an article. I said I would be delighted. The next day he asked if I would mind if his wife and son came in the car too.

'For heaven's sake, Manion, it's your car – of course I don't mind.' It was a very pleasant journey. We stopped on the way at Seringapatam and went to see Tippoo Sahib's exquisite little pleasure palace, where the walls were decorated with enchanting frescoes of battle scenes of the eighteenth-century wars; the French soldiers all with little pointed beards and moustaches and the British with brick-red faces.

We had made an early start and reached Mysore at lunch time.

'I expect you'd like a European meal,' Manion said, 'I'll drop you at the hotel and pick you up in about an hour. Okay?' I felt I ought to refuse but I had eaten a lot of curry in the last days and the idea of having Western food again was tempting. I said I would do as he suggested. After lunch the Subramanion family came to pick me up and we wandered all through Mirza Ismael's splendid gardens with their artificial waterfalls and lakes. Then we toured the city and when dinner time came Manion said there was a good European restaurant overlooking the gardens where I would get a good meal. Once again I didn't argue, though I felt I was being very rude. Later I discovered that I would have embarrassed him horribly if I had insisted on sitting down to a meal with his wife – even though I was a foreigner and the question of caste didn't arise.

I took the train back from Bangalore to Hyderabad and Freddie, Jimmy and I drove north to Bombay. We managed to get rooms in a kind of dormitory right at the top of the celebrated Taj Mahal Hotel, which was anything but in keeping with the splendour of the public rooms downstairs. The other occupant of our dormitory was a former official of the Punjab Railway called Bumstead, a very amusing and engaging fellow. One day when we were all out together we saw a shop whose proprietor was called Arsiwallah and, from then on, Bumstead was known by no other name.

In Bombay we all went one day to the old part of the city, which few foreigners seem to visit. In the centre of it is a street which must be one of the richest in the world, but nobody would think so at first glance. It is called Sheik Menon Street. Gharry drivers shouted at pedestrians to get out of the way. Bullock carts rumbled by. Sometimes, looking quite out of place, a smart car tried to force its way down the narrow street. Men and women sold every conceivable – and inconceivable – thing. Just off Sheik Menon Street is one of Bombay's most famous Hindu temples the Mumbai Devi. Mumbai is the patron goddess of Bombay and the name 'Bombay' is a corruption of Mumbai. There was a notice outside the temple saying: 'For Hindus Only', but I was invited inside. People were bathing in a large 'tank'. At the side of the 'tank' long-haired, long-bearded holy men squatted, meditating. Just outside the temple a bearded man was dancing to the accompaniment of a slow, rhythmic chant. Sacred cows wandered about as they chose, munching melon rinds or any refuse they could find. It was India as I had always imagined it. Near the temple a lane runs off Sheik Menon Street. It is called Phul Gulley. Here they sell flowers for the temple. In the middle of the lane were huge baskets filled with brilliantly coloured flower petals. The flower sellers picked them up in handfuls, put them on scales and sold them by weight. Little girls were making lovely garlands from roses, tuberoses and marigolds.

In Sheik Menon Street there were shops with painted masks of Hindu deities and tufts of hair from the tails of sacred cows. In other shop windows were marvellous gold-embroidered saris some of which cost a small fortune. Other shops sold cheap plastic goods. None of this sounds as if Sheik Menon Street is a particularly rich one. But at one end of it is the Bombay Cotton Market, where millions of rupees change hands every day. I walked by it and was almost deafened by the concerted roar of a wildly gesticulating, excited crowd of brokers screaming their bids. Further down the street is the Bombay Bullion Market. Inside, there is an even wilder scene of pandemonium. The market is a long room divided up into stalls like a Portobello

Road antique market but with a wide, open space running down the middle. Above each stall a thick rope hangs from the ceiling. A man would suddenly seize a rope and propel himself across the room, shouting an order or an acceptance of an offer to or from one of the crowd of brokers in the centre of the floor. Then he would swing back, raising his legs to avoid hitting people in the middle of the room, and make a neat landing back in his stall. I have never seen business done in such a frenetic manner and I thought the Shanghai Gold Bar Exchange was crazy enough. But Shanghai was sedate compared with Bombay.

Outside this madhouse was a high pile of silver ingots. I tried to pick one up without success. They weighed 140 lbs each. Two men were wheeling a truck stacked with these great blocks of silver. There were no police to supervise this operation. The men were just pushing all this wealth through the teeming crowd.

Shops which were not much more than holes in the wall lined the street near the bullion market. Brokers and merchants were squatting in them on white, cotton mattresses, with telephones beside them. Behind were piles of gold and silver bars. I watched a man hacking a gold bar in half with a hammer and a cold chisel. The bar was the size of a small brick. When he had finished he weighed one of the halves on a pair of scales. It was a little too heavy for his jeweller customer so he hacked a corner off it. It was just like a grocer cutting a little off a piece of cheese that weighed too much. I asked the broker if I could hold one of these gold bars. Smiling, he handed me one. It was so heavy I nearly dropped it. He told me it was worth 35,000 rupees – about £2,600. I thought it was the largest amount of solid gold I was ever likely to hold in my hand. But there were dozens of similar bricks in this one little shop.

The broker introduced himself. His name was Mr Manilal. 'Have you ever seen a touchstone?' he asked. I hadn't. From a drawer he took out what looked like a jet black cobblestone. 'Let me have your gold watch,' he said. I pulled it off my wrist and he rubbed it across the stone. It left a smear of gold on the black surface. 'Eighteen carat,' Mr Manilal said. 'Look, you can compare it with this colour chart of the different grades of gold, but

I know them without having to look at it.' He tried Jimmy's watch on the touchstone. 'Sorry I'm afraid we can't do better than nine carat.' Mr Manilal said these touchstones come from the bed of the Jumna river and they are very expensive. But they are invaluable for grading gold. Then he asked us if we would like to see his silver foundry. He left a boy in charge of his gold shop and we walked along Sheik Menon Street and down a narrow side alley. At the back of a long dark room there was a furnace. In the foreground were a lot of large baskets filled with silver jewellery, bracelets and necklaces and ornaments of different kinds. Some of them were very beautiful. Mr Manilal said he had agents who travelled round the villages buying these silver pieces.

'It seems a shame to melt down some of those things,' I said. 'Some of them are lovely.'

'Pick whatever you like,' Mr Manilal said, 'I'll weigh it and you can have it at the price of scrap silver.' I chose several charming pieces and they cost ridiculously little.

In a side turning running past the Mumbai Devi temple is Bombay's pearl market, which has been famous for centuries. In the old days Arabs used to bring their pearls from the Persian Gulf in dhows to this great centre of the pearl trade. Nowadays they fly to Bombay. It's safer and quicker and anyway what is the price of an air ticket when you are carrying merchandise worth tens of thousands of pounds? And while, in the old days, the pearls were tested by experts who relied on their eyes and sense of touch, now they have become much more up to date and in all these poky little shops they have X-ray apparatus which detect flaws with far greater certainty.

This same little street is also the greatest centre of the diamond trade in India. For three centuries diamond merchants have examined their gems under an old brass lamp on the first floor of a tumbledown-looking old shop. I watched them weighing diamonds on delicate scales and examining them through jewellers' lenses. Some of these merchants didn't look as though they had two rupees to rub together, but in the course of a day they handle jewels worth tens of thousands of pounds.

And there were countless jewellers' shops with vast quantities of cheaper wares – gold and silver rings, bracelets, necklaces and anklets. Nowhere have I seen such wealth concentrated in such a small area. The value of the jewels, gold and silver tucked away in these shabby little shops must be almost incalculable. Sheik Menon Street and the little alleys leading off it would make Bond Street or the Rue de la Paix almost seem like Petticoat Lane in comparison.

I left Freddie Palmer and the others in Bombay and took the train to Delhi. On it I met one of the advisers of the Maharajah of Bhopal. He said why didn't I come and stay for as long as I liked, while it was still possible to offer such hospitality? I have often thought what a difference it would have made to my life if I had accepted his offer. I was greatly tempted to do so. But I thought I should return to Leila. because there was now no obstacle to our getting married. However, I felt I might as well see a little more of India before I left so from Delhi I drove to Agra. I had just finished dinner in Laurie's hotel when the BBC correspondent, who looked like the late Sir Stafford Cripps, came in and suggested that I accompany him to see the Taj Mahal by moonlight. I said I would be delighted to do so if there were any moon. As it was it was one of the darkest nights I ever remember and I proposed compromising by getting up early the next morning and seeing it by sunrise. But over the Taj Mahal 'Sir Stafford' was a purist. It must be seen by moonlight even if there wasn't any moon. So off he went into the coal-black night. He returned in an hour and had the grace to admit that he had been able to see absolutely nothing and joined me the following morning.

I have still not seen the Taj Mahal by moonlight but it could not possibly look more beautiful than it did when I saw it, pale honey-coloured until the sun began to rise and then passing through a series of delicately changing pinks until, when the sun was well up, it shone in all its glory, a dazzling white.

Chapter Nine

Within a few weeks of my return to London, Leila and I were married. After Caxton Hall her father and stepmother gave a reception at the Mayfair, which was a sad affair because I think nobody thought the marriage would last long. Certainly nobody expected it to last so *short* a time. Soon after we had returned from a brief honeymoon, Laurence Gilliam told me he wanted me to do another 'spot' in his Christmas Roundup. This time it was to be a report from the most damaged city in Europe, Warsaw. So I flew to Warsaw, where I was met by the *doyen* of BBC Engineers, Harvey Sarney, who had made the journey by road in the old recording van which had been his since the landings in Normandy.

On Christmas Eve Harvey and I were recording carols sung in the Church of the Holy Cross. We were sitting in the van outside the church in the bitter cold, listening to the music on the loudspeaker, when a girl came up. She looked only about seventeen. She told us her father, mother, brothers and sisters had all been killed in the 1944 uprising. She looked more like a peasant than a city dweller, with her high cheekbones and apple cheeks. Without being in the least abashed, she told us she was a street walker. But she was alone on Christmas Eve and she had come to have a bit of company. We gave her a drink.

'You want something warm on a night like this,' she said and scurried off into the darkness. In ten minutes she was back with a steaming can of coffee. She left us when we went to get a couple of hours' sleep before going to record more carols in another church at six o'clock in the morning. Once again we were listening to the loudspeaker when we saw a familiar figure coming down the road carrying a large can.

'You told me you'd be down here and I thought you could do with another hot drink,' she said. She had walked nearly two miles on this bitterly cold night to bring us a can of coffee. It was infinitely touching. But it was typical of the friendliness of the Poles and of the terrible things that had happened to them during the war. We gave her a warm jersey and a pair of thick woollen gloves and she went off delighted.

The Polish carol singing was wonderful and it made the background to a moving Christmas broadcast. Laurence agreed to my staying on in Poland and doing a New Year's broadcast from the High Tatra Mountains, down by the Czechoslovak border in the south.

After a few days' stay in Krakow, the lovely old Galician capital, which had been totally undamaged in the war, we drove on south to Zakopane, Poland's great winter sports resort in the High Tatra. In Zakopane I forgot completely I was behind the Iron Curtain. It might have been Switzerland except that it was much more fun. We spent New Year's Eve in a little inn high up in the mountains and made some wonderful records of the Gurals, the highlanders of Poland, who wear narrow white trousers made of a thick homespun, with black stripes down the seams, and pom-poms on their shoes. The rest of the costume consists of a short embroidered jacket, a hat like a shallow bowler with a string of cowrie shells instead of a ribbon and a magnificent wide leather belt decorated with silver and brass.

They played their strange, wild music on fiddles, 'cellos and bagpipes, they danced and they drank – they certainly drank! And we drank level with them. We left the inn at three in the morning and drove erratically down to the town to end up the night at the 'Gong', Zakopane's best night club. There we met two girls from the British Embassy in Warsaw who were on holiday. We didn't go to bed at all. We took the funicular straight up to the ski-ing slopes and in the crisp, cold air we all felt wonderful. Later in the day we discovered we had made quite a reputation for ourselves. We were still up and about, but the party in the mountains had been too much for the tough Gurals and their orchestra had already missed two appointments.

We stayed several days in Zakopane and in the course of them I once again fell in love – with one of the girls from the British Embassy. I had to leave Zakopane at last but we arranged to meet in a week's time in Warsaw.

We drove a little way from Krakow to see the famous salt mine where a group of workers spent years carving a cathedral out of the solid salt. Like the sculptures at Ellora in Hyderabad, which are carved in one piece from the living rock, so this cathedral, chapels, altars, figures and everything is cut out of the solid salt.

I found a telegram waiting for me in Warsaw telling me to go to Gdynia to cover the story of a shipment of Polish coal to England. Harvey Sarney and I had a date that night with the girls from the Embassy and several other people. But we were told it only took six or seven hours to drive to Gdynia so we planned to leave directly after dinner and drive through the night. In the end we didn't get away until after midnight. By breakfast time we hadn't even reached the old frontier of East Prussia.

The road northwards was good and there seemed to be no hurry to cross the Vistula. We reached a place where a bridge was marked on the map and we headed for it. But the bridge had been destroyed and a new one was only half finished. A man said he believed there was a car ferry about twenty miles further north. There were no more bridges; they had all been destroyed. We had passed the last one over a hundred miles back at a place where we had stopped for breakfast.

We drove on northwards through the lovely old East Prussian villages, with their black and white timbered houses; through the wonderful old town of Marienburg, where the medieval castle of the Teutonic Knights was half smashed by shellfire. The Germans had held out in this ancient fortress and the Russian artillery had in the end blasted them out of it at point blank range.

Return to the P.O.W. camp Sulmona. My old hut

Naples 1948

It wasn't all work – Venice, 1948

From the top of a high embankment we looked down on the grey, sluggish Vistula. There, sure enough, was the car ferry. It was already past noon but we had almost reached the Baltic. We were only thirty miles from Danzig and Gdynia was not much further on. But the car ferry was not working. Pack ice had broken the chains that pulled it across the river. There was nothing to do but turn back. At last we crossed the Vistula on a temporary wooden bridge built by the Russians and reached Danzig in a state bordering on coma at 5.30 in the morning. We had been driving off and on for over thirty hours. Danzig was in ruins and there wasn't a hotel in the entire city. In Zoppot, a seaside resort half way between Danzig and Gdynia we fortunately found a first class hotel. We booked a room and told an astonished hall porter to call us in an hour.

The coal ship was still in Gdynia. Its captain was an old Scotsman and when I produced the microphone he started off in fine style. In a broad Glasgow accent he almost spat into the instrument:

'Coals to Newcastle! Little did I ever think it would come to that!' This was not, perhaps, quite the line the BBC wanted for their *Progress Report* on coal, but it seemed to me to be an admirably concise summing up of the situation.

We started on our return journey at four o'clock in the afternoon, expecting to be back in Warsaw some time in the early hours of the following morning. After a series of black mishaps we didn't arrive until 9 the next evening.

I spent a wonderful week in Warsaw. I was very much in love again and convinced that this time I had found the real answer and that my marriage to Leila had been a terrible mistake. The latter assumption was a true one. I arrived back in London late at night and took a taxi to our flat. There was, inevitably, a painful scene, made far worse because Leila said she was expecting a baby. I felt that it would be impossible to carry on, however, and we parted. I went first to stay with my sister, Mary, and from there to my old friend from Finland and Western

Desert days, Richard Busvine and his wife Gina. Over the weeks that followed there were many telephone conversations between London and Warsaw. I also became involved in a series of programmes for the BBC on British industry called: *Progress Report*, which from a public relations point of view did little to endear the Corporation to British industrialists.

At Stewart and Lloyd's steelworks at Corby, for example, they went to immense trouble to cut a huge iron cylinder in half so that the recording van could get near enough to the coke ovens for a recording to be made. I realized that it would be impossible to hold the microphone when the white hot coke was pushed out into waiting railway trucks, so I tied it to a pole and for safety's sake wrapped a piece of wet cloth round it. The heat was so tremendous when the ovens opened that there was a puff of steam from the microphone and then the instrument caught fire and started burning merrily. The engineer, inside the van, saw none of this.

'Recording all right?' I asked.

'First class.'

'You astonish me. Come and have a look at the mike!' He was horrified and begged me not to tell the story over the air. It wouldn't have made any difference if I had included it in my script or not because the whole coke oven sequence was cut by the producer, W. Farquharson Small, who had told me to record six minutes. One and a half minutes were used.

When I went to Rolls-Royce I was determined this should not happen again. One of the head engineers recorded an admirably concise piece that lasted exactly one minute; and an old Rolls-Royce fitter summed his feelings up in the following brief sentence:

'Well, when you've been with the firm, as I 'ave, for thirty years, you begin to get a bit of a Rolls-Royce complex.'

'You can't cut that, Mr Farqhuarson Small,' I thought to myself. Back in London, as usual, I played back my discs to Farqhuie. He was quite pleased with the engineer's contribution.

'Did you get anything from a workman?' he asked. I played back the fitter's piece.

'Is that all?' Farqhuie said. At which I hit him and he fell off the music stool on which he had been sitting onto the floor. I think he thought it was just a playful shove, but it was nothing of the kind.

Progress Report dragged to a close and one day I had a telephone call from Laurence Gilliam, asking me to come along to his office. There was an attractive woman there whom I knew vaguely by sight.

'I don't think you've met Eddy, Marjorie,' Laurence said. It was my first meeting with Marjorie Banks, one of Laurence's top writers and producers. Laurence wanted us both to go to France to do a kind of 'progress report' on the recovery of that country.

Marjorie and I went to France just at the time that tourist traffic to the Continent was starting again after so many years and most people were thinking in terms of hotels and night clubs, of different food and the sunny shores of the Mediterranean, rather than Communism and de Gaulle, production figures and achievements of reconstruction. But we had to think of these things, too. We found a lot of changes. But we had already been conditioned to these changes. The forms to be filled in, the papers, the red tape in general, the grumbling about the government, the rising prices were not much different from what we had become accustomed to reluctantly in our own country. But besides all this we found a great deal that seemed surprisingly as it had been before the war. The gaiety of Paris at night, with the restaurants open and the *boîtes-de-nuit* flashing their signs until long after London was dark and dreary. So much of the Paris scene that tourists love and expect was still there. Even the Spanish gipsies.

Sitting in a *bistro* one evening, one of these women in a long, flounced dress came up to our table. Feeling in a good mood we 'crossed our palms with silver' and she told our fortunes.

'You will marry,' she said, 'and you will be together for the rest of your lives.' We paid her her money and smiled. My heart was still in Warsaw; Marjorie was married. We were getting along very well together and both looking forward immensely to our journey across France but . . . Half way through the trip I began to wonder whether perhaps the gipsy's premonition might not have some substance in it. So much so that I began to regret perhaps a tiny bit that I had arranged to meet a plane from Warsaw in a fortnight. But that was some time ahead.

We drove southwards down the valley of the Yonne and our first main stop was at Beaune, the wine capital of Burgundy. We had an introduction to the well-known wine shippers, Pierre Ponnelle and we lunched with Henri Ponnelle at his charming house at Vergelesses just outside Beaune, where our hostess was his fourteen-year-old daughter, home on holiday from a convent in Dijon, who acted with an *aplomb* only possible with a well-brought-up French girl. As befitted the daughter of a well-known wine grower she sipped a little of four or five different wines that accompanied our admirable lunch and which had such a stimulating effect on me that after the meal I climbed to the top of a tall tree in the garden. In Beaune we stayed in the enchanting Hôtel de la Poste, where we met for the first time, its proprietor, Marc Chevillot, whom we have since come to know well.

Marc Chevillot comes from an illustrious family of *hôteliers*. His grandfather Victor Chevillot was a renowned chef and the most French of all the French things we saw on our trip was his epitaph which hangs in the hotel. It is called: '*Le Tombeau de Victor Chevillot*' and it was written in exquisite French by a journalist who was a frequent visitor. My English translation does not do it justice but at least conveys something of the spirit of the original.

'Victor Chevillot of Beaune has died at the respectable age of eighty-two years. I hope that he will have been buried in his vestments of office; in his tall chef's cap and white tunic, wearing his apron, with his carving knife hanging at his side. I hope too that on the day he is laid to rest, all Burgundy will put on mourning – all Burgundy, that is, which rejoices in eating and drinking. I hope that in the fields, in the coppices and thickets that surround that little town of Les Hospices, the very animals which Chevillot so often sacrificed on fires of vine twigs will mourn his passing. Those hares, whose saddles he larded with shallots and garlic and left to steep for days on end in the *eau-de-vie* of Burgundy. Those plump partridges, which he knew how to baste and roast better than any man on earth. Those thrushes, which he served on beds of grapes. Those trout which frolic in the waters of the Armençon and the Cure, which he prepared *au bleu*. Those voracious crayfish, which he entombed in shrouds of cream. I hope that all game, whether furred or feathered, all fish, even those stupid barn-yard fowls, upon whom he conferred immortality by sautéing them *à la Jean-sans-Peur*; even those snails, albeit soulless, meditating eternally on their trails of transparent slime, nearby in their hermitage of Chenove; I hope that all that is living yet worthy of the table, within a radius of fifty miles will have experienced an infinite sorrow upon learning that this gentle executioner, who knew so well how to render the supreme honours to his lesser brethren, has left our mundane sphere for the kitchens of Elysium.'

Near Grenoble Marjorie and I conceived the notion of injecting a little tourism into this story, which seemed to be getting somewhat overloaded with the economic facts and figures we had been collecting on our way. We would, we thought, branch off to the east a little and climb the Alps by Napoleon's summer route to the south, crossing them by the Col de Galibier. It was still early spring but in Grenoble we were assured the road was open. We travelled along by the icy, grey-green waters of the river Romanche, until the mountains rose steeply on either side, slatey-grey and bluish and tawny gold in the sunlight. By the time we began our first real climb up and round in hairpin bends along the narrow mountain road, dusk was already beginning to fall. It grew bitterly cold and the ice and snow from the peaks seemed to menace the road on both sides. We began to descend again, driving through a cosy little mountain village and then began the second climb up to the Col de Galibier itself.

When we began the first steep ascent we noticed a snow plough lying at the side of the road. This should have been the signal to turn back. We went on. Half way up the precipitous road, with a sheer drop to the right and the mountain towering on our left, we were faced with a high bank of frozen snow, which completely blocked the road. Somehow we slithered back down the road; and somehow, on a jutting-out ledge, we contrived to turn the car, With teeth chattering we reached the mountain village we had passed through on the way up and in the little inn there drank hot brandy toddy and ate fried eggs and ham and listened while they explained that it would be impossible to drive over the Col de Galibier for another couple of months. 'It is a pity you didn't stop and ask on your way through the first time. You would have saved yourselves a lot of trouble.'

But warmed by the brandy and the delicious, simple meal we felt it had all been well worth while. If we hadn't attempted the Col we should never have found this charming little hostelry or felt the extraordinary sense of well-being that the happy outcome from our ordeal had brought about. It was in this mountain inn that I – I think both of us – began to think that maybe there really was something in the gipsy's prophecy.

The next morning we looked out on a white world of snow and ice, but within a few hours we were driving through Provence, through the hot scrubby land of the Midi, where the vines grew in gnarled rows, still unclad by the leaves that make this desiccated land look so un-naturally green in the summer. We drove to Marseilles and worked interviewing dockers and trades union officials and had a wonderful interlude, spending a whole Sunday on M Ricard's estate on the Camargue, that wild section of the delta of the Rhône, until recently populated mostly by wildfowl and flamingos, herds of black fighting bulls and wild, white horses.

M Ricard is the immensely wealthy manufacturer of the *pastis* bearing his name, *pastis*, the great aniseed-flavoured drink of the south, which is automatically brought as an *apéritif* unless you ask for something else. He lived in an almost feudal style and his estate might have been a South American *hacienda* a century ago. A self-made man, he believed in sharing with and looking after the people who work for him. When we arrived late in the morning, his employees were crowded into the vast, barn-like school house, which he had built right alongside his own and which he used, at week-ends, for large communal meals in the style of some medieval nobleman. Long tables running down the school house were already laid for the midday meal and at one end was a bar, where enormous quantities of pastis were being consumed by us, our fellow guests and by the workers on the estate who, for Marjorie's and my benefit, danced and sang the songs of Provence.

After a gargantuan lunch we staggered out of doors into the hot sunshine and went to see M Ricard's fighting bulls and wild horses.

We stayed on for dinner and late in the night drove back to Marseilles in an extremely erratic manner.

Soon after we returned to Paris my girlfriend from Poland arrived according to a plan we had agreed upon long before I set out on this journey and which, if I had had any sense at all, I should have cancelled. An agonising week followed. I decided once and for all that unlike many of my friends I was a one-woman man – at least a one-woman-at-a-time man (this was my only digression in a lifetime from this principle). Once again a romance faded and another began – or, more accurately, continued on its interrupted course – and this time, and at last, stayed on it.

Chapter Ten

Marjorie and I, after this brief journey through France, which had resulted in only one BBC programme, had established ourselves as a 'team'. Marjorie wrote the scripts and I filled the comparatively easy role of narrator of the programmes. We both interviewed people we met on our travels and any skill I developed as an interviewer – and I ended up as a pretty good one – I owe to Marjorie. Laurence Gilliam had some more ambitious plans for us. He wanted us to do a large scale programme about the children of post-war Europe, and to collect material for any other programmes we thought fit as we went along. The scope of the 'children of Europe' programme covered about half a dozen countries.

We decided we would try and make this journey on our own, without help from recording engineers or being followed by a cumbersome recording van. This was in the days before tape recording. (It wasn't, in fact, because the Germans had produced the magnetophone even before the war had ended and the French had since then made considerable developments in this new technique, but the BBC still stuck rigidly to the old disc cutting method.) So we went to EMI to see what they could suggest in the way of small disc recording machines. We had to have a small one because our car was a Standard Eight. They had the very thing; they even let us have it free for the publicity value such a journey would provide for the machine. We learned how to work it; how to cope with such hazards as 'swarf', the black, hair-like stuff that comes out when the needle cuts the grooves in the disc, and which wrecks a recording if it is allowed to wind itself round the needle, and all the other complications that, in these days of tape recorders, happily no longer exist.

We drove through France to Switzerland. We crossed the frontier between Gex and Geneva and there was trouble with the Swiss Customs over the recording machine. They wanted the equivalent of £250. We couldn't spare it. We left the machine in bond and the next morning went to Radio Geneva. A charming official there readily agreed to guarantee the duty on our recording machine. When I said I thought the Swiss Customs seemed to be a bit tough he smiled:

'Oh, you know, what's happened to you is nothing, really,' he said. 'It wasn't many years ago that a Swiss archaeologist came back from the Middle East. He had been doing some excavations at Ur of the Chaldees and he was bringing back with him a Sumerian skeleton, carefully packed in a long box.

' "Have you anything to declare?" the Swiss Customs asked him.

' "Yes, I have a human skeleton, some five thousand years old." The Swiss Customs official looked puzzled. He spent half an hour looking through books and ledgers. Understandably enough he found no rate of duty on prehistoric skeletons. The archaeologist waited patiently while the Customs official telephoned Berne to obtain a ruling. Needless to say nobody in Berne knew what the duty on such an unusual thing should be. A long conversation followed. At last the Geneva Customs man hung up the receiver, turned to the archaeologist and smiled.

' "I am happy to inform you," he said, "that it has been decided to permit you to import your – ah – object, free of duty as "used personal effects".'

Marjorie stayed in Geneva to make necessary arrangements with the World Health Organization and UNICEF – the body which organized the United Nations children's fund, while I drove to the eastern end of Switzerland to see the children's village of Pestalozzi, near Trogen in the Appenzell. This village, named after the famous Swiss educationalist was and still is a curious experiment. An Utopian experiment many people said because the idea was to bring up groups of children together from as many different countries as possible and the fact that they all got on well together – which they did and do – would sow the seeds of international tolerance and understanding. Whether there was any hope of such a small unit as Pestalozzidorf bringing about anything so desirable or not, at least a number of children did have a very happy childhood. And maybe some Polish boys and girls did go back to their country to spread the word that there were at least *some* nice Germans.

The different national groups all lived together in their own houses, built in the Appenzeller style, with steep shingled roofs and each had a 'house father' and 'house mother' of their own nationality. They did lessons in their own languages but they also learned 'Switzer Duitsch', so that when they met children from other houses for games or winter sports or walks in the countryside they had a common language.

At that time there were many volunteer workers from different countries, including Britain, who were helping with building and the general running of the village. But as time went on, under the able leadership of Herr Arthur Bill, things became so well organized that outside help of this kind was no longer necessary. I have since been back to Pestalozzi several times and have been able to watch it grow and the number of different nationalities increase to include even a British 'house'. But I found it more interesting in the early days when, for example, the Polish children in their art class drew and painted almost exclusively scenes of violence, bombs exploding, tanks firing shells, people being machine-gunned. This happened again among the Hungarian children who came to Pestalozzi after the revolution in 1956, but children have been coming to Pestalozzi for many years now who, happily, know nothing about war at first hand.

We travelled by car through the Simplon Pass and drove along the shores of Lake Maggiore along a white road that ran between pink and yellow villas and the deep blue water and we stopped for the night at a hotel with a broad terrace built on piles over the lake. As we stepped on to it with the idea of having an *apéritif* before dinner, we saw an infuriated man with a bristling moustache, holding a fishing rod and shouting at the top of his voice at a passing motor boat in a curious mixture of English and Italian.

'Hey you *barco* there! God damn it *attenzione mio* bloody lino! Keep a bit *piu lontano*! *Ha capito* damn you?' He turned round and saw us.

'Ah, scusi—' he began.

'It's all right, you can talk English,' Marjorie said.

'Eh? Well thank God for that! But these damned boats. Here I am peacefully fishin' before me dinner and they come roarin' by and nearly foul me line. They've done so several times, blast 'em. Well, anyway they've scared all the fish away so what about a drink? Eh?' We joined him. He was an ex-major in the British Army who, like hundreds of others, had preferred to chance his luck in post-war Italy rather than return to an England of rationing and restriction. He had his 'little filly' as he called her tucked away in a nearby villa and he had about a dozen irons in the fire 'and one of them is sure to turn ups'.

Milan was a nightmare. We had a hundred different people to see: consular officials, bankers, industrialists and journalists. We searched for workers who could speak some English and for unemployed who could tell us their sorry story.

During those days we talked and talked and talked. We were given the Communist point of view by Rafaele Miella, editor of the Communist newspaper *l'Unita.* Miella was an elegant, very well dressed man in his middle thirties and unlike many Communists was not in the least afraid of talking – in excellent English. He of course blamed the capitalist system – and particularly the exaggerated form of it existing in Italy – for the state of the country. When, later, we were talking on more general terms I said I thought it a sad thing that communism should have first flourished in Russia. Marx, I said, had always envisaged it beginning either in Germany or England.

'You're quite wrong,' Miella replied, 'Russia is the only

country in Europe brutal enough to have seen Communism through its inevitably bloody early stages.'

It was in Milan that we compiled our second chapter in the story of the children of Europe. In the outskirts of the city was the *Casa di Don Orione*, called alternatively *La Casa dei Piccoli Mutilati*, a home for children who had been mutilated in the war. We both rather dreaded our first visit. Marjorie felt it would need all her courage to see and talk with little boys who had lost their arms, their legs, their sight through the appalling violence of war. The boys were all in the yard of the home when we went in. Somehow it was impossible to feel distressed by the cheerful, noisy scene that met us and it was not until later that we had time to realize the pathos of it. We recorded them singing and we played the record back to them. They crowded round the car astonished, excited, listening to themselves. A little boy had his face turned to the loudspeaker, a face criss-cross with deep, red scars. A boy in blue listened leaning on a crutch, one of his trouser legs folded over a stump. A tall, thin boy without any hands had another boy hoisted on his back – a boy without any legs.

The *Padre*, Father Giulietti, his round, gentle face beaming with pleasure, told us that at first they arrived frightened, difficult, miserable.

'But after a few weeks, after we have treated them in the best way we can – we don't control them too much, we leave them free, as you see, to play, to shout, to do anything that a boy can do which isn't any harm to him – then they open like a flower. They smile and don't shout any more at night – when perhaps they are remembering the impressions they had during the war, of the bombs and so on.'

After a short time, no matter what their handicaps, the boys start to play football. One boy with no legs was the team's goal keeper. Father Giulietti became almost as excited as the boys themselves when he described their enthusiasm. He told us, how all the boys help one another, how the boys without legs wash the boys without hands and how the boys with legs carry those who haven't any.

'And so they help themselves all day long. Whatever they can do for one another they do it because they have a great spirit of generosity one for the other.'

'But it is very difficult,' he went on in his gentle voice, 'because they are growing. So these poor boys, every five or six months have to go to hospital to be operated on. Also the artificial legs and hands, we have to change them every five or six months because their legs and hands grow. It's a great problem which will cease only when they are twenty years old.'

It was an appalling thought. For ten or twelve years these boys would have to suffer operations and all their lives they would suffer from terrible handicaps. Because war had come to their fields and playgrounds. Most of them were hurt by picking up hand grenades or unexploded shells.

Once in the Via Manzoni, to our delight, we saw four young Italians looking into the window of an antique shop, where an illuminated Gregorian chant, painted on parchment was displayed, and singing the chant in harmony. That, we thought, could only happen in Italy. Neither can I imagine a garage attendant anywhere but in Italy saying, as Giovanni did when we parked the car:

'You are fortunate indeed in coming to Milan just now. The Brera Gallery has just reopened and you have the opportunity to see Mantegna's *Cristo*.' And when we told him we were going on to Genoa in a few days he said:

'Then you must not fail to go by way of Pavia and see the Certosa.' And in due course we took his advice and saw this marvellous Carthusian monastery.

Once again, in Genoa, it was an economic story we were out to get, a story of the reconstruction of a great port which at the end of the war had been left paralysed with the docks wrecked, a hundred-metre gap blown in the breakwater and the harbour littered with countless mines. One evening we drove to a village called Quarto del Mare, perched on the heights a few kilometres outside Genoa, where a number of dockers and seamen live. There is a workers' club there which has a remarkable choir and they were giving a recital that night. We could hear them singing as we climbed the last few yards of the steep hill. A group of men was huddled in the middle of the club hall. Paying strict attention to their conductor they sang a succession of traditional Ligurian songs, some of them very ancient ones. In every song there was a part for a falsetto voice and this, too, is a tradition that goes back for centuries to the days of Christopher Columbus. When a Genoese ship put to sea it always carried a falsetto as a member of the crew. This was purely to give an illusion of a woman's voice to men who might not see a woman for months on end. Some of these falsettos became very prima-donna-ish, refused to do any work, expected the other members of the crew to wait on them and, strangely enough, got away with it.

We drove on to Portofino, where we looked up Alan and Lucy Moorehead, who were staying in Alex Clifford's house on the summit of the steep promontory that rises above the beautiful little harbour, a house which Alex bought for a song just at the end of the war. We wanted to get further south so we went on our way to Sestri Levante, which in those days was a charming little fishing port. The fishing boats with their high, raking stems were lined up on the beach and the fishermen were mending their nets, which were stretched out over the sand. A short general strike left us stranded there. We spent a very pleasant day lying in the sun and swimming. It is very agreeable sometimes to have all initiative taken away from one and to have to give in to *force majeure.* Particularly when it means lazing in the sun on a sandy beach.

The next day the strike fizzled out. We drove on down the Via Aurelia, past the crowded beaches of Viareggio, through Pisa and on through Livorno to Rome.

We spent five crowded days in the Eternal City, working like maniacs. Everybody in London used to envy us these journeys enormously. I think they imagined we spent our time lying on beaches and eating in expensive restaurants. We loved the journeys but sometimes we worked eighteen hours a day and it was hard, hard work. But it was fun and these journeys have completely spoiled me as far as travel is concerned. I don't want to travel any more without an object, simply moving from one place to another sightseeing. Even though at times it is a bore to interview mayors and businessmen, shopkeepers and housewives, there is other work that is completely enjoyable.

Our second evening in Rome they were giving an open air performance of *La Traviata* in the Baths of Caracalla. We went by arrangement with the management and in the interval, between the acts, hid our pathetic little microphone in a far corner of the stage behind the scenery. An operatic production is usually recorded with the help of several microphones, with at least one slung high across the front of the stage. We couldn't do anything like that. The car was parked on the rough gravel at the side of the stage near the refreshment buffet. We lurked there, waiting for the more familiar arias and dropping the cutting needle on the disc whenever a minute or two worth recording seemed to be coming up.

It was a wonderful scene in the ruins of the Baths of Caracalla, a confusion of dark shadows and yellow lights. Battered, immense, the fragments of Roman walls reared up to a blue-black sky. One could imagine those Romans of the Third Century having their hot, cold and vapour baths, their massage and exercises. The disc spun, recording Violetta's aria and the last, passionate scene with Alfredo; recording the applause, too, the roaring, shouting Italian appreciation of good singing. We recorded, sometimes quite long extracts, for several hours and in the programme that we broadcast eventually we only used a minute or two for a 'colour' description of the scene. But it was all well worth it and to our utter astonishment the quality of the recordings was remarkably good.

To add to the children story we went to the Villa Savoia, once a royal summer palace, then a home for twenty-eight boys and girls who, like the boys at Milan, had been hurt and maimed during the war. One of them was a beautiful little boy wearing striped cotton rompers called Vittorio. He was nine years old and completely blind because in the battle in his village between the Americans and the Germans he had been shot in the head.

'Signora,' he kept saying to Marjorie, *'non puo vedere* – I can't see, I shall never be able to see any more. But I can sing' – and he sang a song: *Quanto s'è bella Roma, Quanto s'è bella Roma prima sera* – How beautiful Rome is. How beautiful Rome is just at dusk. And little Vittorio will never see Rome. But when we played the song back to him he laughed with delight and he kissed Marjorie and clutched her hand and he didn't seem to know how to be sad.

Down the Appian Way and through the Alban Hills we took the road south. South to Naples, city of the very rich and the abjectly poor, of the great hotels and the luxury restaurants of Santa Lucia and of the most ghastly slums you would find anywhere. And beyond along the loveliest road in the world through Sorrento, Positano and Amalfi. On to Salerno with its acres of war cemeteries and on again to Eboli. At Eboli we sent Laurence Gilliam a telegram consisting of only four words: 'But we went on.' And we were very disappointed later to learn that he hadn't seen the point of it. It had only been a year or less before that the Italian author Carlo Levi had written a book called *'Cristo s'è fermato a Eboli'* Christ stopped at Eboli, which meant, quite simply, that everything worth while stops after Eboli – culture, education, development of land and industry, almost life itself.

We went on. We went on to a terrible village called Campagna. It is a village in its size because it is not much more than one steep main street high up in the hills. But crowded into its narrow, tall tenements, which looked quite out of place in such a country setting, are thirteen thousand people. One of them was Mike Palladino, once a prosperous barber in the United States, who decided to return to his native Italy with his dollar savings, marry and build a home. In the dark little café in the main street Mike Palladino was half in tears as he told us his story. There was no window, no electric light and no one else in the café. Nothing on the floor and the dull pink walls were chipped and stained. Mike sent a ragged boy to order food and cigarettes. We ate *pasta asciutta*, the kind of macaroni the Italian soldiers are given, and Mike talked long and bitterly in a rich American voice.

The trouble was his wife went on having one child after another. When the Allies landed in Italy Campagna was cut off from all supplies and Mike went almost mad trying to find milk for his children, walking miles up into the hills to try and beg a little from the *contadini*. One after another four of his children died before the British and Americans arrived. For a while he had a job as an interpreter. Since then he had been unemployed.

'And the only prospect I got now,' he cried bitterly, 'I gotta sell every damned thing and I gotta go some part of the world and I don't know where but I gotta go.' There were hundreds of thousands of Mike Palladinos in Italy then.

On our way back to Naples we spent a day swimming at Positano and a night as the only guests in the little hotel down on the beach. We've never been back. We'll never see Positano like that again. In Naples one day we were lunching at one of the expensive restaurants in Santa Lucia, down in the old port. Fishermen in tattered jerseys sat in their boats a few yards away mending their nets. Some of the more enterprising paddled their boats past the tables inviting the diners to come for a row round the harbour. Ragged urchins scampered between the tables selling newspapers, or just for no particular reason at all. They didn't see as much money in a whole year as a party of four was spending on a single meal. And yet they didn't seem to show any resentment at the glaring inequality of this state of affairs. A row of beautifully kept racing yachts lay alongside the jetty. The sunlight sparkled on their vivid reflections in the blue water. A group of half naked little boys were catching shrimps from a wooden raft moored close alongside the restaurant. One of them had only one leg and was using his crutch to disturb the shrimps clinging to the sides of the raft so that his friends could catch them. A dead-end-kid in an American sailor's hat, whom we had recorded a few days before sidled up to the table. His name was Enzo.

'You don't want that roll of bread with all that spaghetti,' he said to Marjorie. 'I haven't had anything to eat since yesterday morning.' Marjorie gave him the roll and he wolfed it down. A few minutes later he chipped into our conversation again.

'Ask the waiter to bring you another roll. He'll bring it if you ask him. I'm still hungry.' I got him another piece of bread. It seemed terrible to be sitting there eating a big meal with so many hungry people almost at your elbow. It couldn't have happened in any country in Europe except Italy.

An Italian ex-Army officer who had been lunching with us was mildly amused at the episode of Enzo and the rolls.

'Those kids,' he said, 'what an upbringing! They can swear in English just as well as they can in Italian. They "sonofabitch" each other just like a GI. You should have seen Naples during the invasion. It was one big brothel. It was beyond belief. By the time your troops got to Rome your command had had some experience and they'd been given some directions about how to behave. But here – it was terrible!'

On our last night in Naples we went to hear the open air opera performed by the San Carlo Company in the Villa Floridiana. As we spiralled up the steep hill above Naples, we kept looking back at the lights twinkling over the bay. The beautiful gardens where they were giving a performance of Bellini's '*I Puritani*', are high above the city and you can look out, past the stage, though a magnificent framework of trees, across the Bay of Naples and see the lights of Capri and Ischia glittering on the black, velvety water.

We drove north, through the Abruzzi, entirely forgetting that some of the bitterest fighting in the war had taken place north of Naples in this wild, rugged country. We reached Isernia as it was getting dark and stopped to ask a boy where the hotel was.

'*Albergo? Niente albergo. Albergo distrutto.*' But his aunt could put us up. We were not sorry to make an early start the next morning. The main object of driving through the Abruzzi was to make a return journey to my old prison camp at Sulmona. We plunged again into the wild, majestic country, the jagged lines of mountains stretching away to a blue horizon.

Long before we reached Sulmona I found myself beginning to get strangely excited. It surprised me because I had never expected to feel nostalgia for a prisoner of war camp. And when the road wound round a bend and I looked down on the Sulmona Valley my excitement rose. I began to pick out half-forgotten landmarks. The pass through the mountains, up which Bob Ross, Neil Currie and I had planned to go on the first stage of our escape. All the plans for that escape came back to me vividly. The painful saving of food; the miles we walked daily for training; the improvised civilian clothing; the forged passes; the skill with which Bob wrote our scheme for escape in the correct military jargon to satisfy the colonel in charge of the escape committee. It had all looked so good on paper. But the *carabinieri* discovered our tunnel.

Away on the other side of the valley I could make out a cluster of red-tiled roofs. That was the POW camp – Fonte d'Amore – the Fountain of Love – a fine name for a prison! In the main square of Sulmona we sat down in a café. Before leaving London George Eisel, who at that time was a waiter in an Italian restaurant told me that if I went to Sulmona I must meet the baker who had supplied all the bread to the camp. George had been one of the supplies liaison men and had known him well. I asked the café waiter if he knew the baker. Everybody knew the baker and a small boy went to fetch him. A large, prosperous looking man arrived. I explained who I was.

'Ah one of the *Inglesi* from Fonte d'Amore! It is a great pleasure! And what will you drink?' We asked for campari sodas and the drinks came. We talked about the old days and I asked what had happened when the Germans came.

'And now another drink,' I said. 'What will you have?'

'No, no, no, no. You are in Sulmona. It is my pleasure.' And he insisted on buying the drinks again. After ten minutes more conversation the glasses were empty again and I insisted upon buying the next drink. I held out a note to the waiter. The baker seized my hand and put it on the table with his own on top of it.

'Now listen to me,' he said. 'For three years I delivered on an average three and a half tons of bread daily to that camp. Thanks to you *Inglesi* I became a rich man. And now, if you please, permit me to repay just a little of what you and your friends brought to me. And let us please have no further arguments about paying for drinks!' We had several more while the baker said that the *Inglesi* were very popular all over Sulmona. It was not only he who had made money out of the *prigionieri-di-guerra.* He pointed out the hosiery shop, which had sold many thousands of shirts and pyjamas; the jeweller's which had made a big profit out of watches. I may have felt curiously nostalgic but there was no mistaking the baker's nostalgia. For him, those beyond question had been the days.

I drove down the main road and wondered if I should remember the turning down the little lane that led to the camp. Heaven knows, I thought, I ought to. I'd walked along it often enough. We used to be sent out on walks, about once a week, with almost as many guards as POW's and we invariably went the same way: down the lane as far as the main road, turn about and back again. Those awful, shuffling walks!

It was almost with a thrill that I found the lane. From then on it was like seeing a film that one has seen a hundred times. The little, battered shrine at the corner; the same fields of lucerne; the farmhouse where we used to watch them drying tomato purée, a red, sticky mess, spread out on sieves to dry in the sun; the tumble down little hamlet of Badia, with the same Mussolini slogans stencilled on the walls: *'COMBATTERE, OBBEDIRE, VINCERE!'* Fight, obey, vanquish! They didn't do any of those things. There they were, still on the walls, nobody had bothered to whitewash them over. Every house I knew and the stream where the village women used to wash our tarpaulin-like bedsheets. I turned left over the little bridge to the entrance of the camp. There was the commandant's house. Strange how much smaller and less important it looked. And there was the commandant's garden and a silly memory came back to me of the British soldier who had been caught killing a chicken there and his excuse had been that the chicken had attacked him and he had only killed it in self-defence.

And now, on the steps of the commandant's house stood a peasant woman with a baby in her arms. Apart from that it all looked the same. The barbed wire fence still ran round the camp. The alley between the wire and the outer wall was overgrown with weeds. 'Stone walls do not a prison make, nor iron bars a cage.' Not much they didn't!

Suddenly I realized that an Italian officer was talking to me. I came back to reality with a start. I felt almost guilty at being the wrong side of the wire. He was in charge of the camp. Did I want to look round? He'd be glad to show me the way. I said I thought I'd remember, I used to know it pretty well. He smiled. Things had changed; there had been much damage.

I walked through the gate – still a network of barbed wire. Strange not to see a sentry there. Difficult to find one's way about. The Gerries had torn down all the walls between the compounds. A little Italian workman stepped up.

'I remember you, *Signore*, you were one of the *prigionieri*.' He had been one of the guards.

No. 3 compound was built on the slope of a steep hill. I wondered what had happened to the concert hall – first hut at the bottom on the right. Dirty and dusty with a great jagged hole in the roof. And that alley to the side of it – the only one that wasn't festooned with dhoby, where Godfrey Anderson and I used to go through our Italian grammar together: *Avrei, avresti, avrebbe, avremmo, avreste, avrebbero.*

No signs of the garden that used to be ablaze with zinnias – nothing but a jungle of ragweed and thistles. How about the sergeants' mess? Oh, that previous stove smashed to pieces and lying all over the floor. No furniture. None of Jack's beautifully made cupboards. And the cricket pitch? Is it possible that they played on such a steep, rocky hill? Anyway the cricket pitch was nearly waist high in weeds. Weeds along every pathway where once hundreds of feet had tramped and given them no chance to grow. Hut 64 and how big it looked with none of the double-decker 'castle' beds. It didn't seem very big on a hot summer's night with about seventy men in it. And the hole in the wall where we had slipped messages to and from the officers' compound. No hole in the wall. No wall at all.

Over into the officers' compound. Another scene of desolation. In the room Andy and I had shared somebody had smashed the terra cotta *stufa* to pieces. (The amount of wood I had chopped for it!) Nothing left of my garden under the window. No sign of the tunnel beside the badminton court. Nothing but weeds and rocks. Slit trenches zig-zagging over the space outside the mess where Tenente Graziani used to keep us waiting for roll call in the snow. Sergeant Briggs' frescoes in the mess of Captain Cook's landing at Botany Bay and scenes of Australian life still looked as fresh as when they were first painted for the Australian officers. They were about the only things that did. All the fine steel ranges where Captain Fitzhardinge used to turn out such remarkable meals – smashed to bits.

Outside in the hot sun I walked across the dreary, dusty compound, looking at row upon row of battered, dirty huts, and the only sound, the whining of the grasshoppers in the wilderness of weeds. I remembered it all as such a scene of noise and activity. I almost felt nostalgically sad seeing the place so quiet, so utterly derelict. There had always been such crowds; such teeming crowds of people.

We travelled up the 'leg' of Italy from Sulmona, through Perugia, Florence, Bologna, Ferrara, Padua and at last drove into Venice down the broad, straight road that links the mainland with that unbelievable city of islands and canals.

'Is there anyone,' wrote Thomas Mann, 'but must repress a secret thrill on arriving in Venice for the first time – or returning thither after long absence – on getting into a Venetian gondola? Black as nothing else except a coffin – what pictures it calls up of lawless, silent adventures in the plashing night, or even more, what visions of death itself, the bier and solemn rites and last soundless voyage.'

We parked the little car in the largest garage in the world and took a gondola to the Danieli, surely the most beautiful hotel in the world. We idled in Venice for a few days, sitting at Florian's in the Piazza San Marco, drinking and listening to the orchestra. And one day we wandered through the Doge's Palace. I do not remember much of the great dark rooms with their crowds of sightseers. But what I do remember was seeing, once again, the *piccoli mutilati* from Milan, who were being taken on a sightseeing tour. One of the boys couldn't see, he could only feel and he was running his hands over the shape of an old cannon. We watched the other boys struggling up the stairs on their crutches, and one or two, who had no hands, were carrying the legless boys on their backs. In Milan, when we had first seen them, the sight had been bearable, so cheerful were they in the Casa di Don Orione. Here, in Venice, it was more heart-breaking, their tragedy was more apparent, as the crowd of sightseers fell back to let them pass by, and watched them with astonishment, sometimes tinged with horror.

Chapter Eleven

When I had arrived in Vienna for the first time in 1936 I thought it was wonderful. All the older people said it was awful. Vienna had never been anything since the days before the First World War. In 1948 I found English people enthusing about a Vienna where the Opera House was in ruins, where half the houses in the Kärntnerstrasse were destroyed, where there wasn't a decent hotel or restaurant.

'It's frightful,' I found myself saying, 'you should have seen Vienna in the thirties.' Worst of all it was an occupied city – and occupied by the troops of four countries. There was a feeling of bitterness against all the occupying powers particularly the Russians, who had been the first to enter and terrorise the city. The Russians had put up a monstrous statue of a Red Army soldier in the Schwartzenberg Platz, re-named the Stalinplatz – but not, fortunately, for very long. The Viennese said that if you took off the soldier's steel helmet you would find the whole statue filled with watches. All over Europe watches were irresistible to Russian soldiers. A story going round Vienna at that time was of a British officer who was held up by a group of Russians who demanded his watch. When he proved he really hadn't one, a Russian roared with laughter, fished a handful out of his own pocket and gave him one.

We added to our programme on the children of Europe in Vienna and then headed on for Czechoslovakia. A Red Army soldier examined our passports in the Austrian Customs House. He only looked about eighteen years of age and the documents probably meant very little to him; but he looked through them slowly, page by page, determined to show his authority. At last it came to the turn of two Englishmen, who were also on their way to Prague. One of them had told us he was in charge of transport at the British Embassy and the other was his assistant. They had driven a truck that morning to Vienna to collect stores at the NAAFI, and were making the return trip. The Russian started to look through the assistant's papers. The Englishman stood this for perhaps a minute. Then he slapped the Russian hard on the back.

'Now come on George,' he said in a rich, loud Cockney voice, 'we've been through all this lot once already today. We don't want to waste a lot of time again, do we? We've got to get back to Prague this evening, see?' The little Russian didn't understand a word he was saying, but he was so surprised by this direct method of approach that he let both the Embassy officials through without further delay.

On the other side of the barrier we came up against the Czech Customs. One of the Englishmen pulled a bottle of sherry out of a bag, uncorked it and passed it round. We got through all the necessary formalities in a most cordial atmosphere, were given ration cards to last us three days, petrol coupons, a complimentary map of Czechoslovakia and we went on our way.

Even in those early days, when the Communists had only been in power for a relatively short time, Czechoslovakia was a sad and dreary country. Wenceslas Square in Prague was crowded with people, drab, shoddily-dressed people, who looked as if they belonged to some mill town rather than to a European capital. There was nothing remotely interesting in the shops.

An American woman, Mrs Glassey, was doing wonderful work with her team of Czech assistants, distributing food and medical supplies to tens of thousands of children all over the country, who badly needed it. Mrs Glassey worked for UNICEF, which at that time was doing great things for the children of Europe.

'All I ask you,' she said to us, 'is don't for heaven's sake tie up our work in any way with politics. An American journalist came out a few weeks back, under our auspices, and I'm pretty sure she'll go back to the United States and build up a political story around what we're trying to do. That's just the best possible way to get us thrown out of the country.' She arranged for us to visit a Danish team of doctors, who were testing children for tuberculosis, vaccinating them if their test was negative and if it was positive arranging for them to go to a sanatorium – if possible.

When we set off for Germany we drove through Carlsbad – or Karlovy Vary. It was dreary and deserted, its great hotels, once filled with rich foreigners, almost empty. It was the same at Marienbad, renamed Marianske Lazne. We spent a day and a night there as the guests of an old fellow prisoner of war, Dr Gottlieb, whom I had not seen since the Germans took him away from *Oflag* XIIB for an unknown destination that we, and I think possibly he, too, feared would prove to be a concentration camp. For Doc Gottlieb had done little to endear himself to his captors. He could be seen dancing with delight when the news of the bombing of German cities came over the radio; and the Gestapo had found an outspokenly critical diary during one of their searches. If it had not been for the kindness of one of the German camp officials who burned most of the worst parts of the diary, Doc Gottlieb would probably have found himself in Auschwitz.

However, he had been sent to a *Stalag*, where he found an incompetent Polish doctor butchering British and American airmen daily. From the day he arrived until the end of the war he was seldom far away from the operating table.

Doc Gottlieb returned to Prague to find that his clinic, which had been seized by the Germans, had been re-confiscated by the Czechs. As a slight compensation for this he was given the job of medical officer of health in Marienbad. He showed us round the pleasant spa before taking us to the King Edward Hotel where he had booked rooms for us. There was a fine, faded flavour of Edwardian vulgarity about Marienbad with its ostentatiously ornate hotels and baths. I liked to imagine it in its hey-day, thronged with the middle-aged aristocracy and plutocracy of Europe, who congregated there to work off the effects of their gargantuan eight course meals. Marienbad specialized in the cure of obesity, which is why King Edward VII was a regular visitor. The King Edward Hotel, where he always used to stay must have been exactly the same as it was when he and the Emperor Francis-Joseph drove through the streets of Marienbad in an open landau. There was a splendid picture of this royal pair in the lobby and a great many pictures of King Edward on his own. But if the hotel still looked the same, the atmosphere of Marienbad was sadly different.

'There's been hardly a single foreign visitor this year,' Doc Gottlieb said, 'and last year the place was packed. That's what this Communist Government has done to one of the best spas in Europe. As for me I've practically nothing to do now. I sit in my office with a bloody great picture of that bastard Gottwald on the wall – they force me to have that, they wanted me to put up a picture of that even greater bastard Stalin but there I drew the line – and I do damn all. Of course I don't need to work from the money point of view. What can I do with money? I'm not a collector of Bohemian glass. And even if I were I'd have to buy it with foreign currency. I used to run this spa. I ran it well because I know how to run a spa. Now I've given it up and the Government has appointed an idiot who has no idea how to run things. So Marienbad will be ruined. Why should I care? The sooner I get out of this damned country the better I shall be pleased.'

Doc Gottlieb and his wife drove ahead of us in their car to the German frontier and waved goodbye sadly. We hated leaving them behind without being able to do anything to help them. Not long afterwards, however, they managed to leave Czechoslovakia and came to England. It cost them a high price. They had to leave everything they possessed behind, even Doc Gottlieb's surgical instruments. Although he was once at the top of his profession in his own country with his own clinic, when he came to England the authorities would not recognize his medical qualifications. After some trouble he achieved a partnership with another doctor in Brixton, where he is still practising.

We arrived in Nuremberg in the late afternoon and after some difficulty found rooms in a small hotel. I had known this marvellous old medieval city quite well before the war and I wanted to show Marjorie the sights. Of course, I knew it had been badly damaged in the war.

'Let's go and see what's left of the main square,' I said. 'I don't know what it's called now. When I was last here, of course, it was called the Adolf Hitlerplatz.' We drove down a narrow lane, that had been bulldozed through the ten-foot-high rubble of century-old bricks. At last we reached a large, open space. I was horrified.

'This must be it,' I said, 'yes it is. That's all that is left of the church where the figures used to come out and strike the hours. And that pile of bricks was the café where I used to sit watching them. That ruin there was the Rathaus. It was such a lovely building with its steeply sloping roof and little, slit-like dormer windows.' We searched for the fifteenth-century Bratwurstkeller, where one used to get wonderful fried sausages. We tried to find Hans Sach's house in vain. Albrecht Dürer's house had been smashed beyond recognition. The old *Burg* had been bombed to bits. But it was the same all over Germany then. Almost every town in Germany – almost every village, even, had been more or less destroyed. At the time I wondered how they would ever repair this fearful wreckage. Returning to Germany only a few years later I saw what the Germans' capacity for hard work could achieve.

On our way back we went to see a camp near Frankfürt that was euphemistically known as 'Boys' Town'. Here, living in tattered tents, a group of refugee German boys, aged from ten to twenty years, were struggling to build homes for themselves. They all came from the Russian Zone of Germany – as it still was then – and from the territories annexed by Poland.

A youth of nineteen, who had escaped from Berlin and found his way to West Germany, begged us not to give his name.

'You see, my mother is still in Berlin and my father is in Buchenwald.'

'In Buchenwald?' I said, hardly realizing what the boy was saying. 'You mean the old concentration camp near Weimar?'

'The very same, except now, you see, it is a Russian concentration camp.'

'Do you have news of your father?' Marjorie asked. A little shrug of the shoulders that was the answer to so many questions in so many European countries.

'We've only had one little bit of news,' he said at last. 'From a man who came back to Berlin from Buchenwald. He was all right, quite decently dressed; well fed. He told us that only a few of them were specially treated and then released. He said my father was a sick man and for him and the rest conditions were terrible. There had been about twenty thousand people in Buchenwald and now there were only eight thousand.'

'Do you mean the others have been deported or moved somewhere else?' Again the shrug.

'This man didn't think anyone had been taken away. But still twelve thousand had disappeared. What can one think?'

Back in London Marjorie wrote a brilliant, poignant radio documentary on the state of the children of Europe and a joyous travelogue of our adventures in Italy. We were well established as a team of BBC reporters.

Chapter Twelve

In the nineteen forties and fifties I travelled a great deal. When I met people in the entrance hall of Broadcasting House, they were always asking me where I had just come from or where I was going to next. But I did a lot of work in London too. When BBC Television started up again, a regular programme was 'Picture Page' which was introduced by Joan Gilbert. Freddie Grisewood did the interviewing. For some reason Freddie was not able to do this for a month or two and I stood in for him. All Television came from Alexandra Palace in those days and it was a somewhat rough and ready affair. In 'Picture Page' they always, quite logically, had one or two essentially 'pictorial' contributions – a painter or a sculptor showing and talking about his work; a breeder of tropical fish or a craftsman of one kind and another. And then there were celebrities of different kinds, authors, travellers and so on. I had to interview them. There was a rudimentary run-through by way of a rehearsal and then we all went to the 'hospitality' room for sandwiches and various kinds of alcoholic refreshment.

One week the old author, A. E. W. Mason, appeared as a celebrity. There wasn't much time left when it came to the rehearsal of my interview of him. There was a team of researchers who provided me with scraps of information about the people I had to interview, most of which I usually disregarded. But this time I did ask one of the suggested questions.

'Mr Mason,' I said, 'you have written a large number of books in your time. How many, in fact, have you written?' The old man, who looked very like the actor C. Aubrey Smith, glowered at me under his beetling eyebrows for some seconds.

'Young man,' he said at last, 'I haven't the slightest idea!' Before either of us could say anything more Joan Gilbert called out:

'That's all the time we have for rehearsal. Back in the studio in half an hour's time. Thank you.' As we made our way to the 'hospitality room' I said to Joan that she might have given me a little more time with Mason.

'Oh it'll be all right on transmission,' she said airily. Everything was put out 'live' in those days and I had great doubts about everything being all right at all. I thought I might as well settle the answer to the one question of how many books A. E. W. Mason had written, so I asked his secretary, who gave me the number. Then I saw to it that the old gentleman was given an enormous whisky and soda and hoped for the best.

When it came to the interview he answered that question quite satisfactorily. I happened to know one of the cameramen who had shot the film of his book, 'The Four Feathers', in Khartoum and I asked him several questions about that. And then I was given the same glowering look again and the old man rapped out:

'Young man, you've been askin' me a lot of questions. Now I think the time has come for me to ask you one. What was it like on the Bishop Rock Lighthouse? Always meant to pay it a visit meself, but never seemed to find the time. So I'd like to know, what was it like there?' I had been marooned on the Bishop Rock only a few months before and it seemed to have stirred the public imagination to an almost absurd degree, not only in Britain but all over the world. To this day people remember me as 'the chap who got stuck on the lighthouse' to the exclusion of a great many other exploits of mine which to my mind counted for much more. At any rate, as far as A. E. W. Mason was concerned, from then on he interviewed me instead of my interviewing him and it was a great success.

A year later, as a result of my growing reputation as a traveller,

I was asked to do a series of TV programmes called 'Foreign Correspondent'. The idea was that I should go with a cameraman to different capitals and important cities in Europe and give an account of what life was like in them and in particular, how they had recovered from the war. The trouble was that it scarcely ever seemed to be possible for the cameraman, Charles de Jaeger, to accompany me. He would go off on his own and take a lot of always excellent pictures. But often – and inevitably – there was no film of something I really needed to talk about. So every now and then the camera would switch to me, sitting in an armchair, and I would say:

'And then there's another extremely interesting thing that's going on in Milan now . . .' and elaborate on this interesting but unillustrated matter. Fortunately nobody seemed to think of writing to the BBC to ask why, if it was all that interesting, was no film made of it.

However, for a few of these programmes Charles and I did travel together and collaborate on the spot in building up the stories. A notable occasion was our visit to Vienna. The Austrian capital was still occupied by the four powers and every evening soldiers of the four countries used to make a ceremonial patrol of the city in a jeep. On the bonnet of the vehicle were the flags of Great Britain, The United States, France and the Soviet Union. This international patrol used to set out in turn from the headquarters of the different occupying powers, where the four men ate before leaving. Charles and I thought this would make an excellent sequence. It so happened that on the evening we had chosen, the party was being entertained at British Headquarters. We obtained permission from the British commander who was enthusiastic about the idea. To be on the safe side I asked him if he would be kind enough to check with his Soviet opposite number that he had no objections. He did this.

Charles set up his lights in the dining-room and worked out his angles. Everybody was there except the Russian soldier. At last he turned up. When he saw the lights and the camera he was furious.

'What's all this?' he wanted to know. I explained to him in

Russian. He refused to be photographed or have anything to do with the idea.

'I come here, expecting to have a quiet meal before setting out on the patrol and I find you English want to make propaganda out of it; *'Eto nyekulturni'* he kept saying – this is uncultured, the worst thing a Russian can say about anybody or anything. And he would have nothing to do with it and refused to be filmed, although I assured him that his general had not only given his permission but would be angry if he didn't agree. All we could do was to film the empty jeep with the four little flags. When the programme went out the camera switched to me in my armchair and I told the story. For once this was something that couldn't have been filmed.

'Foreign Correspondent' was produced by Mrs Grace Wyndham Goldie and I shall never know how we managed to get the programmes on the air. I would be in her office half way through writing a script without having seen the film when Grace would come in and say:

'Come on down and see the "rushes".'

'Give me half an hour to finish the script first.'

'No, it's got to be now. This is the only time we can get the theatre.'

'But it won't be much use – oh all right, let's go.' And we'd go down to the theatre and I'd take some notes as best I could of the length and content of the sequences. Then I'd go back and probably have to rewrite what I had already written and try to write as far as I could to fit in with the film for the rest. By some miracle it usually worked out fairly well. I was never very satisfied with these programmes myself because given a little more time I knew I could have greatly improved them, but they were on the whole a success.

I did another weekly radio programme about this time called 'Thanks for the Memory'. It was Marjorie's idea. Everyone, she said, is reminded of some event in their lives when they hear a certain piece of music. So, using the old song 'Thanks for the Memory' as a signature tune, I started the ball rolling by playing half a dozen records and telling the stories of the events in my life which they brought to mind. I then asked listeners to write in and tell stories that certain tunes reminded them of. I made it clear that the music must be accompanied by a good story. It wasn't of any interest that a tune should remind a listener of Dad's birthday or the time Grandma came to stay. We had an enormous response. At least half of the letter writers paid no attention to what I had said and the stories accompanying the requests for tunes were of the 'Dad's birthday' type. But we always got enough good stories to make very good, well balanced programmes. We got funny stories and sometimes poignantly tragic ones. One was so macabre that we didn't dare use it though it had a horribly comic side to it.

'I was in Petrograd,' the writer said, 'at the time of the Russian Revolution. We had a ground floor flat and one night there was a knocking at the front door. I opened it and the Secret Police burst in. They didn't pay any attention to us because we were English. They went upstairs and burst into the flat of a Russian family and evidently started to butcher them right away. To drown the noise of the screams we put this tune on the gramophone' – it was some completely banal piece of music – 'and turned the volume up as high as possible. I shall never hear that tune without remembering the screams and the blood dripping down the walls – it wasn't a well-built house. Please play it for me.' We didn't.

In between my travels I filled in time in London narrating feature programmes and adapting books and stories for radio features. In the early 1950s I began another regular series for the overseas service of the BBC which was called 'Commonwealth Club'. This was a kind of magazine programme in which, again, we invited anyone living in the Commonwealth to write to us and tell us how they lived in Ceylon or Trinidad or the Falkland Islands. We got actors in to read these letters (I wonder if David Jacobs or Derek Hart remember doing these humble jobs), we had an expert who talked learnedly about megacycles and ionospheres and gave advice to listeners about how to obtain optimum reception. We had guests of greater or lesser celebrity whom I interviewed; we introduced some light relief with some music, which had to be provided by someone from the Commonwealth. This seemed to be shared out largely between the West Indies and Australia and the most frequent contributors from these two opposite ends of the commonwealth were Cy Grant and Shirley Abicair.

In the late summer of 1949, after I had finished my TV series, 'Foreign Correspondent', there didn't seem to be any immediate prospects of travel, so Marjorie and I went to Paris to see what we could do for ourselves. The Marshall Plan was in full operation at this time and Laurence Gilliam told us that the head of the department of 'mass media' – which meant films, radio and so on – was in Paris. Our plan was to meet him and persuade him to let us do a series of radio programmes. His name was Al Friendly and he, Ed Gruskin, who ran the radio programmes for ECA – the European Co-operation Administration, which administered the Marshall Plan, Laurence Gilliam, Marjorie and I all had lunch together. The upshot was that we got the job. In the next few months we visited eight European countries from Norway to Greece and travelled something over ten thousand miles.

The ECA 'mass media' establishment in Paris bordered on the surrealistic. It was housed in a long brick and wooden building in the Avénue Gabriel, nearly opposite the American Embassy which, in the Edwardian days of the *Belle Epoque*, had been a fashionable *bordel.* It wouldn't be fair to say that the tradition had been carried on, but one could claim that there was a certain continuity of atmosphere. They were a wonderful collection of types in the Avénue Gabriel. Artists, dipsomaniacs, nymphomaniacs to a greater or lesser degree. Ed Gruskin, the head of radio division had a wife who was a very good blues singer – she was always a great success at the *boîte* 'Chez Inez'. Inez was a Southern Negress, who had married a Danish count and ran this night club near the Panthéon in an admirably economical way. Her guests provided the cabaret, free. But her Southern American cooking was better than anything I have ever eaten in the United States. There was a non-stop game of musical chairs and general post as people dashed in and out of offices with ideas, suggestions, queries, alterations in plans and cancellations. We escaped at intervals to the nearby Crillon Bar, but it was hard to make anything like a clean break from the mad-house atmosphere. It always astonished me that anything was ever done there. And yet a great deal of work somehow was done.

The first country Marjorie and I were to go to was Holland. There was always a great complication about money. We never were able to draw the necessary amount of funds in Paris. If we were to work in Holland then we had to draw our expenses from the ECA office in The Hague. We didn't want to go to The Hague but we had to in order to be able to eat and pay our hotel bills. We always seemed to arrive in a country either after the ECA office had closed or, even worse, at a week-end and then we had to live on credit and eat exclusively in our hotel until Monday.

In Holland it was a story of the rehabilitation of the low-lying country that had been flooded in the war that we had to tell. The Dutch at least were grateful for what Marshall Aid had done to help bring this about – and said so. This was not always the case in other countries. We went first to the island of Walcheren whose dykes had been blasted by the British Navy in 1944 to flood the Germans out. We were told of herrings swimming in the ditches and mussels clinging to the wheat stubble. And then we went on to the Wieringermeer Polder which the Germans, in a wanton act before they left Holland, flooded with sea water.

The days we spent on the polder were rather like a collection of typical Dutch paintings, of flat Dutch landscapes alternating with bright Dutch interiors. Henk Vandraager, the polder farmer whose story we were telling, drove us for miles over farmland which looked exactly the same. We never knew for sure in which direction we were going because the scene was always wide and clear with great, open skies above the flat land and the straight, endless roads.

Henk drove us at tremendous speed over the flat country. The monotonous landscape slipped past. One remembered little variations. A heron standing beside a canal. A flight of curlew; the time when Henk crammed on the brakes to avoid a covey of partridges scuttering across the road – 'They are so small they can walk as quick as a mouse'; the ragged skeletons of the great Dutch barns – the 'floating roofs' as they were called when flood water was still there and all the walls had been swept away. We climbed a steep grassy bank to the top of the dyke and Henk told us of the day when his farm was lost. The Germans had been working on the dyke for some days saying they were strengthening it in case the allies bombed it. But the day before they left they planted a lot of bombs and gave Henk two hours' warning to get what he could out of his farm before they blew up the dyke.

'I loaded a little bit of food and some clothes on the car and drove off the horses. I saw my wife and children safely away and then stayed and watched. I saw the dyke go up and a raging flood of water pour over my home.' We drove out to the great dyke across the mouth of the Zuyder Zee – twenty-two miles of road, running along the top of a high steep bank, with the North Sea on the far side.

We flew into Norway over Oslo Fjord and I don't remember ever seeing anything more beautiful with the sun glinting on the water and the little islands with their pine and birch trees and painted houses. We drove into Oslo along a winding road through a landscape of fir trees and oaks and maples, blazing in wonderful autumn colours. Our objective was the whaling port of Sandefjord.

In the little town of Tønsberg we met Finn Bugge, a director of one of the big whaling companies and brother of Bobby Bugge with whom years before I had done a tour of Spain together with Rupert Bibby. Bobby had been at Cambridge and his name, which was pronounced as it would have been in Lancashire if it had had an 'r' at the end of it was a source of some embarrassment to the college authorities. After a meeting they decided it must be pronounced 'Bewje'.

Before the war this company had had three big whaling factory ships. They had all been sunk. At this time they had only one, the *Balaena*, the finest and most modern afloat. We were lucky to be there just before she sailed for the Antarctic. We went aboard in a launch and just had time to meet the captain and his English wife, the factory manager and one or two others before going down to the saloon. It was a scene of great gaiety but we felt that the gaiety was a little on the surface because the women knew they wouldn't see their husbands and sons for at least seven months. We were there until the early hours of the morning and we returned to this huge 25,000 ton ship a few hours later.

'There's not much left from the whale these days,' the factory manager said. 'We boil down the blubber for oil. We get oil from the bone, too. We get oil and liver extract from the liver. We grind up the bone for bone meal. Hardly anything's wasted.' There was a laboratory where they extracted insulin, and vitamin 'A' which they put into margarine. The factory manager had been in whaling for many years. He had seen the shore factories in South Georgia; then the small 4,000 ton factory ships, where they had to tie the whale up alongside, cut him up there and haul him aboard in pieces; and finally the big factory ships, where the whole whale was hauled aboard up a great hole in the stern and cut up on deck.

We met a whaling man, Herman Hermansen, who had started at 17. He worked all through a winter in South Georgia and at last returned home with a lot of money saved. (The scenes in Sandefjord when the whaling fleet returns have to be seen to be believed it seems.) During the war he was lucky to escape to Liverpool and joined the Norwegian commandos, returning home just before the end of the war. In Herman's house in Sandefjord we drank *akvavit* and beer and he showed us some of the things he had made while he was away on his long, seven months' voyages: lamps made of whales' eyes, round things as big as a large orange and parchment coloured; and sperm whale's teeth formed the stand for the lamp. And Herman had engraved sperm whale's teeth with whales and sailing ships. His wife brought in supper, herrings and fried rissoles and a big jug of fresh milk.

We spent the night on a big factory ship the 'Empire Victory' which was due to sail the following morning. We went up on deck before turning in and saw a man leaning over the rail looking over the fjord. He was an engineer in one of the 'catchers', one of the little tug-like vessels, which chase the whales. He told us about the gunner – who harpoons the whales and also is skipper of the 'catcher' – with whom he had sailed the previous season.

'He killed 495 whales,' he said. 'A good day would be fourteen or fifteen and that kept us very busy.' A good gunner like this was very popular with the crew of the 'catcher', he said, because not only did he receive a bonus for each whale killed but so did the crew, too. A good gunner might make as much as £6,000 or £7,000 in a season.

The whaling men spend seven months of the year on the job and five months at home. Most of them have little farms and occupy their time at home farming and fishing. In any case they earn far more in their seven months at sea than they could ever make staying at home.

Next morning, with the sun rising over the unbelievable loveliness of the Oslo Fjord, we flew to Copenhagen. In Denmark it was to be a farming story. When we arrived at a large pig farm they were very apologetic over the fact that we had missed slaughtering day. We were enormously relieved. We had to make do with seeing the pigs being weighed – very unwillingly. We spent a couple of days with a Danish farmer and then returned to the lovely city of Copenhagen. This was my first visit and apart from the architectural beauties of the place my chief memory is of the restaurant where they produce something over one hundred and fifty different kinds of sandwiches, listed on a menu about six feet long; and of going behind the scenes there and watching an old woman shelling shrimps. She had three large piles in front of her on the table. One of unpeeled shrimps;

one of peeled shrimps and the third of shells. She had been doing this unbelievably monotonous work for nearly forty years!

Back in Paris we set out for Lorraine in a large and rather old Cadillac. The chauffeur-owner drove it tenderly and with caution. When we stopped once some small boys asked in awed voices what the horsepower of the car was.

'*Combien de chevaux?*' the driver replied, '*mon Dieu, elle a toute une cavallerie!*' In no circumstances, however, was he prepared to permit the cavalry to charge, and we ambled quietly along the straight wide avenues that cross France from Paris to Germany.

We had decided that it would be appropriate to do a story about the country of Joan of Arc and so we headed for the little town of Neufchâteau and the nearby village of Domrémy, where Joan of Arc was born. In Neufchâteau we stayed with the *sous-prefet* and his wife and in the course of our researches attended a concert given by the band of the *sapeurs-pompiers* of Neufchâteau. From time to time, at a signal from the gold-braided bandmaster the *cors-de-chasse* threw their instruments up in the air, caught them dexterously and gave a concerted blast. This was all right for 'The Gladiator's Farewell'. But when it was announced that the next number would be 'La Symphonie Inachevée de Schubert' we felt they had taken on a little too much. It was a valorous if not a very 'finished' performance of the Unfinished Symphony.

The next morning we recorded the mass in the little church at Domrémy and went back for breakfast afterwards with the curé, who, at eight in the morning, offered us glasses of *mirabelle*, the plum brandy of Lorraine – but hid the bottle when I took a photograph later. I was charmed with the curé's lavatory. Above the seat was a picture done in pokerwork. It showed a prelate sitting 'at stool' saying his rosary. Behind him the devil asks him if he is not ashamed to be saying his prayers in such a place.

'Not in the least,' replies the prelate. 'For *le bon Dieu* knows that my prayers, which rise, are for him and that everything that falls is for you!'

Everything possible went wrong with our trip to Austria. We thought for a change that it would be pleasant to travel by train – and in particular on the Orient Express to Vienna. Unfortunately we mistook the time of its departure from Paris and were only just in time to catch the less romantic Arlberg Express. Of course, our sleeper reservations had gone on without us and we had to spend almost our last penny to pay for other sleepers. When we were half way across Austria I looked at the 'grey cards' which one had to carry then in order to cross the Russian zone to get to Vienna. They were made out to cross from the British zone to the Russian zone at Semmering. We were heading for Ens, the frontier between the American and Russian zones. I felt a fool not to have checked earlier because we had had exactly the same trouble a year before when driving to Vienna. That time we had got away with it. So, instead of getting off the train at Salzburg and making the roundabout journey to Vienna through the British zone, we decided to chance our luck.

At the American side of the bridge over the river Ens the American frontier guards looked at our papers.

'You'll never make it. Those Russkies'll turn you off the train sure's can be. Still, if you want to, go ahead and chance it. But we'll be seeing you back here before long—.'

The other side of the bridge the Soviet guards boarded the train.

'*K'Vyenu? Da? Eto vash bagazh?* Ah, but your passes are for Semmering. You must travel through the British zone.'

'*Nyevozmozhno!* It isn't possible! But we are so near Vienna now and we have urgent business there.'

'Ah I think the business is not so urgent. I regret but you must leave the train and return to Linz.'

They were most polite about it all – but equally firm. We had to scramble off the train with all our baggage and go into a little guardhouse beside the line. A red-hot stove was blazing. A

Red Army non-commissioned officer was sitting at a desk. He took our particulars and looked at our passports. I looked at the stove. I remembered a story I had read once about a Czech who was returning to his country from Russia. The Soviet frontier guard had looked at his passport and then tossed it into the stove. Nothing like that happened. In fact once having thrown us off the train the Russians couldn't have been more helpful. They stopped a goods train going back into the American zone, told an Austrian railwaymen to put our baggage aboard it and said goodbye in the friendliest possible manner.

The American frontier guards were not surprised to see us back. In their guardhouse was a former Austrian, now a British subject. He had not chanced crossing the bridge. After a long wait we caught another train back to Linz. We had to wait there from 11 that night until nearly 6 the next morning. We had no money and were very hungry. At last I steeled myself to ask our fellow traveller if he could lend us some money. He had dollars which he was prepared to lend at the very favourable rate of exchange (to him) that he claimed he could get in Vienna. We'd have paid any rate. We had to change trains three times before reaching Vienna late in the evening. Then, early the next morning, were heading back over exactly the same route. We were to visit a forestry estate in Styria, near Brück, the first town where we had changed trains the day before.

It was unfortunate that our host, an agreeable Austrian baron had had his spendid *schloss* occupied by British troops. During their Christmas celebrations the previous year they had contrived to burn it to the ground and the baron was obliged to live in the dower house which, by comparison, was a modest sized building. We tried to pretend we were Americans for a while, but then I made some remark which gave the show away. However, the baron seemed to bear us no ill will and with him we trudged up a steep mountain path to watch his men cutting down tall fir trees. With lightning speed they stripped them of branches and sent them hurtling down a slide to the valley below.

* * *

The next evening we waited on the cold platform at Leoben station for the express from Vienna to Italy. At least we'd have our sleepers this time, I thought. But our bad luck stayed with us. The train got into Leoben at two minutes after midnight. It counted as Wednesday. Our sleepers were booked for Tuesday. This time we had no money to pay for others. We sat up all night in a dirty Yugoslav carriage. It was a dismal farewell to Austria.

That evening we were in the teeming noisy city of Milan. Our hotel was just opposite the famous Scala Opera House, right in the centre of the city. The trams clattered down the Via Manzoni. The cross traffic waited impatiently for the lights. All drivers in Milan are always in a particularly tearing hurry.

We were to tell the story of a typical Milanese working man. His name was Arturo della Barbera and he worked in Snia Viscosa, the huge man-made-fibre concern. The della Barberas invited us to dinner in their flat in the outskirts of Milan. They had gone to such trouble with the meal. We started off with mountains of spaghetti; then came veal escalopes with a monumental salad lavishly adorned with an intricate design carried out with beetroot and mayonnaise that must have taken hours to make. And then, when we thought we had finished, a huge piled-up dish of *gnocchi* those little paste dumplings that are about the most filling dish imaginable. The meal nearly killed us because we had to plough through it. It must have been a considerable strain on their modest weekly budget.

The following evening we took them out to a first class Neapolitan restaurant because we thought it would be a change for them to eat a different kind of food. When the waiter brought the menus we told them to choose whatever they liked. They both scanned the menu for some time.

'Cos'e spaghetti alle vongole?' Arturo asked. I explained that it had a sauce made with little shellfish and was very good. His wife asked what some other well-known dish was. It made us feel ashamed that we, as foreigners, seemed to know more about Italian food than they did. The menus were written in Italian.

They don't go in for that nonsense of writing everything in French like the English do. The dinner was a great success and I think our friends enjoyed their evening.

Unfortunately there was no opera at the Scala, but a friend telephoned us just before we left to say that he could arrange for us to hear an audition. We stepped on to the vast stage on our way to the room where the audition was being held and looked across to the magnificent auditorium – eight tiers of boxes rising in an elongated horseshoe, all crimson, gold and white. The Scala was gutted by fire during the Allied bombing of Milan and it was characteristic of the Milanese that it was the first building they put in order again. A year or so later I was in Milan on my own and they were playing la *Tosca.* I asked the hall porter at the same hotel what the chances were of getting a ticket and he said it was quite impossible unless I were prepared to pay a ridiculous price on the black market. I went out to have a drink with some friends and returned to the hotel about nine o'clock.

'Do you still want to see *Tosca*?' the hall porter said. I said I certainly did. 'Well, if you don't mind escorting the manicurist from the hotel hairdressing salon, you can go for nothing. She has complimentary tickets. Well, if you were to give her a thousand lire she would be very happy.' To my astonishment I found myself sitting – admittedly with a number of other people – in what had been the royal box. The manicurist, although of what the French would call a respectable age, evidently feared I might have designs on her because she refused my offer of a drink in the interval. I went out into the foyer on my own and I never remember seeing such an elegantly dressed crowd.

Whenever we arrived somewhere on this ten-thousand-mile journey it seemed to be our fate, as soon as we had installed ourselves in a comfortable hotel, to have to repack our bags immediately and set out for some remote spote where such a thing as a comfortable hotel was unknown. In Greece it looked as if we were going to be lucky. It seemed that the best thing we could do was to see the work of the health service at Thebes, within easy distance of Athens. Next day we saw the Chief of the ECA Health Mission. He said there was no doubt at all that if we really wanted to report on the work being done in Greece we had to go up into the mountains of Thrace and Macedonia.

We travelled north on what we called the 'Milk Run'. It was the daily Dakota trip taking personnel, mail and supplies to the American missions in the little mountain towns of northern Greece. Trussed up in uncomfortable parachute harness we, a nurse officer of the ECA Health Mission, and five American soldiers squatted along the sides of the bare military plane. During the war the RAF had a saying: 'All Greeks clouds have hard centres.' After we had twice attempted unsuccessfully to land on misty airstrips among the mountains, we saw the point of this only too clearly. When we finally landed near Kozani, after a couple of attempts that involved, at one point, hurtling by the mountainside with the wing tip almost touching the unfriendly rock, we understood why the 'milk run' was unpopular.

A splendid little Greek doctor met us at the airstrip. That evening he took us to eat at a local café, an experience that was torture to the ECA nurse who, like many of her countrymen and women was convinced that all European food was poisonous. Throughout the whole of our trip she was miserable eating anywhere except in a PX or American army canteen.

Early next morning we set out in Dr Michopoulous' Red Cross ambulance for another mountain town, Kastoria, further to the north, near the Albanian border. The driver of the ambulance had spent about twelve years in the United States. Then his mother became very ill so he returned to Greece. But she lingered on for several years and his permit to return to America expired. Ever since he had been trying to go back but his chances were very remote. Meanwhile he drove the ambulance and the mobile dispensary that travelled between the mountain villages.

We watched the mobile dispensary working in a village called Nestoria. It was tragic to see the number of children who had been orphaned by the civil war; and the children who had lost hands and feet from picking up hand grenades and other explosives; and those suffering from skin diseases caused by malnutrition. We had to drive back to Kozani in the dark and when we arrived the Doctor confessed that he had been quite a bit worried about the bandits. It was the first night drive he had done in Macedonia since the civil war with the Communists which was only just over.

The following morning we went to a refugee camp where men, women and children who had been in hiding in the mountains and forests had with great difficulty been rounded up. Now they were being sent back to their villages, back to houses that had been burned down and only roughly patched up; back to fields neglected and unplanted; but going home.

In all Europe, where there was still so much suffering, we had seen nothing to equal the suffering of the Greeks after nearly ten years of brutal civil war; nothing worse than the terrible poverty of the patient, enduring Greek peasants and their children.

Back in Paris the radio people at the Avenue Gabriel decided to dramatise the material we had gathered in the course of our four months' journey through Europe. We left them to it and returned to London, where Marjorie wrote a series of scripts and we broadcast them as documentaries.

Wherever we had gone we had asked people about Marshall Aid, how it had helped, in what way it had done most good. Before we left Paris we put forward the idea that we might go to the United States under the aegis of ECA to find out how the American people felt about giving Marshall Aid. To our astonishment, after thinking about it for a few months, they agreed and in the summer of 1950 we flew to New York.

Some time before we were due to go to the United States I was talking to the actor, John Slater, one day and telling him about our forthcoming journey.

'You could do with a car over there, couldn't you?' he said. I said I hadn't really thought of this but, of course, it would be very pleasant. 'I'll have a word with John Parkes, the head of Alvis,' John said. A few days later we all lunched at Mr Parkes's club.

'Yes,' he said. 'We missed the New York Motor Show; I think it would be a very good idea to send one of our models over.' A week later I was asked to go down to Coventry to have a look at the car they had chosen and try it out. To my consternation it was a very low two seater sports car, painted a bright red with room in the boot for a minimum of luggage. As we had to take with us not only enough baggage to keep us going for several months, but also a fairly bulky tape recorder and quantities of tapes, this was anything but an ideal car for the job. However, I couldn't very well look a gift automobile in the carburettor, so I thanked Mr Parkes, who made arrangements to ship it to New York right away.

Chapter Thirteen

We flew to Washington, steamy in the June heat, arranged a terrifyingly comprehensive programme with the Marshall Plan people and flew back to New York to collect the Alvis. The Americans don't recognize an international driving licence, so the first thing I had to do was to qualify for an American one. At the Police Commissioner's office I filled out papers, was given car plates and fixed an appointment for an immediate test.

I picked up an engaging character called Lou at the garage and he drove me to a point just off the East River. There was no office. The inspector drove up in a car.

'Now first there'll be an eye test,' Lou said. 'I didn't see so good with my left eye when I took my test, so when they tell me to hide my right eye with my hand, I leave a little chink, see? Then there's the written examination--'

'Yes, I've got the paper here, there's twenty questions—'

'Well, let's have a look at them. We gotta get 'em right.' I was a bit anxious about the inspector seeing, but luckily he went off to give someone else a test. So I settled down with the paper. A Negro truck driver came up; then another; a man who evidently had nothing else to do either. Every question was debated vigorously.

Question: If your brakes are in good condition can you pull up in 80 feet travelling at 40 m.p.h. True or false?

Me: I should say, yes.

1st Negro: Why, sure you can.

Lou: I dunno so much.
2nd Negro: It says if your brakes are good.
1st Negro: Sure it does. Sure you can – put it down for True mistah!
Lou: Yeah. I guess that's right.
Me: Okay. True it is.
Question: Can you see a child at night with good headlights at 500 feet. True or False?
Me: I'll have to figure that out in yards.
Lou: I guess not.
1st Negro: Why, at 500 feet, sure you can.
Onlooker: I guess so.
Me: That's about 170 yards. I think so.
2nd Negro: Sure you can see a kid at dat distance. Put it down for True.
Lou: Aw, I suppose you would.
Me: True it is.
Question: The minimum distance you may be behind a street car is four feet. True or false?
Me: I'd say false. I think it's 10 feet.
1st Negro: Then four feet'd be okay.
2nd Negro: Put it down for True.
Lou: Don't you guys understand what minimum is?
1st Negro: Ah don't know about that but Ah guess four feet's surely too close.
2nd Negro: Yeah, dat's right.
Me: I'm sure it's ten feet. We'll put it down for False.

And so it went on. At the end Lou said

'You'd better let me dope it over and see if it's all okay.' He did. 'Yeah, I guess it's all right.' I thanked our collaborators. At this point the inspector returned and I took a ride with him. The previous one had lasted (fortunately) about twenty minutes.

'I guess you've had a British licence for a good few years,' the inspector said. 'Oh, over twenty, anyway. Well, take a sharp turn at the end . . .' All went well and I was back in four minutes feeling pretty confident.

'I guess you're okay, bud,' Lou said. I got my licence the next day.

We had an appalling time packing our baggage and tape recorders into the Alvis before we left our hotel. Throughout our journey of nearly five thousand miles we were never able to close the boot properly. We always had to lash it down with nylon cord. The entrance to the petrol tank was inside the boot and every time we filled up we had partially to unload the car. It was anything but a suitable vehicle for the purpose. The Alvis was very much a sports car, very close to the ground. Driving through the streets of New York we felt almost in danger of being run over by the leviathan trucks that towered above us.

We planned to reach the town of Harrisburg in Pennsylvania for our first night. I was bowling along a splendid two track highway at something over eighty miles an hour in spite of constant notices saying that there was a speed limit of fifty. On such a fine road I couldn't believe they were serious. A Ford shot past us, pulled into the side of the road ahead of us and waved for me to stop. He was a traffic cop. He told me to follow him and I drove behind the Ford along miles of small country roads until we stopped at last outside a small general store in a village. The cop made his report.

'Have you anything to say,' asked the old storekeeper who, it seemed, was the local magistrate. I said I was a foreigner and I didn't believe it possible that they would have a speed limit of fifty miles an hour on such a fine road.

'I can't take that as an excuse,' the old man barked, 'Will you take three days jail or a fine of thirteen dollars and seventy-five cents?' He rattled it out as if he had often done so before.

'I'll pay the fine,' I said, though I thought it was a stiff one for a first offence. Once he had my money the old man became quite human.

'Waal, I'm sure sorry you got such a bad welcome to the State of Pennsylvania,' he said, 'but it's that old Governor of ours. He lives just above the highway and I guess he just don't like to see all these people buzzin' by all day.' We reached Harrisburg to find the best hotel completely occupied by a convention. It was the first of many similar experiences in the future. We were in the height of the convention season, when every hotel in the United States seemed to be packed with representatives (mostly Babbitts) of every imaginable industry. After a while this didn't dismay us any more. We simply made a point of finding out what the 'checking-out' time of the hotel was and then reported at the desk. There were always one or two conventioners who were recalled home for one reason or another and we always got rooms.

On the Pennsylvania Turnpike to Pittsburgh they had a more generous speed limit of seventy miles an hour, and we reached America's steel town without mishap. Although our purpose on this journey was to find out what Americans thought of handing out aid to Europe – if they thought about it at all, we also wanted to find out how they lived, and compared with England which was still wallowing in austerity, they certainly lived well. We were constantly astonished at the number and variety of material things that the Americans not only had but took for granted. Things have levelled out a lot since those days, but then it astonished us to find a car park with around eight thousand cars belonging to the workers at the steel rolling mill of Jones and Loughlin. I had an appointment to visit the steel firm of E. D. Mesta, source of the wealth of 'Call me Madam' Pearl Mesta, America's first woman Ambassador. I wanted to sound the opinions of some of the workers there about Marshall Aid, but a young member of the family who was a junior vice-president, said that would be quite out of the question. Nevertheless I had to go over the whole, blazing-hot plant and the only thing that made my day was to see one of the unapproachable workers toasting a hamburger at the end of a piece of wire which he had poked through the little window of a 400-ton open blast furnace. Marjorie had had a better day visiting Pittsburgh University with Austin Pardue, the Bishop of Pittsburgh, a charming man to whom the actor Leo Genn had given us an introduction.

At first we were charmed by the little towns we drove through in Pennsylvania and later Ohio. The broad, dead straight main street with its shops and drugstores; the residential sections as one entered and left the town, with their white frame houses, their porches, their green lawns sweeping down to the pavement. But as we continued our journey through the States of Michigan, Illinois, Kentucky, Tennessee, North Carolina, and Virginia these little towns became deadly in their sameness. An English student in the State University of Ohio in Columbus agreed.

'Each of these little towns,' she said, 'is a place that hasn't been there very long; a kind of mushroom in this wide and lovely and tolerant countryside, where the town seems to bear no relation to the soil it's on; it's just popped down there as if it had grown up overnight.' Driving through any of these little towns on a Sunday morning, one would have thought the place had been evacuated. Everybody was in church – a remarkable contrast with Britain!

Before we had left Paris, Bill House, who worked for ECA there, had left a note for us.

'If fate should ever play you the dastardly trick of landing you in Cleveland Ohio,' it said, 'you must look up my father.' We arrived in Cleveland as we supposed at lunch time, but Cleveland perversely used Eastern Standard Time as opposed to the rest of the State of Ohio and we were an hour later than we had thought. Lunch had finished in the hotel we went to so we took refuge in the bar and ordered double dry martinis. We got into conversation with the barman. Marjorie asked him what Cleveland was like. He looked at her for some time before replying.

'I despise this city,' he said at last. We were inclined to agree with him. We revised our opinion a little after an excellent dinner that evening with Bill House's father; and an interview with the president of an enormous machine tool factory the next morning helped further to restore us. He was furious because the United States Government had refused permission for him to complete several important deals with countries behind the Iron

Curtain. I put a microphone in front of him on a table and asked him his opinion on Marshall Aid.

'Our Government,' he began and gave the table such a thump with his fist that the microphone jumped into the air and landed on the table again; 'in its benign wisdom' – another thump and the microphone miraculously landed 'on its feet' again, 'has seen fit' – thump. Further thumps punctuated the president's lengthy diatribe against his Government. It was great stuff and I thought what a shame it was that it would all be unusable on account of the thumps. When I played it back later it was marvellous. The thumps sounded like small bomb explosions and expressed the President's outraged feelings admirably.

We paused in Dearborn, just outside Detroit, the headquarters of the Ford Motor Company; stayed at Ford's lavish Dearborn Inn; were given the full treatment and drove on to Chicago. Chicago we loved – city of 36 different national groups speaking 62 different dialects, as the Mayor of Chicago told us, adding that Chicago had the largest Polish population outside of Poland and the largest Czechoslovak population outside Czechoslovakia. Chicago is a great city for statistics. By making use of our 'check-out' routine we succeeded in getting rooms in the Stevens Hotel, where an immense convention of furniture makers had gathered. The Stevens then – and maybe still – was the biggest hotel in the world. 3,000 guests could be accommodated in 5,000 rooms on 36 floors and 5 sub-basements. 328,000 pieces of linen were used every day and 50,000 pieces of china and glass at a single banquet. If you slept one night in every room it would take you 8 years to sleep in all of them. If the carpets were all made into 27 inch strips they would stretch for 40 miles. The 25 elevators had travelled 3 million miles since the opening of the hotel (God knows how far they have travelled by now!) and lots more fascinating and endearing stuff like that.

We once sat down to dinner in the Stevens and on the table was one of those foldover cards saying 'Drink our Californian Wines' or something to that effect. We thought it was a good idea. So we said to the waitress – no waiters in the Stevens – that we'd like a bottle of Californian red wine. She looked at us as if we had ordered vitriol and soda and disappeared. When we had half finished the meal she reported that the barman didn't seem to have any Californian wine. I said that didn't surprise me and told her to bring beer and forget it. She still thought it eccentric that we didn't want coffee to wash down our Chicken à-la-King.

Having reported fluctuations of the Chicago grain markets for months when I worked for Reuters in Shanghai before the war I looked forward to seeing how things worked in the Chicago Board of Trade, where all these dealings take place. We had, an introduction to one of the vice-presidents, who put us on to his alarmingly efficient public relations officer, Mrs Dustin. She said she thought we could do no better than to start off by attending one of the lectures she gave to visitors to the Board of Trade. This explained the whole process of dealing in 'futures' in the different commodities. I already knew only too much about dealing in future deliveries of commodities, having once been nearly cleaned out by selling short in cotton for delivery some months ahead on the day that almost the entire Argentine crop was destroyed by frost. However, I sat through the well-delivered lecture and then we were taken, with our fellow visitors, to view proceedings 'on the floor' from the 'visitors' gallery'. This marked the end of the routine visit and the others left. Mrs Dustin asked what more she could do for us.

'If we could bring our tape recorder to this gallery tomorrow,' I said, 'we could record the noise of all the dealings down in the grain pits below. Would that be possible?' Mrs Dustin looked puzzled.

'Why, sure,' she said, 'but wouldn't it be better right down on the floor?'

'Oh, well, yes of course it would. But, do you mean – that would be possible?'

'Of course! Whyever not? And I'll fix for you to do the cash market as well as the futures markets. It's quieter but interesting just the same.'

We got on the floor just before the market opened. When it did it was a fantastic scene. In the circular grain pits, which rose above the floor in concentric circles, hundreds of men, mostly wearing white jackets, were shouting and gesticulating with their hands. They were buying and selling – corn in one pit, wheat in another, rye in a third – to be delivered at a later date agreed by both buyer and seller.

'Do you see that man flashing two fingers in the air, with the palm of his hand outwards?' Mrs Dustin asked. 'He's offering ten thousand bushels of wheat. Sell – palm out; buy – palm towards you. Get it?' It was clear once you knew. Then she took us to a line of small tables running along one side of the football field-sized room. Men were pouring little heaps of corn or wheat on to the tables out of little canvas bags. Others were picking up small handfuls of the grain, looking at it, appraising it and then buying a car-load or more maybe as a result.

'Those little bags,' said Mrs Dustin, 'are samples taken right from the centre of a car-load of grain, just like you take a sample from the middle of a cheese. Now, let's get organized.' She turned to a couple of grain dealers and explained that we wished to record on tape how a cash transaction was made. They began to carry out the deal as I switched the recorder on. 'No! No!' cried Mrs Dustin. 'Can't you understand? This is for broadcasting from London, England. Put a little life into it can't you? You don't want them over there to think that the cash market in Chicago is some kind of a mortician's business do you?' The two dealers, both of whom were probably millionaires, apologized and said they'd try to do better. And, indeed their second attempt, which was entirely fictitious, did sound a little more lively.

We were invited to dine one evening at a restaurant attached to the Ambassador East Hotel called the Pump Room. It was, indeed, inspired by the Pump Room at Bath. The owner had seen this once and had been so impressed that he had set about building a replica as near as possible. The walls of the room were dark blue; the paintwork white. The waiters were dressed in hunting pink tail coats, white breeches and black silk stockings and buckled shoes; and little coloured boys were dressed in striped silks and turbans like Regency blackamoors. The food was admirable – and we were about ready for some good food after the rigours of small hotels and restaurants in Ohio and Michigan. One of the specialities of the Pump Room was a kind of outsize *shashlik* brought to the table with a flourish on a rapier and blazing with brandy which had been added a few seconds before. After dinner we were invited to take coffee with the owner in his private apartment. We complimented him both on the cuisine and the décor and remarked in particular on the 'flaming sword' dish.

'Well,' he said, 'the customers seem to like it and it doesn't do the meat much harm.'

We met the chief of the Chicago Crime Commission and learned from him that although gang warfare and gang killings had become unfashionable, every kind of graft and racket were still thriving in Chicago, where the Capone syndicate was as active as ever. We spent a morning in Maxwell Street, Chicago's Petticoat Lane. We talked to Mr Skerman, head of Marshall Field's, the first of the great department stores in the world, who said:

'I've often wished I could transplant bodily a large group of those excellent salesmen and saleswomen who have waited on me in your shops and stores' – and having already decided that American service was the most casual and off hand in the world, we were inclined to agree with him. We were just able to see the Chicago Fair, a lavish display, held on the lake shore at which we learned to our astonishment that all the scientific inventions and discoveries that we had hitherto believed to have been made by Europeans, had their origins in America. And then we packed up the Alvis with customary difficulty and headed south.

In Lexington, Kentucky, Professor Steele of the University of Kentucky, summed up the philosophy of his State.

'The Kentuckian's idea of Heaven,' he said, 'is sitting on the front porch on a Sunday afternoon, with a mint julep watching the mares and foals in the lower paddock.' Kentucky is a charming State. In the so-called Blue-Grass-State there are narrow hedge-lined country lanes like England, with tall, shady trees and rich *green* grass. It seems that the grass is only bluish for a week or ten days in the year, when it comes into bloom. We drove through this lovely countryside, past horse-breeding farms with their white race-course railings curving over the rolling meadows. We visited one of the most famous of them, Calumet Farm, near Lexington, owned by a Mr Wright, of Chicago, manufacturer of Calumet baking powder and one of the most beautiful and wonderfully run horse-breeding establishments in the world. We liked everything about Kentucky except the fact that so much of the State is 'dry'. Which, in a State famous for the production of Bourbon whisky seems curious, if not downright hypocritical.

Through the hillbilly country of Tennessee – and we saw the shacks and the gaunt figures of the comic papers back in the forest off the road – we came to the town of Gatlinburg, a nightmare of tourism, a single street of hotels, motels and olde log cabins, selling every kind of folksy, crafty, mountainy and Indian junk. But the mountain folk in Gatlinburg are smart. They are the real thing. The older ones, at least, were brought up barefoot and tough in shacks in the forest. But they had the sense to move with the times and cash in on the tourists, selling their knowledge as guides, their skills as craftsmen and their mountain hillbilly songs.

Wiley Oakley was one of them. He was part Yorkshire by origin as his name proclaimed, and part Indian. He had been a celebrated mountain guide, who had conducted Henry Ford and John D. Rockefeller through the Smoky Mountains.

'I've never been to school in my life,' he said, 'but that don't mean to tell you I'm dumb though. I'm just partly dumb.' He wasn't dumb at all. He was a very smart old fellow, making a small fortune out of his store where he sold Smoky Mountain souvenirs to the tourists. His son had got together what would now be called a 'group', who sang hillbilly songs every evening in the store and drew crowds of customers.

We drove on through the Smoky Mountains, a botanist's and a zoologist's paradise. We were delighted to see a beaver washing its face by the roadside and stopped once to watch a black bear padding gently towards us. We drove on into North Carolina and passed through a Cherokee Indian reservation. Outside a shop – describing itself as a 'Trading Post' and selling a lot of tourist junk, stood a magnificent Indian brave with his full feathered headdress. The effect was somewhat marred by the fact that below this finery he was wearing a rather dirty white T-shirt. I wanted to take a photograph of him, but I wanted a close-up so that I could end up with only the splendid head. I went up to him and asked his permission to take the picture. The noble savage shifted the gum from one side of his mouth to the other.

'Be a quarter,' he said.

We sweltered in the heat on the borders of North and South Carolina on a vast farm where they were carrying out experiments with hybrid corn. We spent an evening on a big tobacco farm where, when we arrived, we found the owner, his wife and three families of sharecroppers, one white, two coloured, putting tobacco leaves into 'hands' and fixing them on wooden bars, where they hang for 'curing'. We talked to Julia, the enormously fat wife of one of the coloured sharecroppers. Didn't she get bored in the off-season when there was nothing to do? A great smile spread across her face.

'Ah's nevah happier,' she said, 'then when Ah's jest piddlin' around doin' nothin'.'

North Carolina is the great tobacco State where nearly all the 'Virginia' tobacco is grown. Wilson is the centre where it is sold. Everybody enjoys the big tobacco markets – especially the thousands of visitors who come to watch and to hear the famous auctioneer's chant. Ted Leeper, who ran the tobacco farmers' own radio station described the scene to us.

'All night long the farmers are heading towards the market unloading tobacco on the warehouse floor, and by nine o'clock the farmers, warehousemen, buyers and tourists gather in the warehouse to watch the auctioneering begin. On one side of the first long row of baskets of tobacco is the auctioneer, assisted by two keen-eyed warehousemen; and facing the auctioneer on the other side of the row are the buyers, who in an instant must be able to judge the quality of the leaf and make their bid; because the rapid chant of the auctioneer is not just a stunt. A good auctioneer must sell a 300 lb basket every four seconds.' Ted Leeper turned to Tom Burton, a nationally-known auctioneer, who was with us and shouted: 'And now let's sell tobacco!' And Tom Burton opened up with the quickfire, rhythmic chant that sells 300 lbs of tobacco every four seconds.

We left the Alvis in Washington and took the train to Chicago. From there we flew to Omaha, just caught a connection to North Platte and from there caught a train to the small Nebraska wheat town of Ogallala. That same afternoon we were on one of the Middle West's biggest wheat farms, thousands of acres of rolling prairie, vast workshops, quantities of machinery, a light aeroplane for crop-spraying and a gigantic grain silo.

'On this whole farm,' the owner, Mr Shelbourne said, 'we only employ two men – of course we've got about a hundred thousand dollars worth of machinery. It used to take ten horses and six men to cut and stack twenty acres of wheat in a day,' he went on. 'Now one man in a combine can cut fifty acres in a day and thresh it at the same time.' Mr Shelbourne employed what are called transient harvesters, teams who start cutting wheat in Texas in May and finish the season in Canada in early October. After that they take a well-earned rest in Florida. We met two of the transient harvesters, the Pesters, he a tall, stringy Oklahoman, she plump and jolly-faced, wearing blue jeans and a checked blouse and apron. If the men had a tough time with the combines, she hardly had a moment to herself, cooking, marketing, fetching spares for the combines if necessary, driving the car that hauled the trailer in which they lived.

'Oh it's hard and hard and hard to keep those combines a-rollin' ' she said to Marjorie. And those combines are a-rollin' sometimes from five in the morning until after eleven at night. We drove out into the endless wheatfields and watched the giant machines cutting the wheat and threshing it as they went along. We were over five thousand miles from the nearest point of Europe. Standing there, looking into the limitless distance, one could see and feel those five thousand miles. Europe might have been in another world. Even the eastern seaboard of the United States seemed infinitely remote. Mr Pester, when we talked to him about aid to Europe was frankly an isolationist. He thought Europe should solve its own problems and that America should do nothing about it and furthermore should not get herself mixed up in any more foreign wars. It was a senseless argument, of course, but it was easy to understand a feeling of isolationism in a place like Ogallala, Nebraska.

We intended to go on by train to Denver and to fly from there to San Francisco. Somehow we got aboard the wrong train and ended up in Cheyenne, Wyoming. It turned out to be a felicitous mistake. The Plains Hotel was enchanting. The bar was decorated like an outsize Indian wigwam and the barman mixed the best dry martinis I have drunk before or since. It was a happy change from the semi-dry rule in Ogallala, where you could only get beer. We were both much too concerned at first with savouring this return to a life of luxury to pay any attention to the other people in the bar. It wasn't until we were well into the second martini that Marjorie suddenly said:

'Did you ever see such incredible men. Gary Coopers, every one of them.' I looked up. She was right. Leaning over the bar and sitting at the tables were the most magnificent specimens of manhood, dressed in tight jeans, fringed leather shirts and high Texan boots. When the barman came with the third martini we asked him who they were.

'Why, it's Old Frontier Days,' he said.

'Old Frontier Days?'

'Yeah, it's our annual rodeo. These folks come from Texas, Oklahoma, California, Nevada – from all over the West. Starts day after tomorrow.'

'Too bad we'll have to miss it, we've got to move on to Denver tomorrow.'

'Well, that sure is too bad.' I then began looking round the room with more interest and it wasn't long before I stopped concentrating on the cowboys and started looking at the girls. One and all they were the most beautiful collection I had ever seen congregated together. Why, I wondered, should this small cattle town produce such remarkable women. Just then the barman came for further orders. I asked him.

'Oh well,' he said, 'I don't think Cheyenne can quite take the credit for this bunch. You see – well – it's a convention of air hostesses.'

We took a Greyhound Bus to Denver and drove through magnificent country with, on our right, the majestic frieze of the Rocky Mountains, impassable barrier to the West that the covered wagons had somehow contrived to pass. It was 100 in the shade in Denver. When we got off the plane at 9.00 that evening in San Francisco it was bitterly cold and we shivered in our tropical clothes.

San Francisco seems to be most foreigners' favourite American city and we were no exceptions. As Al Hyman, of the San Francisco Chronicle said to us:

'People here seem to take more time to live than to make a living.' I think there is a great deal of truth in that. Conversely in many other cities in the United States people concentrate on making a living to the exclusion of anything else. We did all the things the tourists do in San Francisco. We ate in Chinatown – surprisingly badly, as it happens. We ate at one of the restaurants on Fishermen's Wharf – extremely well. We rode on the famous cable cars. And, best of all, and most memorable of all, we had a drink in the 'Top of the Mark', the bar at the top of the Mark Hopkins Hotel, with a panoramic view in all directions. We went there at sunset and we watched the sun go down over the Bay and then the lights came on across the lovely span of the Golden Gate Bridge so that it looked like an inverted diamond necklace, suspended in the sky; and the whole long length of the Oakland Bridge glittered across the Bay. There are a few things I should like to do again before I die and one of them is to have a drink at sunset in the 'Top of the Mark'.

Mile after mile of fruit trees as we sped southwards down the San Joaquin Valley on the Santa Fè Railroad. Mile after mile of sandy, yellow hills dotted with scrubby green trees as we continued our journey through the Mojave Desert. And then the landscape changed again to a flat wasteland dotted with tumbleweed; and then to a tableland with desiccated cactus and scrubby, round blobs of tumbleweed with rags and pieces of torn paper (from where?) caught on their prickles. At seven the following morning we were looking at the miracle of the Grand Canyon, that most spectacular example of erosion in the world, where frost and rain, wind and river have carved the rock into massive temples that stretch away into the distance in a sea of colours, ever changing with the light from the soft greens and greys of morning to the brilliant yellows and oranges and reds of midday and the misty blues and rich purples of late evening. Even the blatant tourism of the hotel with its Hopi Indian dancers and Navajo jewellery couldn't spoil the wonder of the Grand Canyon.

And then it was Houston, Texas, a big, brash city, where the oil millionaires kept permanent penthouses in the Shamrock Hotel, costing hundreds of dollars a night. It was to find out about the oil industry that was the chief reason for our going to Houston. We were taken to oilfields on land and we went in a speedboat 6 miles out into Galveston Bay where they were hauling up two miles of drillpipe to change the bit; and we were taken round refineries, where with ingenious models they attempted to explain to us the chemical properties of petroleum. It was my first but by no means my last acquaintance with the oil industry.

It was tropically hot in Houston but every hotel, restaurant and bar was air-conditioned. It seemed almost hotter when we returned to New York where air conditioning was the exception rather than the rule. Our hotel, which was a good one, wouldn't even provide fans in the bedrooms. Cornelia Otis Skinner, whom I had known years before in London and whom we had seen in New York when we first arrived, invited both of us to stay for the week-end at her place on Long Island. It meant waiting in New York for several days. We were so exhausted by our travels that all we really wanted to do was to go home. We were very sorry to miss the week-end on Long Island but we refused the invitation with regret, packed our bags and flew back to London.

The tomato-red Alvis had caused quite a sensation wherever we had gone in the United States and numbers of people urged us to exchange it for their Buick or Pontiac – which frankly we should very much have liked to do. Every time we stopped for gas the men in the filling station wanted to know all sorts of details about the car's engine and performance. I told them what I could. When we got back to London I saw Mr Parkes who had so generously lent us the car and said it was a pity that he hadn't had a few hundred cards printed, with a picture of the car and a certain amount of information about it. I said I thought I could probably have sold quite a number of cars for him without any trouble.

'Oh well,' he said, 'it wouldn't have been much good. We're discontinuing that particular model and it might have been a bit embarrassing to get orders for it.' I said nothing. But what had been the purpose of the exercise?

Chapter Fourteen

In the late autumn of 1950 I had to hurry over to Castle Ward. My father was very ill and I arrived only a short while before he died. It came as a tremendous shock to me. I had no wish to become Lord Bangor – not then at any rate. I had made something of a name as Edward Ward and I was right at the peak of my professional career. I flattered myself that whatever else I had done, far more people had heard of me than they had of any of my forebears. I was very grieved by my father's death. We had never had much of a conventional father-and-son relationship, but he had been an excellent companion and we had always been the best of friends.

All the family came over for my father's funeral. As he had been so passionately fond of the sea we thought it would be appropriate to give him a sea burial in Strangford Lough, under the waters he had sailed so often. My father in many ways had a very conservative outlook on life and I have often thought since that he might well have been outraged at such a bizarre arrangement and would have far preferred to have lain with his ancestors in the dank churchyard of Ballyculter. However, at the time the whole family agreed that a sea burial was a wonderful idea. We found out later that the people of the neighbouring villages had been deeply shocked by what we had done.

Nothing had been done about making over even a part of the estate to me, so I immediately found myself faced with the

Holy Week, Seville

French officers' mess on the Black River Tongking
(now North Vietnam) 1951

Ankoli cattle (I courageously walked through a herd of a couple of thousand of them)

Edward Ward by the oil derricks on Lake Maracaibo, Venezuela

prospect of enormous death duties of some £80,000. Even the archaic and paralysing entail, which had been introduced at the time of the re-settlement of the Bangor Estate when I was 21 years of age could easily have been broken by my father and myself. I blamed myself bitterly (and still do) for not having taken a more constructive interest in the estate. In a ridiculous, ostrich-like way I had chosen to ignore it; to consider it as something not directly to do with me.

Right away there was the problem of what to do with Castle Ward. There were about a dozen workmen on the place and I hesitated to get rid of them *en bloc* right away (which is precisely what I should have done). I thought it might be possible to make money by selling firewood, so I set the men to felling trees and cutting them up into logs at the old Victorian sawmill in the farmyard. It didn't work. I stopped farming altogether, sold all the tractors and agricultural implements and let as many of the fields as possible. Meanwhile the overdraft on the Estate account was increasing at an alarming rate. After several months I dismissed all the men except a gardener, Bob Skillen, and a garden boy. Skillen had been very worried about the future after my father's death and had asked me what the prospects were. I told him he would be all right anyway.

'I'm very glad to hear it, Mr Edward,' he said, 'for, let me tell you, I'm a man of apprehension!'

Looking back on that chaotic time now, everything seems to have been done in a headlong manner without proper thought being given to anything. In order to find some of the money to pay the death duties, I decided to sell Castle Ward and the surrounding land and woods to the Northern Ireland Government who, in turn, handed it over to the National Trust – the idea being that the Ward family would always be encouraged to live there and look upon it as their home. I now bitterly regret having taken this precipitate decision. I wish I had turned Castle Ward into some commercial project, such as a hotel, in which I would have retained a personal interest.

Meanwhile the sale of the property in Bangor and the small town of Killough to meet the crippling duties began. Back in

London, wondering how I was going to pay an electricity bill of £17 10s. 9d., I would get a letter from the Estate solicitors saying that they had sold a piece of Bangor property for £4,000. But of course none of it came to me. I got letters, too, from our Estate agent, who was in his nineties, on the subject of the sale of some pathetic little scraps of property bringing in a ground rent of £7 or £8 a year. 'We have had an offer of £100; this represents over 14 years' purchase which, given the present state of the property market, is favourable and we advise acceptance.' These letters from Mr Burke Murphy always ended on a chatty note. 'Changeable weather we have been having. Frost at night, turnabout with rain,' was the peroration of one of them. But the point was did I accept an offer of £100, representing 14 years' purchase. I had to say I did. And as it turned out I was right because a few years later the property market slumped and the best one could get was ten or even fewer years' purchase.

It was in the middle of all this turmoil that my divorce from Leila became absolute and Marjorie and I got married. The early days of our married life, living in a top flat in Harley Street, were troubled by having to make decisions about things that I didn't really understand and a succession of letters from Belfast urging this and advising that. Among the ten pound gas bills and the electricity account for £22 and the modest bills from the grocer and the butcher, arrived one day a little account for something over £3,000 from the Inland Revenue – or whoever it is that deals with death duties. This was stated to be for interest on unpaid estate duty. In a panic I telephoned Lennox Cotton, the Estate solicitor in Belfast.

'Ah yes,' he said soothingly, 'that is quite in order. You see if we had sold additional property to pay the duties, you would have had much less income. In fact the income you have received has been well in excess of £3,000.'

'But, damn it, I haven't had any income at all from the Bangor Estate,' I shouted into the telephone.

'True, but the income has gone to reduce the estate overdraft, which would have been correspondingly higher if this income had not been used to reduce it.' In desperation I raised a capital sum from a reversionary company to deal with my large personal overdraft. But this £3,000 had to be deducted before I received a penny.

Meanwhile I had to carry on with my professional life. At least so it seemed to me at the time. Looking back on things it is quite clear that what I should have done was to concentrate on the Irish estate and do everything possible to put it on to some rational basis. But I still looked upon Ireland and everything to do with it as something divorced from what I considered to be my real life. The money from Ireland was quite different from the money I earned by my own endeavours. It wasn't, of course; it was just money, but it took me a long time to look on it in that way.

Looking through my old passports, which I have always kept as a record of my travels, I find entries for several trips to Europe in the beginning of 1951. But the next notable journey I made for the BBC – one of the most concentrated journeys I ever made – was for the Overseas Service to the Middle and Far East.

I had been doing my weekly programme for the General Overseas Programme of the BBC for some time. One day the Overseas Service decided to give me a holiday from 'Commonwealth Club' and instead send me on a tour of the Far East, taking in India, Pakistan, Persia and Libya on the way home. I was to concentrate on the 'trouble spots' – of which in the autumn of 1951 there was no lack, with the war in Korea still raging, the French fighting the Communists in the Red River Delta in Vietnam – it was still Indo China then—, a bloody guerrilla warfare dragging on in the jungles of Malaya and a coup d'état in Thailand.

I set off from London airport in a fearful old four-engined BOAC plane called an Argonaut, which was so noisy that I was quite deaf for a long time after every landing.

Tokyo was still occupied by Allied troops. One of the sights of the times was the daily triumphal progress from his residence to his office of General MacArthur. Motor cyclists, blaring sirens, cleared the streets along the route and MacArthur's car hurtled through Tokyo at seventy miles an hour. It was most impressive.

I did a good deal of recording out in the streets – the noise of the traffic had to be heard to be believed. I made an especially good recording of Tokyo traffic policemen. These courageous men perch on platforms and never remove their whistles from their mouths. They pretty nearly talk on their whistles. Sometimes they make a slow, coaxing, encouraging noise; sometimes they berate the traffic with staccato, strident blasts. A Tokyo driver knows exactly what a traffic policeman wants him to do.

Looking back on things I wonder why I worked so hard on this journey. I'm sure I sent back far more material than anyone in London ever expected. Apart from my recordings in the streets and interviews in people's homes and offices, I recorded long pieces two or three times a week. The US Marines let me use their studio to do this and at least there I didn't have to bother with the 'Booster' which I had bought to increase the strength of the Tokyo electric current. But there was another factor which is very important in recording and that is 'cycles'. The machine was designed to record at 50 cycles but this was often beyond the resources of the Tokyo power supply. A Marine sergeant used to look after me during these recording sessions. I would arrive and ask him how things were.

'Can't do no better than forty seven cycles this morning, Mr Ward,' he would reply cheerfully. This gave them plenty of trouble in London when they received my tapes.

I had a lot of fun in Tokyo. I went to the Kodokan, the great Judo hall, where I watched husky US Marines being thrown about by sixty-year-old, pot-bellied Japanese 'black belts'. I went to the Kabuki Theatre and to balance this cultural experience spent one hilarious evening with a Japanese variety impresario, who took me round all the Tokyo strip-tease places. They were not in the least like the dreary affairs for tired businessmen that seem to be so popular in the West. There was an extraordinarily comic quality about these Japanese shows that was something quite special.

I had a letter of introduction to Frank Hawley, the *Times* correspondent in Tokyo, who knew the city as probably no other Westerner knew it. He had lived there for almost twenty years except for the war break and spoke Japanese better than most Japanese did. Soon after I arrived he asked me to dinner, and brought along an American radio correspondent named Richard Harding Davies Rendell, an appropriate, if somewhat exacting name for a journalist.

'I hope you like Japanese food,' Hawley said, 'because I'm taking you to a restaurant where you get real Japanese food – the best by far in Tokyo – not the sukiaki and stuff that passes as Japanese food that you get in most places.'

It was a tiny little place. There was a semi-circular bar. Behind it stood the cook. He had a large wooden tub filled with live fish and prawns and a big copper bowl standing on a charcoal fire and filled with boiling oil. On a shelf was another bowl filled with batter.

'Have you ever eaten raw prawns?' Hawley asked. I said I hadn't.

'Right, we'll start with raw prawns.' He gave an order in Japanese to the cook, who put spoonfuls of what looked like some piquant sauce on our three plates. Then he plunged his hand into the tub, pulled out a large prawn, deftly broke it in half, pulled the shell off it and put the tail, still twitching, on my plate.

'Dip it in the sauce and eat it,' Hawley said. I have eaten a remarkable variety of strange things at one time and another including even dried water beetles in South China, but this twitching prawn demanded a certain amount of courage. However, I felt I was being subjected to a critical test, so I dipped it in the hot, spicy sauce and bit a piece off. It was quite delicious. I ate three more as well as other little bits of raw fish that are among the specialities of Japanese cuisine.

'Do you like *tempura*?' Hawley asked. I said I liked it very much. 'You've almost certainly never eaten properly cooked *tempura*,' he said and gave another order to the cook, who took another live prawn from the tub, subjected it to the same treatment but this time dipped it in the batter bowl and then plunged it into the bowl of boiling oil. Hawley was right. I had never eaten proper *tempura* before. We drank saké with this admirable meal and when we had finished Hawley proposed that we should do the round of a few geisha houses.

'A little culture would do us no harm at this stage,' he said. There was no irony connected with this remark. A geisha house is in no sense a house of ill fame. Geisha girls are cultured, charming people and Japanese go to geisha houses to hear poetry exquisitely recited and classical songs beautifully sung. They also go to them for romantic reasons because the girls are usually extremely beautiful and romance, where marriages are usually family-arranged affairs, is something that most Japanese men have to go out and look for.

We continued to drink saké at the geisha houses. Rendell and I drank it from the usual little porcelain cups but Hawley said they annoyed him and drank his in pony-sized glasses, each of which held at least six of our cupfuls. At the third geisha house we went to, the girls, who were exceptionally lovely, had sung three or four plaintive little songs when Hawley, who was beginning to show the effect of his high consumption of saké, turned to me and said:

'Enough of all this damned culture. I'm going to get the girls to sing the Japanese Army song about the fall of Singapore! I'll bet they know it.'

'You can't do that, Frank!' Rendell said.

'Can't I bloody well?' Hawley replied. 'You watch me!' He turned to the leading Japanese Geisha girl and spoke to her in Japanese. It was clear that she and the other girls not only knew the song but were more than ready to sing it. And out it came, a slightly orientalized Western marching song which the girls sang *con molto brio.* They evidently hadn't forgotten a note of it. Richard Harding Davies Rendell looked uncomfortable during the rendering of this martial air and kept murmuring that Hawley shouldn't have asked the girls to sing such a thing. When the song came to an end Hawley applauded loudly.

'Well, you see, Richard, Eddy and I can take it. Let's see if you can!' He shouted something to the geisha girls and they started another even more spirited song. After they'd sung a couple of verses Frank shouted over the singing:

'Know what that is? It's the Japanese Navy song celebrating the fall of Manila!' Richard Harding Davies Rendell didn't say another word for the rest of the evening.

One day I lunched at the British Embassy. Among the guests was an extremely pleasant young man who was exceptionally tall for a Japanese. His name was Tokugawa. I told him that after I had finished my work in Tokyo, I planned to travel down to Nagoya and Osaka and, indeed right down to the south to Sasebo.

'Nagoya is my own home town,' he said, 'if I can be of any help please don't hesitate to get in touch with me,' and he gave me his telephone number. During the next few days I visited the Nikon camera factory and if it hadn't been for the fact that the Americans were controlling its entire output I could have bought for £18 a superb lens that conveniently fitted a Leica camera and which in England cost over £200. I spent a week-end at Nikko and then, one evening. I took the night train to Nagoya, the Stoke-on-Trent of Japan. I arrived at four o'clock in the morning, went to a hotel, slept until eight and then I remembered Tokugawa. I wanted to visit some of the potteries and I felt sure he could help me. I telephoned him. He answered the telephone himself and said he would come right over. In my hotel room he put through several telephone calls and at the end of it all wrote out the names of the managers of two potteries and said he was sure they would be able to provide me with all I needed.

'I wish I could come along with you,' he said, 'but unfortunately I have to go to Tokyo in an hour. One thing I do hope you will find time to do before you leave Nagoya and that is to visit the Tokugawa museum. I'll telephone the curator and tell him to expect you some time in the afternoon. Once again he dialled a number. I thanked him for all his kindness and we said goodbye.

'Do have a look round the museum if you can,' he said again as he left. Thanks to the introductions I had a most successful and speedy trip round the potteries. I had several hours to spare before taking the train on to Osaka and so I thought that in view of Tokugawa's kindness the least I could do was to take a look at the local museum, which he had seemed so anxious for me to do. I was met by the curator and spent the next half hour looking at showcases containing objects of remarkable banality. There were indifferent Balinese masks; bits and pieces of Egyptiana; some very ordinary Chinese and Japanese porcelain; some African drums and weapons. It was a lot of what I call 'sea-captain' stuff. After a while the curator could scarcely fail to see that I was not much impressed. He smiled and sucked in his breath with a loud hiss.

'Tokugawa Museum contains many thousands of items,' he said. 'Is not possible to show all items at same time. There is good treasure and bad treasure. What you have seen is, frankly – ah – bad treasure. I now show you – ah – good treasure.' He led me into a small room, where a succession of works of art of quite incalculable value and beauty were brought in for me to look at. Priceless Sung Dynasty paintings from China; a fabulous collection of seventeenth-century scrolls showing the early history of the Kabuki Theatre; an exquisite bridal suite made for one of the bygone Tokugawa daughters in lacquer inlaid with gold. And while I was gazing at these unbelievable 'good' treasures, I realized what a consummate fool I had made of myself. Of course it was partly General MacArthur's fault for having abolished titles in Japan. But my friend who had so obligingly made business appointments for me at eight o'clock in the morning was the Duke of Tokugawa, whose family had been the ruling *shoguns* of Japan for three centuries. Only a few days before I had seen the tombs of his ancestors at Nikko, which the Tokugawas had built. It would have been much the same if a visitor to England had telephoned the Duke of Devonshire and asked him to fix up a round of visits in the Potteries, and then had rather grudgingly agreed to have a look at Chatsworth.

Right down in the south of Japan, between the two World Wars, a man called Mikimoto – who was still alive at the age of over ninety, when I was there, invented the 'cultured' pearl. His industry was flourishing. There was the little factory on the seashore. In the sea were moored countless metal baskets of oysters.

'No trouble,' the Japanese guide told me. 'Not necessary to feed oysters. They obtain all nutriment they need from "prankton".' They could grade a necklace as they wished. The smaller pearls nearest the clasp came from oysters that had only been in the baskets a comparatively short time. The bigger the pearl, the longer the oyster must stay in the basket. They could make any shaped pearl purely by inserting the right shaped grain in the oyster. A round grain – a round pearl. A curiously shaped grain – a so-called 'baroque' pearl. What nonsense, really. The grain of sand or whatever it was goes into the oyster by mistake – a valuable 'natural' pearl. It is put in on purpose – a 'cultured' pearl, worth far, far less. The oyster, at least, doesn't know the difference.

From the south I flew over to Korea. I stayed there a little over a week, driving up near the front line, if there could be said to be such a thing in that wild, uneven country. Were they fighting where I had spent that wonderful holiday before the war in the Diamond Mountains, I wondered? One day, as mortar shells landed and exploded all around us, I found myself becoming furious. What's the sense of this? I thought. I've had my war. I've been nearly killed many times. I was taken prisoner. I didn't come over to this lousy little war to get hit by a mortar shell. And then I thought of all the magnificently heroic episodes of this extraordinary, political war. I thought of some of the valiant things the Americans had done. I thought of the bravery of the Turks. I thought of the epic deeds of the Gloucesters. And it beat me. I could understand heroism when you are fighting directly for your country, when if you lose your country gets overrun and occupied by the enemy. That's worth laying down your life for. But not, surely, this ideological conflict at the back end of the world in Korea. And yet, there was just as much heroism there as there had been in France and Italy and Germany and the Far East in World War II.

In Hong Kong, I had the good luck to be offered the loan of his flat by John Keswick, the head of Jardine Matheson. Keswick said: 'I think I can make the extravagant claim to having the best cook in Hong Kong – and that's saying something these days when most of the best cooks in China are here. My Number One boy will look after you very well I think. And so – well, treat the flat as your own, give dinner parties. Do whatever you like. I'm delighted to be able to help.'

I had really forgotten that it was possible to live so well. I was rushing round collecting stories and I would go back to the flat to write them up. I would be sitting at my typewriter and at about four o'clock, as if by magic, tea and sandwiches were at my side. Two hours later the tea things would disappear to be replaced by a decanter of whisky, ice and a siphon. My clothes would be spirited away some time during the night and would be back in the morning pressed and ironed. The air conditioning would be turned off just before I got up in the morning because in November it was becoming a little chilly. I did give a couple of small dinner parties and they were superb.

I made friends with the Hong Kong Chief of Police, Mr Mackintosh and with him made many trips to the islands and to the New Territories on the mainland. One day we went to the village of Shatoukok where, five years before, I had got to know the old East River Guerrillas, good, honest Communists, armed to the teeth with Mauser pistols and belts slung with hand grenades. The fact that one side of the main street of Shatoukok was Hong Kong Territory and the other side Chinese hadn't mattered in those days. It certainly did on this visit. Grim, humourless Chinese sentries stood on guard and there was no possibility of re-visiting the old Customs House that had been the headquarters of the East River Guerrillas. Mackintosh insisted on staying on the 'Chinese' side of me as we walked up the main street. He spoke fluent Cantonese but it amused me that when it came to trying to buy some silver ornaments from the Hakka merchants, I managed better than he did. They could understand my fragmentary Mandarin. The Hakkas came originally from somewhere in Central China.

The difficult thing about this whole journey was that I always had to fly between one country and the next. I never had more than a matter of hours to forget about one set of political or military conditions and get ready to assimilate the next totally different ones. In Hong Kong I had been concentrating on the recovery from the war years; the influx of refugees from China; the general threat of Communist China. A few hours away I found myself involved in the war in Indo China. I stayed a couple of days in Saigon, where I had been before, briefly, in 1946, and then flew up north to Hanoi which is a charming town, much pleasanter than Saigon. It was like Aix-en-Provence in an oriental setting. There were the same avenues of trees, the same fountains.

The British vice-consul in Hanoi asked me to dinner one evening.

'I thought you might like to meet one or two intelligent Vietnamese who can tell you how people think these days,' he said, 'so I've asked a journalist, a doctor and a lawyer to come round later on. It won't be until about eleven o'clock because they don't want the French authorities to see them calling on me.' They turned up about 11.30 and we talked for hours. What it all boiled down to was that there was an extreme right wing group who were pro-French; an extreme left wing group who were pro-Ho Chi-minh; and the great bulk of the population joined one side or the other depending upon which they considered the lesser evil. What they all really wanted was independence.

'Personally I would be quite happy for us to be part of the French Union,' the lawyer said, 'if it worked on anything like the same lines as the British Commonwealth. But it doesn't. We should simply remain a French colony.'

'The French point of view,' the journalist said, 'is that we can go to Paris; we can study at the Sorbonne or at any other French university; we can have French citizenship and what on earth more do we want? Well, we want our freedom even without all these advantages.'

At this time the French had pushed across the Red River Delta and had just established themselves on the far bank of the Black River. I registered myself at French Military Headquarters in Hanoi and it was only a couple of days before I was able to fly out to the Black River in a little Piper Cub. The Red River Delta looks quite extraordinary from the air. Limestone formations erupt from the flat plain, rising sometimes in steep pinnacles, sometimes in high, round humps, sometimes looking like fairy tale castles. Sometimes these *calcaires* as the French call them have been eroded into weird, animal-like shapes. But the *calcaires* are at their most remarkable just off the coast in the Bay of Along – a vast archipelago of these limestone eruptions that rise steeply out of the sea. To attempt to sail between them would be a nightmare.

Strongposts had been established on some of the larger *calcaires* on the plain and we flew over several of them. Then we had to fly higher to get over a range of craggy hills. On the other side the character of the country changed completely. The Black River wound its way below us through thickly vegetated country and we landed on the far side of it on a little airstrip that had been made on a comparatively level piece of ground. I was taken to the officers' mess, which was an open building made of rough branches, with grass-thatched roof. They were just about to sit down to lunch. Two bottles of champagne were on the trestle table – one of the officers was going on leave and was celebrating the occasion. We sat down to the exquisite meal that the French seem to be able to conjure up no matter where they are. It was a Foreign Legion unit that was holding this westernmost outpost the French forces had reached. Over coffee and brandy I asked the colonel if by chance he had any former members of the Afrika Korps in his regiment.

'You see,' I explained, 'I was taken prisoner in the Desert by the Afrika Korps and it would be very interesting for me to talk over those days with one of them – in happier circumstances.' The colonel looked at me solemnly for a few moments.

'I don't know,' he said at last. 'It is possible that if you stayed with us for a few weeks you might find a former member of the Afrika Korps. But I don't know. You see, we ask no questions in the Legion.' It was pure *Beau Geste.* After lunch, in something under five minutes I found a Westphalian sergeant, who had served with the Afrika Korps all through the desert campaigns. We had an enjoyable, nostalgic talk about North Africa.

I had to spend a couple of days in Saigon before catching a plane to Singapore and one evening an American I had met in the hotel suggested we go to a vast amusement park that existed in Saigon in those days and see a Vietnamese opera. I said I'd seen a good deal of Chinese opera before the war and I'd be interested to see if a Vietnamese one was much different.

'Well, they have women actresses,' my friend said, 'which is more than they do in China. Very good looking ones, too.'

'You should have seen Mei Lang-fang playing a woman's part,' I said, 'he looked exquisite and I don't believe any woman could have moved with such consummate grace. Anyway don't let's get too near the orchestra; if it's anything like a Chinese orchestra we'll be deafened.'

'Oh no, they have a kind of Western orchestra, saxophones and trumpets.'

The play turned out to be classically traditional in the Chinese manner. The central figure was a king. A group of traitors was planning to assassinate him. But the king was wise to their plot. He had his own men in hiding, very obviously, in the wings. The climax of the play came when the traitors started to surround the king, while at the same time his henchmen attacked and routed them. Now in China the orchestra would have accompanied this stirring scene with a deafening crescendo of noise from the cymbals and drums. In Saigon the orchestra marked the occasion by playing, *fortissimo*, 'Alexander's Ragtime Band'. We were the only members of the audience to think it a comical choice of music.

A week later I was having tea on the lawn outside a rubber planter's bungalow, not far from Kuala Lumpur, talking with Mrs Lucy, his wife, about Malaya.

The garden with its brilliant tropical flowers and shrubs and a tall tulip tree blazing with flame-coloured blossom was exquisite and the view beyond was astonishingly lovely. You looked out over the plantations of rubber trees, with their pale grey mottled trunks to a jungly, mountainous valley.

Our conversation was constantly interrupted by the Lucys' three-year-old twin boys, who kept coming up to show me their toys. I asked Mrs Lucy how she managed with the twins, cut off from the outside world as she was by the high barbed wire fence that ran round the garden.

'Oh well, they play about in their nursery in the early part of the morning. It's just like an ordinary nursery in most ways, but it is surrounded by a two-foot-wide barricade of sand, so that no possible stray bullets can come into it. It's difficult to imagine that the twins never go for a walk,' she went on. 'They never go anywhere outside the barbed wire, unless they go in our armoured car. Since, about a year ago, a small girl, the same age as the twins, was murdered on an estate near ours, I've never left them alone without a European in charge.'

Some months previously the Lucys were attacked by bandits almost every night for several weeks.

It began to get dark and we went inside, into the screened verandah that was like a large porch. Mrs Lucy fixed *stengahs* –

long, weak, whiskies and soda. I looked across to the little circular bar. Above it were hanging three hats. One was a topee with a big chunk missing from the front as if it had been bitten out. Beside it was a home-made military cap with a tin star and the third was similar but with a red star embroidered on it.

'What's the history of the hats?' I asked. Mrs Lucy laughed.

'Well, the topee's my husband's bandit and the other two were shot by our Malay special constables.'

'And you hang them up like sporting tropies – like deers' antlers?' Mrs Lucy wrinkled her brow and paused before replying.

'You know I've never thought about it like that before,' she said. 'Yes, I suppose we do.' And then her voice hardened. 'And very appropriate, too, if I may say so. Those terrible Communists are just like wild beasts. They haven't shown any mercy to anybody. They've committed such terrible atrocities they don't deserve any mercy. I can tell you I was quite envious of my husband when he got his terrorist. I've always felt that I could repay the deaths of my various friends, by getting one or two of them myself in return!' For a moment it was astonishing to hear this charming, normally gentle woman speaking with such venom. But only for a moment. I had even felt a little nervous driving the few miles to the Lucys' estate from Kuala Lumpur, with the dense jungle coming down to the road on both sides, where you wouldn't see anyone even a few feet away. Never to go to bed for month after month without knowing that you may be roused by a volley of bullets during the night must have been an unnerving experience, made all the worse by having children to worry about. One would not be likely to have any charitable feelings towards the terrorists.

The arrival of Mr Lucy interrupted my thoughts. His wife made the introductions and poured him a drink.

'Mr Ward was interested in your bandit, darling.' Mr Lucy downed half his *stengah* – it was a very hot evening.

'Oh, I was inspecting an estate one day and coming back I was passing another of my estates and I thought I'd stop the car and have a look into one of the fields. I took my shotgun with me – rather automatically because I wasn't expecting any danger.

One of the special constables came with me. I was walking up the terraces looking at the rubber when suddenly, out of the corner of my eye I saw a terrorist in a lying-low position, with his rifle pointed at me. Luckily I'm fairly useful with a shotgun and I quickly aimed and shot him and luckily got him in the head.'

I arrived in Bangkok just at the end of a revolution. It had been an entirely bloodless affair, all very civilized. For many years the Navy had run Thailand. Admirals and captains had filled all the top political jobs and now the Army and the Police had forgotten their past differences and had joined together to throw out the Navy. Between them they had taken over the Government. All the admirals and captains were in hiding in the jungle. Of course Thailand still had a Navy and one of the first things the new Government had to do was to find a new commander-in-chief for it. They dug up a harmless old admiral, who had been on the retired list for over twenty years and had forgotten practically all he ever knew about naval affairs and made him commander-in-chief. For good measure they also made him Minister of Agriculture, about which he knew absolutely nothing whatever. It was all pure Gilbert and Sullivan.

The revolution had been bloodless, but the new régime was acting in a fairly tough manner. The former Chief of Police had made himself Minister of the Interior as well as holding on to his old job. As a policeman he had had a reputation of great ruthlessness and when I went to see him I could well believe this was true. He had been known as 'The Tiger' and he evidently appreciated the title because he had a huge tiger-skin rug on the floor of his office. One of the first of his rather high handed actions was to put all members of the Parliamentary opposition under house arrest. It didn't appear to be a very strict measure because I had no trouble in going to see the Leader of the Opposition, an extremely charming Prince. He had been educated in England and spoke absolutely perfect idiomatic English. We sat on the verandah of his house drinking lager beer, and in true Oriental fashion talking about everything in the world except the subject I had come to discuss with him – what line was the opposition going to take?

I had always rather enjoyed these delaying tactics in China and was delighted to find they were the rule in Thailand too. The thing the prince had loved above all else in England were the pubs. He had become extremely knowledgeable about English beer and he was very anxious to know whether this or that pub in London was still going and if the bitter was as good as it had been in his day. Meanwhile we consumed bottle after bottle of lager.

'Poor stuff,' the prince said, 'but it's the best we can do here.' At last I felt the time had come to get to the point. I asked the prince what the policy of the opposition was going to be. A look of utter incomprehension came over his face.

'I don't think I quite get your meaning,' he said.

'I mean what are you, as leader of the opposition, going to do?'

'Do? Do? Why, nothing of course!'

'But surely the opposition must have some policy, must take some kind of action mustn't it?' The prince looked pained.

'My dear sir you cannot seriously suppose that a man in my position could possibly have anything to do with the type of people who have taken over our country? I mean one couldn't bring oneself to speak to them, even.'

'But if the opposition does nothing surely there'll be nothing to stop the Government doing exactly what it likes?' The prince looked at me sadly.

'Absolutely nothing. But I repeat you cannot possibly expect me to associate in any way whatever with such people. One can only hope that, given enough rope, they'll hang themselves. But that, I fear, is unlikely. The trouble is, you know, that Thailand suffers from the curse of plenty; our people are so rich that they are simply not interested in politics and will do nothing. And now another bottle of this execrable lager, I think.' And I was able to get nothing further out of him.

I saw a good deal of Geoffrey Wallinger, the British Ambassador to Thailand, and he very kindly checked the articles

I was writing before I sent them back to London. One evening I was invited to dinner at the Embassy. When I arrived I learned that the Ambassador had been detained at the airport, where he was waiting to meet some visiting notability. We went in to dinner without him. The Wallingers had inherited a Chinese butler from the previous ambassador and Mrs Wallinger couldn't bear him. By the time we had reached the main course Geoffrey Wallinger returned. He was not feeling very well and he excused himself and went to bed, saying he would only have a bowl of soup. Mrs Wallinger rang for the butler and said:

'His Excellency only wants a bowl of soup. Will you please have one sent up to his room.' The Chinese looked distressed.

'No can do missie,' he said.

'What do you mean, no can do? There's plenty of soup isn't there?'

'No, missie, soup no have got.'

'Well there was plenty left when it left the dining-room what happened?'

'Coolie have eat,' the butler blurted out. After that the dinner party became a riot.

'I say, go easy on that soufflé,' one of the guests cried, 'the coolie'd be sure to like it.'

I arrived in New Delhi on Christmas Eve. I dined that evening with some friends at Maiden's Hotel. At midnight the dance band suddenly broke into 'Happy Birthday to You'. I looked round the room to see who was celebrating a birthday. And then I realized that nobody was. This was the Indian idea of heralding in Christmas. There was no work to be done on Christmas Day and I stepped out into the crisp winter sunshine and walked miles through Delhi by myself. I recorded (with my camera) one legacy of the British Raj, a group of Indian boys playing cricket outside the walls of the Red Fort.

I stayed in Delhi just long enough to do a social reconstruction story and then flew on to Karachi, a city very different from the one I had known four years before, packed with refugees, with shanty towns mushrooming up outside. I was glad to be on my way to Persia.

I stayed in the Ritz Hotel in Teheran. At one time and another I have stayed at several Ritz Hotels. But the Teheran Ritz was something quite special. My boarding house-like room was heated by a rusty Valor-Perfection oil stove, in the depth of winter – and it was bitterly cold in Teheran. But the Ritz boasted a very good Russian restaurant.

I interviewed several political figures including the leader of the opposition, who was taking sanctuary or *bast* in the Majlis – the Parliament building, where he had retired to bed in a private room. All his friends and supporters visited him there and he remained perpetually in pyjamas. I believe if he had dressed the sanctuary would no longer have held good.

The highlight of my stay in Teheran was my visit to Premier Mossadeq, who had installed himself in a small, red-brick nursing home in the suburbs of the capital, where he, too, remained permanently in bed. Mossadeq had recently been instrumental in throwing the British Petroleum Company out of Persia and was (temporarily) riding on the crest of a wave as a result. I shall always remember going into this nursing home room – a dreary room with a dado round the wall, and Mossadeq, wearing striped concentration camp pyjamas, sitting up in his cheap, iron bed and looking at me with his piercing eyes that flashed under their deep, hooded lids.

We talked in French so there was no need for an interpreter and I was alone with the old man for about three quarters of an hour. He began with a diatribe against the iniquities of BP some of which was founded on a good deal of fact. He talked hard, commonsense for a while and then would fly off into pure fantasy.

'I sometimes think,' he said at one point, 'that it would have been far better if our country had never had any oil at all. It has done us no good so far and we don't need foreign currency. We produce almost everything we need ourselves. The only main raw material we have to import in rather large quantities is sugar.'

'You say you could get on perfectly well without oil, Excellency,' I said, 'but inevitably your whole economy is geared to oil. Just as South Africa, for example, is geared to gold. South Africa could probably get along without gold far better than Iran could without oil.' Mossadeq looked at me for a few moments. Then he leant forward in his bed and gave me a hard slap on the knee. He chuckled.

'You know, you've got something there,' he said. Just at this moment there was a knock on the door and a waiter came in with a tin tray with two white canteen cups of tea and a large bowl of sugar. It was handed to me first and I took a couple of lumps of sugar and put them into my tea. When the waiter offered the tray to Mossadeq he put his hand into the sugar basin, took a large handful of sugar – at least fourteen lumps – and dropped it all into his teacup. The tea, of course, overflowed and slopped into the saucer. I was fascinated.

'You know, Excellency,' I said, 'you were talking a little while ago about the need to import sugar into Iran. I believe you must be largely personally responsible!' Mossadeq let out a great roar of laughter at this sally and leant out of bed and gave me another slap on the leg. I really believe he enjoyed the time we spent together as much as I did. He was an old man of very great charm.

My long journey was very nearly over. I flew on to Cairo and from there to Benghazi and Tripoli. That was before oil had been discovered in Libya and the country was living more or less on charity. I made a few recordings there and flew back to London, feeling more than a little exhausted; ten countries in three months and never more than a day's gap between any two of them. I was suffering from a fairly severe attack of mental indigestion and very much looking forward to seeing Marjorie and my six-months-old daughter again. I had become a father three months before I set out on my travels.

Chapter Fifteen

I had scarcely had time to settle down in London again – oh! there'd been a lot of work, a number of special programmes that I broadcast as a result of my long journey, when the BBC wanted me to go to Finland. The Olympic Games were to be held shortly in Helsinki and the idea was to build up a programme that would give a picture of Finland and at the same time be treated as a 'return journey' to the country where I had worked as a war correspondent during the Winter War of 1939–40.

I had known Finland as a country where the temperature fell to thirty below zero; a white country, where the myriad lakes looked like smooth, white fields, where the fir trees in the unending forests were for ever laden with a burden of snow. I returned to Finland in the heat of midsummer. The shops of Helsinki, which I had remembered half empty and barricaded against the air-raids with stout wooden boards, were full of good things. A fever of the forthcoming Olympic Games pervaded everything.

On my first day I went with a Finnish friend from the war days to the great war cemetery just outside Helsinki. We stood at the top of a rising slope of ground by Field Marshal Mannerheim's grave, ablaze with flowers. And we looked down the slope over thousands upon thousands of soldiers' graves. Most of them had lost their lives in the Winter War; some in the war that followed between the Germans and the Russians. My friend made a sweeping gesture with his hand over the rows of little tombstones.

'That,' he said, 'is the price we have paid for our freedom.'

It was immensely moving. Moving not only because of the gesture towards the price paid but because this Finn beside me could speak with conviction and utter truth of 'our freedom'. Finland was, and still is, free. The Finns live their own lives in their own way and to imagine for one moment that Finland is behind the Iron Curtain – well, you didn't and still don't have to stay very long in the country to realize the absurdity of any such notion. I, for one, am convinced that it was Finland's determined fight for liberty in the Winter War of 1939–40 that was largely responsible for her unique position today as the only European country whose frontiers march with those of the Soviet Union that is *not* behind the Iron Curtain. Finland was the only one of all those countries where I didn't even – and that was back in 1952 – need a visa for my passport.

I stayed in Helsinki a few days and then travelled north to Lapland. I stayed in Rovaniemi, where I had remembered the days as only lasting three hours at the most – when the photographers not only had to work overtime during those short hours of daylight but had to plunge their cameras quickly back under their jackets to stop them from freezing. In midsummer in Rovaniemi you could easily read a book at midnight. The trouble was not the bitter cold but the voracious mosquitoes.

The Finns had done marvels of reconstruction in the seven years since the war. The destruction in Finland had been appalling. In a country where most of the houses in the country towns were built of wood, a few incendiary bombs soon left nothing standing except the monolithic chimneys. Rovaniemi had been almost totally destroyed and evacuated. When I returned such a short time afterwards you would never have guessed there had been any bombing. I spent some days in the North – and for me it was a fascinating 'return journey' and then I returned to Helsinki.

The Finns had built a magnificent stadium for the forthcoming Olympic Games and one afternoon I went there to see a football match between Finland and the Red Army. (The latter somewhat 'loaded' their team by including several Soviet international players and therefore, not unexpectedly, won the match.)

I happened to be sitting behind a group of Chinese, who I assumed were officials in the Chinese Embassy. One of them offered cigarettes to his friends but nobody seemed to have a match. I thought I would surprise them.

'*Ni yao yang huo ma*? – Do you require foreign fire?' I asked. An astonished Chinese turned round and gratefully accepted a light. In the interval I was invited (in my capacity of some sort of VIP) to take refreshments in a large room under the stand. I knew nobody there. They were mostly Russians and Chinese. There was one old gentleman who looked to me to be unmistakably a Japanese. Some months previously in Tokyo I had met a charming young Japanese called Awati who had told me he was coming to the Olympic Games to take part in the yacht racing events. By way of making conversation I turned to the old gentleman and said:

'I wonder, sir, if by chance you know when Mr Awati is arriving from Tokyo?' The old man looked at me and smiled.

'I should hardly be in a position to answer your question, sir. I come from North Korea.'

Early that year our son Nicholas had been born and on my return from Finland we had gone to Norfolk to spend a summer holiday with some friends, when one evening Laurence Gilliam rang up.

'Eddy, how do you feel about going to Egypt,' he said. 'I want a story about how things are going there in these early days after Farouk has been thrown out.' Holiday or no holiday it was something I couldn't miss. And it was a great joy to be married to somebody like Marjorie who realized this just as well as I did.

I arrived in Cairo in high summer with the temperature well into the hundreds. It was a very changed Cairo for me. Shepherd's Hotel had been burned to the ground during the rioting at the time of the revolution. The Continental Hotel, where I had always stayed during the war was no more. The famous Turf Club had been gutted, and several of the members murdered on the spot. There had been a proposal to re-establish the Turf Club on Gezirah Island and one of the oldest members was reported to have said:

'Never heard such a preposterous idea in me life. Might just as well take White's and plant it on Hampstead Heath!'

I ended up in the Semiramis, on the banks of the Nile. This was a hotel used essentially by winter visitors to Egypt. It had no form of air conditioning. It wasn't even possible to get an electric fan in one's bedroom. The only room I could get was an immense double one, which was wildly expensive. I went some way towards getting my money's worth by changing beds about two o'clock in the morning and getting at least a degree of coolness at half time.

Since the fall of King Farouk all the titles, 'Pasha', 'Bey' and so on, had officially been abolished. The press official, with whom I dealt, however, was still addressed by all of us as Mustapha Bey (though I doubt if the 'Bey' meant much more than the 'Esq.' in England). He was a very friendly, nice fellow and one day I said to him:

'What about my having a look at the Kouba Palace?' I knew that the new régime in Egypt was doing everything in its power to vilify and execrate their former King Farouk. Mustapha Bey said he thought it was a good idea and would I call in at 10 the following morning. I did – I made a point of calling a little earlier and Mustapha Bey said he hoped I didn't mind but a number of other members of the foreign press wanted to come too. I minded very much but there was nothing I could do about it.

We drove to the Kouba Palace. Before we were allowed in we had to agree to be searched before we left.

'This is something everybody must agree to – even if he is a high member of the Egyptian Government,' we were told.

'All right,' we said.

The Kouba Palace was – or had been – King Farouk's home. We walked though the beautifully kept grounds, with flowering shrubs and palm trees, and an Egyptian captain taking us round:

'He had four hundred gardeners to look after all this.' Through a big, dark basement room to a heavily barred door with electric gadgets on each side.

'They're invisible rays that used to ring alarms.'

Beyond the bars to Farouk's treasure room – a small room lined with huge safes: Farouk's collection of gold coins, medals and medallions – sovereigns to big saucer-sized discs of gold. And an unbelievable collection of banknotes including ten thousand dollar bills neatly docketed away in files. Jewelled caskets, sweetmeat boxes – seven big safes crammed with treasure. 'How much, for Heaven's sake, is it all worth?'

'Well, his stamp collection alone is supposed to be worth three millions sterling anyway.'

And then the gymnasium – every conceivable weight-reducing machine – body-pummellers, rowing machines, mechanical horses.

'They do not seem to have served their purposes!'

The music room – a vast white room with glittering chandeliers, a white piano with a pianola attached, a mechanical organ and what must have been the original jukebox – I wound the handle and a terrifying blare of early jazz came out – a little electrical music box with Mickey Mouse and Donald Duck inside the lid – a collection of expensive rubbish of almost inconceivable bad taste and banality. The Egyptian captain evidently agreed:

'He was very fond of this room. Unbelievable childishness!'

On through another series of rooms, furnished abominably, hung with appalling pictures. All that money and no taste – but absolutely no taste at all! And then to Farouk's private apartments. Cupboards full of jewelled cufflinks, fitted dressing-cases – others crammed with every gambling device and game imaginable – roulette wheels, baccarat 'shoes', hundreds of packs of cards with naked girls on the back (I put one in my pocket to test the Egyptian security). Chests of drawers full of pornographic statuettes and figures and drawings and books but all of the Port Said 'feelthy picture' class, all ridiculously naïve and schoolboyish, and mixed up with all this all kinds of 'trick' toys and gadgets.

'You see the kind of king we had!'

And then his dressing-room – wardrobes full of army, navy and air force uniforms – one cupboard fitted with specially-designed little racks with a fantastic collection of ties – over a thousand of them ranging from specially woven ones with the royal monogram to the most gaudy American hand-painted 'shockers'; well over a hundred walking sticks with gold and jewelled heads.

'This one with a cockatoo's head – if you press a button it raises and lowers its crest. What nonsense!'

On our way downstairs again we went through storerooms where Farouk's magpie-like acquisitions had barely even been taken out of their packing cases. There was a collection of priceless Fabergé enamels packed on a shelf alongside some awful modern Italian porcelain nudes. Farouk collected everything.

The last room we came to was the audience room, where the King had received ambassadors and distinguished visitors. The date on the calendar on the ex-king's desk was July 24th, 1952. Nobody had bothered to tear off the dates since that day when Farouk had to leave all his palaces and his treasure chests.

I had dinner some days later with Sir Ralph Stevenson, the British Ambassador and we talked about Farouk. Sir Ralph, of course, had known him quite well.

'In some ways,' he told me, 'he was an extremely intelligent man. He was very unfortunate. If his father had lived longer things might have been very different. But he had a very bad upbringing. There were too many sycophants who agreed to everything he said or wished.'

On the subject of Farouk's grossness Sir Ralph said:

'I have gone duck shooting with the royal party at Fayoum and when we have paused about mid-morning for refreshment I have seen the king eat two or three ducks one after the other. He was a prodigious trencherman!'

The visit to the Kouba Palace was an interesting interlude. My great objective was an interview with General Neguib – Nasser was very much a 'backroom boy' at that stage. At last Mustapha Bey succeeded in arranging the interview. Some days before I had had a talk with Eric Downton of the *Daily Telegraph* and when I told him I hoped to get an exclusive interview with Neguib he said:

'Try him out on Kemal Ataturk. They say Neguib's modelled himself on him.'

Neguib's office at Abassia, between Cairo and Heliopolis, was a great contrast to the exotic luxuriousness of Farouk's fantastic palace. It was a simple military room with a big desk; framed quotations from the Koran on the walls; maps; a cubicle leading on to a balcony where the Commander-in-Chief snatched the few hours of sleep he was able to on an austere iron cot. I couldn't help thinking of the childish nonsense of Farouk's personal life – his juke boxes and pornography – when I started talking to General Neguib. I had been a little disconcerted when I had been asked to submit a series of questions to the general the day before. I always hate doing this because one seldom if ever gets a spontaneous answer. The ante-room to Neguib's office was crowded with Egyptian officers and I am sure that Nasser was among them. I plugged in my recording set and put my pre-submitted questions to General Neguib. He replied to them with more life and apparent spontaneity than I had hoped and when he had finished I found myself alone in the room with him and the machine still running. I seized the opportunity.

'You have given me an account of your official policy, General, but now I would like to know a little more about you yourself. What do you do in your spare time, for instance?' Neguib smiled.

'As you may imagine I don't have very much spare time these days. I do some exercises in the early morning just to keep fit. I like to play tennis and to swim but in these last years I've had little time for these things. Perhaps my chief hobby is collecting books.' Trying to lead up to his admiration for Kemal Ataturk I asked him what kind of books he was most interested in.

'I am particularly interested in economics and psychology. I find psychology particularly useful in judging character—'

'And do you read biographies, General?'

'Biography not so much – from time to time but—' This wasn't getting on to Ataturk. I plumped for the direct approach.

'I'm told, general' I said, 'that you are a great admirer of Kemal Ataturk.' Neguib 'gave'.

'He was a great man. Perhaps the greatest man of the century – at any rate in the Middle East. I think we all must admire such a great man and try to imitate him if possible.' Naturally enough I was delighted with this frank interview. I air mailed the tapes back to London immediately. It was a good precaution. A day later I was accused of 'unethical conduct' by Neguib's 'watch-dogs' – Nasser doubtless included.

'General Neguib answered my questions quite freely,' I said. 'He is the head man in this country isn't he?' I added naïvely. It was sad to think that it was only a matter of months after this that Neguib was deposed and that he has remained under house arrest ever since. He was, I am convinced, a good and honest man. He had been put in as a figurehead on account of his general's rank by the junior officers who had staged the revolt. From their point of view he became too big for his boots. He was not content to remain a passive figurehead. With his picture in almost every house in Egypt he began to consider himself as the leader of the country. That did not suit Nasser and his associates. So Neguib had to go.

Chapter Sixteen

Nineteen-fifty-two was a year of exceptional travel – even for me. In the winter of that year I went with Maurice Brown of the BBC to the Lebanon, Syria and Iraq, to report the opening of the great 30-inch oil pipeline from the oilfields at Kirkuk, to Banias on the Mediterranean coast.

Maurice and I stayed a week in the ramshackle old city of Baghdad and amused ourselves collecting material for a joint programme called 'Portrait of Baghdad'. When we began our researches we came up against a great number of difficulties. In order to get permission to wander through the city, we had to call on the Minister of Propaganda and Guidance. He, of course, wanted us to see new bridges and power stations and modern building projects. We said that naturally we should like to see these examples of progress, but that, nevertheless, people in England, ignorant that they are, would expect, in a programme about Baghdad, to be told about the old markets that have been in existence since the days of Haroun al Raschid. The Minister found this very curious, but agreed. He even went so far as to provide us with two members of the secret police – for our protection because he felt the people in the bazaar would not like foreigners with recording machines invading their territory. The two secret police were invaluable. They were a very tough couple of men and everyone in the bazaar was terrified of them. They carried our recording equipment and if we wanted the coppersmiths to hammer away at their work to give us background sound effects, one word from our henchmen set them hammering away as if their lives depended on it – which perhaps they did.

We were discouraged from mentioning animals like camels and donkeys because the Iraqis were ashamed of such primitive means of transport and if you were caught taking a photograph of one of these officially non-existent beasts, you were liable to get into trouble. In the end we wrote a light-hearted programme in which that fine actor Esmé Percy took the part of our guide round the city. The Iraq Petroleum Company were furious about it and felt we had offended the susceptibilities of the Iraqis and embarrassed the IPC because we were in Baghdad under their auspices. Oil companies are always – naturally enough, I suppose – very touchy about what is said or written about a country in which they are operating.

Later in the same year I was one of a large international party of radio reporters who, sponsored by some United Nations organization – I think it was UNESCO – set themselves the task to trace the course of the Rhine – as a great European waterway – from its source to its delta. From the St Gotthard Pass we dutifully trudged up the mountainside until we reached a small, insignificant stream. We followed it down to Liechtenstein and to the point where it flows into Lake Constance. Then we drove along the lake to the point where it flows out – I have never been able to discover who decided that it was the same river. Maybe they have made chemical tests; or maybe someone put a paper boat into the river just before it flowed into the lake and watched it being carried unerringly to the exit point.

From Strasbourg onwards our journey seemed to be a long succession of *vins d'honneur* and *Weinproben*. The German representative, Horst Scharffenburg became our spokesman during the time we were passing through the German part of the Rhineland and made fine speeches of thanks after all the *Weinproben*. Horst had lost a leg at the Battle of Arnhem, but he managed so well with his artificial one that many of us didn't realize that he had one. When we reached Bonn we found the city very crowded and some of us had to share rooms. I was having breakfast the next morning when Samy Simon, from Radio Diffusion Française, came into the dining-room. He looked terrible.

'What's the matter, Samy?' I asked. He shuddered.

'Quelle expérience, mon dieu quelle expérience!' he said. He had had to share a room with Scharffenburg, and when he went upstairs to the bedroom, very late at night and opened the door, there, in the moonlight, he saw Scharffenburg's leg standing at the foot of his bed.

'Ah, cette jambe!' Samy cried, *'c'était pur Kafka!'*

One of our stops on our journey down the Rhine was at Ludwigshafen, opposite Mainz, on the left bank of the river. There we had to visit the Badische Anilin und Soda Fabrik, the largest remaining unit of the dismembered chemical colossus, I. G. Farben. The BASF was an enormous industrial complex covering a large area of Ludwigshafen. It was intersected with streets which bore romantic names like Soda Street or Sulphur Street. We dutifully trudged round this depressing place and didn't much look forward to dining with the managing director, Dr Schaeffer, that evening. Here I was in for an agreeable surprise, however, for Dr Schaeffer was an Old China Hand and we had many friends in common. Over brandies and cigars after dinner, I sat next to this pillar of German industry. As he became mellower and mellower, we reminisced nostalgically about those days in China that we should never see again.

'D'you remember the old missionary hymns?' I asked him.

'What about Jesus loves me that I know?' he said, and together we sang: *'Che ssu nai wo wo chih tao . . .'*

'Remember Baa Baa Black Sheep?' He didn't. *'Pa Pa hei yang . . .'* I began.

'But I'll bet you never heard "It Ain't Gonna Rain No More No More" in Chinese,' Dr Schaeffer said and started off, fortissimo: *'Chin t'ien chin t'ien pu hsia yu . . .'* There were several members of the firm at the party and I wonder if they had ever heard their managing director let himself go like that before.

* * *

Not long after the war I had done a series of broadcasts for the North of England BBC about rivers in the north. I roughly followed the course of a river and talked to the characters who lived near it; told a little of the history and if there were local musicians, so much the better. I had done several of the Yorkshire Dales, the North Tyne and, in the West, the Eden and the Lune. Not having anything particular to do in the spring of 1954, I persuaded the BBC Overseas Service that a similar set of programmes should prove good nostalgic entertainment for Britons scattered over the far flung Commonwealth.

I did more or less a repetition of my earlier series, meeting many of the same people again. One fascinating person whom I met for the first time was Mr Kit Calvert who lives in Hawes, at the head of the Wensleydale, and makes Wensleydale cheese. They gave up making the blue Wensleydale during the war and were only just starting to bring it back.

'I'm doing what they did at Stilton,' he said. 'The mould in the cellars where the cheeses matured had all disappeared. So they had the idea of buying a lot of penicillin from Glaxo and spraying it all over the cellars. It worked fine.' And penicillin prompted Kit Calvert to talk of the old days in the Wensleydale.

'You know in winter time,' he said, 'you just had to stay put when the snow came. There was no doctors in the dale and the dalesfolk had to look after themselves. Well, my old grandmother made a great reputation for herself as a healer. For years she had treated cuts and suchlike with bread poultices. Well one day a lad came to her with a bad cut which he had left to get septic. My grandmother looked around for a bit of bread to make a poultice with and the only thing she could find was half a mouldy loaf that had been left out in the scullery. Ah well, she thought, it'll do I suppose. She made a poultice with it and the septic cut healed up in no time. After that she always left a loaf in the damp scullery to get mouldy for her poultices. Well, that was back in the middle of last century. But, you see, my old grandmother had accidentally discovered a kind of penicillin nearly a century before Fleming.' Kit Calvert was a remarkable man. The bookshelves in his study were stacked with books on

Touaregs. The Unveiled Women

Lalla and Nicholas at Ramatuelle

Edward Ward at TRAD – A screen from the
Fairground Collection

local history and folklore. His great life's work had been to translate the New Testament into Wensleydale dialect:

'For third time the Lord said: "Doost tha luv me Peter?" Now Peter were a bit narked at being asked three times. He said: "Tha knaws ah do, Lord." "Then fother me lambs and yows," ' was one extract I remember.

I went over to Paris to do a programme about NATO later in the year, and General Sir Brian Horrocks and I went out to Versailles to interview Lord Montgomery. In fact Brian and I scarcely opened our mouths and sat at the receiving end of a typical Monty monologue. Brian Horrocks came to lunch with Marjorie and me at home soon after we returned to London. It was at a time that we had the luxury of an Italian *au pair* girl. As soon as we had finished eating Sir Brian jumped to his feet and said:

'Come on, now, let me help with the washing up. Shall I wash or dry. Just say the word.' Marjorie had great difficulty in keeping him out of the kitchen. 'But I always do it at home,' he complained. At that time Sir Brian Horrocks was Black Rod in the House of Lords. He was a member of a football pools syndicate with several members of the staff, including one of the policemen outside the House. While the House of Lords was in session he often used to sit in his corner and pass the time filling up the pools coupons. One day an official came up to him:

'I hope you'll forgive me for mentioning it, Sir Brian,' he said, 'but me and my colleagues really don't think you ought to fill in your coupons in the House. People in the Gallery can see you doing it quite plainly.'

I continued with the NATO programme by going to Germany and Austria later in the year with Dave Woodward, one of the BBC Feature producers. We started off at Kaiserslautern, an important American military centre. We arrived in the evening and stayed the night in a small hotel, where the food had been particularly good. The next morning we reported at American headquarters and were taken in hand by their Army Public Relations Officer, an extremely efficient woman major. When it came to lunch time she said:

'Well, now I'd be very happy if you two gentlemen would come and have lunch with me at our club, out in the country. I can promise you a real good Texan steak. I'll bet you haven't eaten steak in a while!' Naïvely I said that as it happened we had had steak the evening before at our hotel. 'But I can never have too much steak,' I added gallantly. A look of horror came over the major's face.

'You mean you ate German steak?' she said, with a break in her voice.

'Of course,' I said, 'why ever not. It was particularly good as it happens.'

'Well, I think you are taking a very grave risk,' she said with the utmost seriousness. And then she lowered her voice and said: 'Confidentially you run a very serious risk of getting—' she paused, and then came out with it: 'of getting WORMS!'

'Well, I've eaten a lot of German steaks in my time, major,' I said, 'and so far I've been spared such a disagreeable consequence!' We reached the club, a splendid building set among a grove of trees with tennis courts and bowling alleys.

'What do you think of it?' she asked, confident of an enthusiastic reply. She got it. 'The main object of this club,' she went on, 'is to keep our boys out of the "gast-houses".' She spoke of the little local German inns as if they were dens of wickedness. The worst thing that could be said against them would be that they are rather boring. We made no comment. The major went on extolling the glories of the club.

'Only one thing we need here,' she said, 'and that's a swimming pool.'

'Oh well,' Dave said, 'the whole countryside's covered with lakes and rivers. The boys have plenty of facilities for swimming.' The major looked horrified.

'We couldn't go swimming in these German lakes,' she protested. 'Why we'd all be down with hookworm!'

'The Germans do,' I said.

'Oh yes, the Germans do,' she said as if she were talking of Egyptian fellaheen bathing in the ill-named Sweet Water Canal between Cairo and Alexandria, immune from birth to bilharzia. We had a couple of excellent dry martinis and then went up to the dining-room for lunch. The Texan steak had been so long in deep freeze that it had lost most of its taste. A green salad was served with it.

'Don't worry,' the major said, 'you can eat it with confidence!' I laughed.

'Why do some of you Americans think that all food in Europe is poisonous?' I asked.

'Oh that's going a little far, I think,' she said.

'Yes,' I said, 'I suppose it is. I believe you feel reasonably safe in hygienic countries like Denmark and Holland. Germany, I would have thought, was about on the borderline.'

For some years I had been invited by Mr Guy Prince, managing director of Lébègue, the large firm of wine merchants, to their annual wine tasting in their vast, cavernous cellars under London Bridge station. I don't know why I was asked because the invitation was one that was most coveted. I tried to sing for my supper by doing a piece about it for the BBC one year but they were not interested. I never even bought any wine and even if I had my purchase would have been insignificant – the wine tasting was strictly a 'trade' affair with a leavening of celebrities of one kind and another.

All the wine merchants, of course, sipped away at the young clarets and burgundies, rolling the wine around their mouths and spitting it out into troughs filled with sawdust provided for the purpose. I did not waste my capacity with immature wines. I went first straight to the best claret table and then to the best burgundy one. I was sipping a superb burgundy – I remember well it was a Richebourg '48 – when I noticed a clerical gentleman standing beside me. He had that benevolent expression on his face induced by a glass or two of good wine and would have been an ideal model for what I call the 'tipsy cardinal' school of painting. Feeling in an expansive mood myself, I poured a glass of this wine and turned to him.

'May I offer you a glass of this Richebourg '48?' I said. 'I think you will find it good.'

'That is uncommonly kind of you,' the reverend gentleman replied. He held up the glass and examined its contents against the light of one of the candles in the huge iron chandeliers that lit the cellars. Then he took a sip, rolling the wine round with his tongue.

'That is a truly remarkable wine,' he pronounced. Then he turned to a little man whom I had noticed following him like a dog. 'Four dozen,' he said. The little man noted it down in his book. The cleric and I joined forces. Needless to say he was a Roman Catholic.

'You know in my spare time I make a little money out of writing,' he said. 'Articles, you know, and little bits of journalism; and I'm ashamed to say – no I'm *not* ashamed to say – I spend it *all* on good wine. Do you ever go to Paris?' he asked. I said I usually went there several times a year. 'So do I,' he said. 'I go there for one or two *glorious* nights,' he waggled a finger admonishingly, 'not what you think; oh, no, not at all; purely gastronomic.' He wrote an address down on a piece of paper and handed it to me. 'You go there and say Père Bernard sent you. I assure you you won't be disappointed.' Some time later I took his advice; I wasn't.

Chapter Seventeen

Towards the end of 1954 Laurence Gilliam planned an epic series of radio programmes on Africa. He asked Marjorie and me to contribute two on Uganda and Kenya. Our son Nicky had been born early the year before and was almost two. Marjorie hated the idea of leaving the children for several months; and hated, even more, the idea of so much flying. The outward journey to Entebbe in Uganda was an agony for her. Each time we landed and took off at Rome, Cairo and Khartoum, she died little deaths. But after our landing in Uganda we did no more flying until our homeward journey.

The twenty-mile drive from Entebbe to Kampala was a cross section in itself of the wonderful, colourful country of Uganda. I could never do better than quote Marjorie's script for our broadcast.

'Sunshiny black faces smile above the handlebars of sunshiny bicycles, heaped high with enormous loads of bananas, or sacks of coffee or boxes or firewood. There are the women – the gorgeous women – painted by Gauguin against a sky and a landscape by the Douanier Rousseau. Their blue-black skins have a dusty bloom like grapes. Balanced on their heads they carry enormous gourds and bundles of branches and baskets. They walk upright and sedate as goddesses, in flowing robes designed by a Victorian missionary and made of cotton from a Lancashire factory. Unbelievable that such a combination should have produced costumes so exotic. Loose tunic tops, fringed satin sashes, elaborately draped skirts sweeping the road, flamboyant colours of the tropics – purple and scarlet, pale ice-blue and crimson, emerald green and imperial yellow. The women of Uganda are arrayed in all the glory of Solomon.

'The land is humped into little hills dotted with trees and patched with shrubs like a strange, brilliant Provence. And as you recognize this tree and ask the name of that shrub you hear the rhythm of the tropics in the music of their names – jacaranda and hibiscus and tamarisk; poinsiana and oleander and bougainvillea – frangipanni and euphorbia and palmetto.'

Uganda is a lovely, luxuriant country. We stayed a week in Kampala meeting Africans and Asians and building up our picture of the whole political and economic state of affairs. And then we drove south, skirting the huge Lake Victoria. We crossed the Equator – both on foot and by car – and ended up at the Kiwala Hotel seven miles outside the township of Masaka. Looking out over Lake Victoria, the main building is like a comfortable old English inn with roses growing round the windows. But as a reminder that one is in the tropics one sleeps in a long hut of pink mud and wattle outside which – to quote Marjorie again – hibiscus and jacaranda drop their lovely blossoms over the 'inconvenience'. The bar was a great meeting place for the local European population and for travellers passing through Africa like ourselves. A bank manager, a police inspector, an Austrian professor, an American missionary, an oil company representative, a tourist, and officers – district, educational, medical, always officers of the Government on safari.

The conversation turned on the perils of driving in Uganda. We said we'd never seen so many bicycles.

'They all buy the same make of bike,' the professor said. 'You see this firm came out here first and they had an enormous poster showing a lion chasing an African on his bicycle and the African was quite happy and smiling because he was easily gaining on the lion. So they all rushed to buy bikes. After all you might get chased by a lion. Well, then another firm came along and they saw the Africans carrying their wives and great sacks of coffee on the back of their bikes so they thought they'd stress how strong their bikes were and they put up huge posters showing an elephant riding one of their bikes. And the Africans thought that was just silly because everyone knows that elephants don't ride bikes. And you know they just won't buy that make! Advertising's a funny thing.'

We began to talk about wild animals.

'Oh the last place to find Darkest Africa is in Africa,' the bank manager said. 'Of course there's plenty of game in the game reserves, but here the animals are mostly white ants. You should see the bank notes the Africans bring me. They always used to bury coins, so now they bury banknotes. The ants get at them – and then they bring me a fistful of white powder and expect money for it. Still, as long as you can find one of the two figures on them it's okay, I'll change them.'

'You might meet a hippo one evening if you're keen on that kind of thing,' the hotel owner said. 'We had an *ayah* here once when the children were small. The second day she came to me and demanded a pot in her room. I said nonsense and she said "If I don't get a pot I'm leaving. I'm not spending another whole night out in that shed with a hippo just outside the door, and that's that." '

'There are crocodiles of course,' the oilman said. 'You know, these people go out fishing on the lake in these little reed rafts of theirs and they'll come back with a foot and say: "That's all that's left of my brother." '

Among the Europeans in Uganda who worked with and for the Africans there was nearly always this tone of amused, exasperated affection. There were never any white settlers in Uganda because in the early days there was a lot of malaria and sleeping sickness and the country on the whole was not suitable for Europeans.

By the lake shore and on the islands the people earn their living by loading ships or by fishing. Thirty miles inland a man reckons his wealth by the number of cattle he owns. Out on the rolling plains to the south-west of Masaka are vast herds of the famous Ankoli cattle, splendid beasts with immense sweeping horns four and five feet long. They are owned by the Bahima tribe, a tall, lean Hamitic people, with fine cut features. They are immensely rich on paper, but as nothing would persuade them to sell a single animal, they live, nomadically, in a very simple way. Like the Masai in Kenya they live entirely on milk and blood, which they draw from a cow's neck by piercing a vein with a sharp pointed little tube. In those days, at any rate, the Bahima were not allowed to carry firearms. At nights they drove their herds inside large *koralls* surrounded by fifteen-foot-high thorn bushes as a protection against lions. If a lion does succeed in getting over this formidable obstacle – which happens sometimes – they have to kill him with spears.

I spent an hour or two in one of the *koralls* and the Bahima sang some of the boasting songs of their fathers and grandfathers. They were a warrior tribe in the old days. Then I had to walk back to the Land-Rover I had come in through a herd of some two thousand Ankoli cattle. This required some courage at first because a cow only had to shake her head and one would have been dealt a fearful and possibly lethal blow with one of those great horns. But they were very quiet and gentle beasts and I pushed my way for about a quarter of a mile through a tightly packed herd of cattle without coming to any harm.

The Bahima herdsmen look upon agriculture as a contemptible occupation, but the green belt all round Lake Victoria is highly cultivated. Uganda is chiefly a country of small peasant farmers. But the area round Masaka is the country of the rich African coffee 'barons'. Yokana Mukasa had 200 acres under coffee and he was planting another 100 acres with seedlings. At the time one bush could produce about £10 worth of coffee and it is possible to plant anything from 400 to 600 bushes on an acre of land, so it wasn't hard to calculate that Yokana was a very rich man. His plantation was fully mechanized. He had sunk deep wells to irrigate the land. He was building a hulling factory which could also deal with the coffee of his neighbours. We all went back to his European-style house and were given tea and biscuits in a large room furnished, like most rich Africans' houses entirely with chairs and small tables like a café. Leopard skins made a decorative, if not cool, covering for the chairs.

From Bukoba in the south we continued our journey round Lake Victoria by water, in the SS *Usofa*. Lake Victoria is roughly the shape of and nearly as large as Ireland. Sometimes the weather can be very stormy and the lake rough. Looking down at the mass of African passengers with their bundles and their babies and their packages of food, lying, sitting, squatting, sprawling, occupying every square foot of deck space, the very thought of a storm was appalling. Every morning at each port of call women in bright cottons disentangled bundles and *totos* from the general chaos on deck and followed their menfolk down the gangway to be replaced instantly and noisily with more bundles and *totos* and men and women.

At Mwanza, on the Tanganyikan (as it was then) shore of the Lake, we had tea with the Assistant Provincial Commissioner who lived in a German Schloss overlooking the Bismarck Rock – reminders of the days of German rule in Tanganyika. Curiously enough many of the older Africans said they preferred German rule to British. For any minor crime the German authorities gave an African a good beating and that was that. He understood this and soon got over it. The British, in their humanity, sent him to prison, maybe for months. He was separated from his family and could earn no money. This he did not like or understand.

At Musoma black men, sweating in the pitiless sun, fastened slings round bales of cotton, the winchman set the engine in motion, the chief officer hurried up and down the deck shouting orders. It might have been a scene out of *Showboat*. We ended our journey at Kisumu, Kenya's port on the Lake.

Across the other side of the Lake in Uganda is the great Owen Falls barrage at Jinja. Like Speke, a century ago, you can stand and look down upon the source of the Nile. But you will not see, as Speke did, the Ripon Falls, and your effort to imagine his feelings when he solved a mystery that had baffled mankind for two thousand five hundred years, is handicapped by their absence. You can only marvel at the ingenuity of man which can, as Sir Winston Churchill once put it: 'make the immemorial Nile begin its journey by diving through a turbine!'

As we walked into the New Stanley Hotel in Nairobi, men and

women were stopping at the cloakroom by the entrance, unstrapping revolver and automatic pistol holsters and leaving them with the attendant, while they went in for a drink or for lunch. One might have been in a frontier town in the old West. With Mau Mau at its height all the white settlers, naturally enough, went about armed and it was a serious offence, punishable by a heavy fine, to leave a weapon in a car even if the car were locked.

Some months before we had left England we had met a distant cousin of mine called Freddie Ward, who had lived in Kenya for about forty years. He had invited us to stay at his farm near Nakuru, above the Rift Valley about ninety miles from Nairobi. Freddie sent his car to fetch us. We stopped for a while to see the thousands of pink and white flamingos on the salt lake by Nakuru and then climbed steeply to Freddie Ward's farm. The house was no farmhouse. It was a very good replica of a William-and-Mary manor house, built all on one floor. Even the furniture was William-and-Mary but made by Arab craftsmen in Mombasa of wood that would stand up to the climate. Though heaven knows the climate was about as ideal as one could find anywhere. We were a little over 6,000 feet up. It was a dry heat and the evenings were so cool that a fire was always pleasant if not strictly necessary.

Violet Ward was apologetic about the servants and in particular the cook. Owing to Mau Mau it was not thought safe to employ Kikuyu servants – and it probably wasn't, because the Mau Mau could bring pressure to bear on them. So the Wards like many other settlers had had to get rid of their well-trained Kikuyus and employ men from the Luo or some other tribe. We both thought the Wards' Luo servants were admirable. It all reminded me of pre-war China days. It was the same kind of unobtrusive service and the food was first class. The trouble with the settlers was that they had had things so good for so long that they had lost all sense of proportion. They were still living in a way that only the immensely rich can live in England, but they really thought they were roughing it. They also had the curious conviction that a fantastic degree of security was due to them.

'We came out here,' they would say, 'and we worked hard and built things up from scratch into what we have now. Surely we can expect our children and grandchildren to enjoy the results of our labours. Surely that degree of security should be there for them.'

'Well, I don't know,' I would say, 'I don't reckon to have much security for myself, let alone for my children and I don't even think about grandchildren.' But they thought it was quite different for them. They were special people; they were pioneers, who had a stake in the country and in its future. The sad thing was that they might have had if most of them hadn't been so greedy – and so stupid. Marjorie and I pointed out that it wasn't intelligent to pay agricultural labour a nominal wage of some eleven shillings a week when they were making so much money themselves. Still less was it intelligent to do this and at the same time send bright Africans back to England to attend universities and then, when they returned to their own country, offer them nothing worth while in the way of jobs. Jomo Kenyatta was the most glaring example of this short-sighted policy. He went to the London School of Economics; then became an anthropologist of world stature and when he returned to Kenya all he was offered was a minor post as a school teacher, earning far less than a second class British teacher. Why didn't they make him Inspector General of African schools at a salary of several thousand a year? They might have saved themselves a lot of trouble in the long run.

Poor old Freddie Ward who, like many of the older generation of settlers, had far more liberal views than their sons – and infinitely more than the newcomers who had flocked to Kenya after the war, thought that Marjorie and I had come to Kenya to write a one hundred per cent pro-settler story, stressing the terrible conditions under which they were living and pointing out what a splendid show they were all putting up. In fact we had come out to Kenya with completely open minds, quite ready to do a pro-settler story if that was the way it seemed to be to us. I think it was the large cocktail party which the Wards gave for us that really set us against the settlers – Marjorie far more than me because she has far stronger and more passionate political views. The scraps of conversation we picked up at that party were sometimes frightening: 'Well, old Bob blooded his gun last week.' 'Amnesty, if you please. If they surrender they'll be all right! Not if they come my way, by God! If I catch one of those Mickey Mice, I'll hang him on the nearest tree!' If we had had a small tape recorder hidden in a vase of flowers we'd have picked up some extraordinary stuff. As it was as soon as the party was over and we had gone to our room, Marjorie laboriously wrote down every scrap of conversation she could remember.

We stayed a few days with Freddie Ward. He had an enormous farm which 'marched' with another large estate belonging to Michael Blundell, a member of the Legislative Council and a man of very far-seeing and liberal views. They had a large canning factory on the spot and between them among other things, grew no less than 140 *acres* of asparagus! Freddie Ward sent us back in his car. Climbing up the beautifully graded escarpment from the bottom of the Rift Valley to the plateau on which Nairobi stands, I remembered the story of the construction of the road. It had been built during the war by Italian prisoners. They had worked on it for a few weeks and then went on strike. The British army didn't quite know what to do. For prisoners of war to go on strike was quite without precedent. While they were pondering the matter the Italians sent a delegation to explain their reasons for refusing to work. It wasn't that they objected to building a road, they pointed out. What they objected to was building such a *badly designed* road. The Italians were a nation of road builders, an art inherited from the Romans. Among the prisoners were some skilled road engineers. If they could work to their own design and abandon the badly conceived Office of Works plan, they would be very happy to continue. The British authorities at last agreed and the Italians built a superb road.

Attached to Kenya Radio in Nairobi at that time was a fascinating character called Peter Colmore. Peter had started up an excellent night club where the orchestra was a group of local Kenyans, who were first class. With all the colour consciousness that was still very much in evidence in Nairobi – you couldn't take an African member of the Legislative Assembly to lunch at the New Stanley Hotel; you could take him to your room for a drink though they didn't even like that much – Peter's night club was proving a great success and the smart place to go. He took us one night to a tremendous party given by the Nairobi police. It was held on an open space in the outskirts of the city, where oxen were being roasted over huge wood fires. The police come from every tribe in Kenya and as far as they could they wore tribal dress for the occasion. While the oxen were roasting they started dancing their tribal dances. Their women were there too and as the drums beat out their compulsive rhythm we saw dancing such as we had never seen before. I have seen a great deal of African dancing and very colourful and exciting it has been. But it was thin and insipid compared with what we saw that night. These African police and their girls really let themselves go. If they ever had any inhibitions they disappeared and we saw an orgiastic performance that was the nearest thing imaginable to a mass, public performance of the sex act. It was fabulous.

Peter Colmore at one stage of his career had taken visitors to East Africa on safari. He spoke excellent Swahili and several tribal dialects. Once, he told me, he was conducting Adrian, the Hollywood dress designer, and his wife Janet Gaynor, the famous star of the silent screen, on a safari through the Ituri Forest in the Congo. Adrian was a compulsive collector of 'Africana' of all kinds and used to return to the United States loaded up with drums, shields and spears. While they were driving through the forest a little pygmy ran across the road. He was carrying a small bow decorated with tufts of monkey fur at each end.

'Gee, that's a swell little bow,' Adrian said. 'Go and ask the little guy how much he wants for it, Peter.' Peter went across to the little man, spoke a few words and then came back to the car.

'He says he won't sell it,' he said. 'He says this is leopard country and he won't move about unarmed.'

'A tough little guy, huh?' Adrian said. 'Go offer him a

hundred francs. He'll take it.' Peter tried again with the same result.

'Gee, he sure is a tough little guy. Offer him two hundred. It's a crazy price but I want that little bow.' Again the pygmy refused.

'Well goddam but isn't he a cussed little guy?' Adrian fumbled for a wallet and pulled out a ten dollar bill. 'This makes no sense at all, Peter, but I kinda must have that little bow. Ten bucks is far too much but what the hell!' Peter took the ten dollar bill to the pygmy. The little man looked at it, turned it upside down and looked at it again.

'But I refused to sell my bow for two hundred francs,' he said, 'why does he think I'm going to take this strange money?' Peter, secretly delighted, went back with the latest news. Adrian exploded:

'Jesus, Peter!' he shouted, 'How goddam primitive can a guy get?'

Everyone agreed that the district of Embu to the north-west of Nairobi would be as good a place as any to get material for a story about Mau Mau. It was quite near Mount Kenya, where many Mau Mau lived in the dense bamboo thickets and it was a well populated part of the country, with all the villages surrounded with stockades of sharpened stakes and patrolled day and night by volunteer home guards. In the neighbourhood, too, were several rehabilitation centres, where Mau Mau prisoners were being put through courses of re-education.

A cameraman had come with us from Nairobi because we were doing a television programme as well and we centred our story on one small Kikuyu family called Secondo – a husband and wife and a couple of children. The husband took his turn at guarding the village by night and his wife ran the home and worked on their acre or two of land, planted with coffee and maize. We built up a good sequence about how the Mau Mau 'emergency' affected an ordinary Kikuyu family.

One evening at the *Boma*, the headquarters of the District

Commissioner, the police asked me if I would like to go with them to a village where a band of Mau Mau was reported to be hiding. We reached the place after dark. I had been given a revolver because 'you never know'. Stealthily we made our way into the village and walked quietly between the circular mud huts with their conical thatch of grass. I had a portable tape recorder with me. One of the police told me to wait near one of the huts and get my recorder ready.

'We'll fire a few shots,' he said, 'and that may flush them.' I waited in the darkness. Suddenly there were two shots, followed a few seconds later by a volley. And then from all the huts came a terrible, uncanny wailing. It was the women making as much noise as they could to cover the escape of the Mau Mau they had been sheltering. I made some first class recordings of this eerie sound and then picked up my machine and walked down the middle of the village looking for the police. I found one of them at the far end of the village.

'We fired a lot of shots at a couple of chaps who were running away from the village,' he said. 'We may have hit them but they got away all right.' And then, suddenly I discovered I had left my revolver behind on the ground – it counted almost as a criminal offence. I made an excuse and rushed back to where I had been lying and by the greatest good fortune it was still there.

We drove to Nyere one day, where we had been invited to stay the night with a settler and his wife. We underestimated the time it would take to get there and we made the last part of the journey in the dark. I confess I was more than a little nervous during the last hour of driving. Of course if the Mau Mau had been in the smallest degree efficient, it should have been impossible to travel at night; it should, in fact, have been nearly impossible to travel at all. If they had been properly organized in the way that, for instance, the Communist guerrillas in Malaya were organized, they could have disrupted all communications in Kenya. They could have mined roads; torn up lengths of railway track; cut telegraph wires. They did scarcely any of these things.

On this evening we were all very glad to reach our destination and I drank three large dry martinis in fairly quick succession. It was a lovely house with beautiful Regency furniture brought out from England. Our hostess carried a large service revolver on a belt round her slender waist. We all went in to dinner. During the meal Mrs Wolferstone (which was not her name) started to talk about the sacrifices she and her husband had made coming to Kenya.

'We had a lovely house in the West of England,' she said, 'and we gave it all up to come out here, because we felt we ought to do our bit to help build up the British Empire. And look at the thanks we get. What help is the British Government giving to people like ourselves, who have sacrified so much?' I found this a little too much to stomach. Emboldened by the dry martinis and the excellent claret we were then drinking I said:

'Come off it, Mrs Wolferstone. Like everybody else you came to Kenya to make money and to live well and if I may say so you seem to have succeeded very well.' It was, I suppose, unpardonably rude on my part, but I couldn't help it. Her husband laughed, then caught her eye and immediately stopped laughing. The atmosphere was a shade tense after dinner and we made our excuses and went to bed early.

Back in London Marjorie wrote a brilliant, tough script about the whole situation in Kenya. It had to be passed by someone high up in the administration of the BBC and, inexplicably he let it go without altering a word. Either he hadn't read it properly or else he was naïvely unaware of the political implications. Somehow word got round, and Broadcasting House was picketed by members of settlers' organizations the evening of the broadcast. One of their great objections was Marjorie's reconstruction of the cocktail party at Freddie Ward's. Of course we hadn't been able to record the actual voices and the parts had to be played by actors and actresses. If these had been allowed to play them as they wanted to, the eventual uproar would have been far greater. As it was Marjorie put a great deal of restraint on them.

The Legislative Council in Nairobi passed a vote of censure on the broadcast and exerted so much pressure on the BBC that it was not put out in their Overseas Service.

On the other side, as a result of the broadcast, we had a succession of letters and telephone calls from different African organizations who seemed to think we could be enlisted as champions of their causes. We kept right out of it. Neither of us had any strong feelings about Africans one way or the other. As with other races we liked a lot and didn't much care about a lot. All Marjorie had tried to do in this programme was to put the case fairly and without bias.

It is a wonderful thing that Kenya, that beautiful country with its incomparable climate, has emerged from the witches' cauldron of African independence far more successfully and with far greater understanding and tolerance on both sides than any of the other new African countries. This is undoubtedly due to the wisdom, tolerant understanding and sound common sense of Jomo Kenyatta, so execrated at the time we were there as the architect of Mau Mau as he languished in prison, and now 'Good old Jomo' to those white settlers who have been wise and adaptable enough to see a future for themselves in Kenya. Jomo Kenyatta has undoubtedly shown outstanding qualities of 'elder-statesmanship' since he has been in power and the only problem – as in so many countries – is: 'after him what next?'

Chapter Eighteen

For some time Marjorie and I had been thinking vaguely about finding a small house abroad, preferably in France, where we could take ourselves and our two children for summer holidays. One Sunday in 1955 we saw, among the houses advertised by Roy Brooks in the *Observer*: 'Old mill with 10 hectares of land including lavender field for sale, £500.' We were at Brooks' office before it opened the following morning. we discovered the mill was in the Var *département* – that meant it couldn't be all that far from the sea. We met the owner, a charming elderly lady, who used to teach in a school in the nearby village of Bargème and take her pupils down to the mill for camping week-ends. She painted a glowing picture of the place. We paid a ten per cent deposit on the spot and she gave me an introduction to her former partner who still lived in Bargème. I flew to Cannes, hired a Dauphine and drove to Bargème. It was possible to drive to within about two kilometres of the mill. After that you had to walk. I followed a rough, winding track leading through what had been forest and was now tree stumps and piles of branches and at last reached some open meadows, with a stream running through them and in the background towering limestone cliffs. In the middle of the meadow was a stone building. There was no door, just an opening. I walked in. The ground – there was nothing that could be called a floor – was thick with cattle manure. I climbed up a dangerously rotten staircase to the upper storey to find the roof had largely fallen in. The setting was quite lovely but it was a completely hopeless proposition. To have put the house in order would have cost a fortune. All building materials would have had to be brought in on mule back.

Back in London we told Roy Brooks of our disappointment.

'I don't know whether this would interest you,' he said, 'but my solicitor has some kind of a place in a village called Ramatuelle, near St Tropez. I think he lets it.' He gave us an introduction to Michael Morris and we rented his house for the month of August.

Lalla was five and Nicky two and a half. We had with us a Danish girl who hated every minute of the stay – we found out later that she was pregnant, which would have accounted for it. There was no electric light – we had to use candles and an old hurricane lamp. There was no water – we had to fetch large enamel jugs full from the village fountain. There was no sanitation – we had to make do with an 'Elsan', which I had the privilege of emptying in a noisome pit a quarter of a mile outside the village. But in spite of all these deterrents we loved Ramatuelle and the lovely sandy beaches only five or ten minutes run in the car from the village. We loved St Tropez and the market under the plane trees in the Place des Lices and we determined to find a house there.

We found nothing the first year. In 1956 we 'bettered' ourselves to the extent of renting a house that had electric light and a shower – but no sanitation, main drainage had yet to come to Ramatuelle. Towards the end of our second visit to Ramatuelle we found a small house for sale right in the centre of the village. We got Bank of England permission to buy it and we persuaded a mason to do some work on it during the winter. God knows it needed it. The place had been occupied for years by a bear-like village character called Marius Moretti. He only used one room on the ground floor. The rest of the house, including the staircase was crammed with firewood. The walls of the 'living-room' were black with tar from his wood fires. The corner of it where he had slept on an old rusty iron bed had partly subsided under his enormous weight and had to be shored up later with a large tree trunk in the cellar.

By the time we reached Ramatuelle the following summer, the house was still not habitable and we rented the same house again and spent much of our holiday working on our own. We got a mason in St Tropez to build a shower room for us and one day, when he was about half way through laying the tiles he said:

'You know, this house is really too small for you. I know of a much better one in the village, which is for sale. I'll go and see the people.' To our astonishment he walked five paces across the little *place* to a house with a balcony where an old man used to sit reading *Humanité* every morning. We had exchanged greetings with him daily for over a month and also with his son, whom we called 'Death of a Salesman' because he looked remarkably like Paul Muni in the part. (He really was an insurance salesman, we discovered later.) It was this house that was for sale but for some extraordinary reason neither its owner nor his wife or son had ever mentioned the fact to us. We were invited in and over a *pastis* we bought our second house in Ramatuelle, having been assured that if we did not come to an immediate decision there was a lady from Paris who would almost certainly buy it. This actually turned out to be true and we were fortunate enough to be able to sell our first house, which we had never occupied, to her at a profit almost sufficient to buy the second. The whole double transaction was carried out in the course of a ten minutes session in the office of a St Tropez *notaire*, attended by us, by the family we were buying the house from and by the Frenchwoman to whom we were selling our first house. It was something that would have been unimaginable in England.

We all came down at Easter the following year and lived for several weeks in appalling squalor, while the house was being put into order and a *terrasse* built on the top floor, an operation involving the cutting off of the end of one room together with its roof and putting in French windows, which we had brought out from England. Everybody says how lucky we are to have a house in the South of France. Lucky be damned, we reply, it's been a lot of very hard work. But it's been well worth it.

We lived in our second house for ten years and then sold again and bought what we think is the best house in the village.

But we never stop doing things to this house. Never a holiday when there haven't been masons in the house and when I wasn't coming back from Stable's in St Tropez with a load of wood to build something with; when Marjorie wasn't painting, or making chair covers or curtains. Some day we'll be finished, though I doubt it. But of course it's not all work; not by any means. We drive down to the beach most days and lunch at the *Club 55*, of which we are founder members. It is run by Geneviève de Colmont and her family and in the early days when things were very primitive there, we used to help with the washing up. The de Colmonts have gone a long way since then and their restaurant, though nothing special gastronomically, is by far the most elegant on that part of the coast. All the patrons of the famous Café des Arts in St Tropez come there for lunch – Brigitte Bardot and the rest. We're lazy. We don't move far from the St Tropez peninsula. Nicky and I go on Sundays to the bullfights at Fréjus and sometimes as far as Nimes and Arles. But otherwise we stay in or near our home. There's always something to do there.

During the winter of 1954–55 Western Germany rearmed. Once again Germany had a *Wehrmacht*, a *Kriegsmarine* and a *Luftwaffe*, less than ten years after the end of World War II. BBC Television wanted to do a programme examining the feelings of the German people about this re-militarization and Anthony de Lotbinière the director of the programme and I, together with the enormous team of technicians that any TV venture demands, set out for Germany.

We went to Bonn, the capital, and it was arranged for me to interview General Heusinger, the commander in chief of the *Wehrmacht.* General Heusinger had been with Hitler in the bunker on July 20th, 1944, when the attempt on the Führer's life failed by a freakish miracle. Everything was arranged for the interview. Behind the C-in-C's large desk the wall was covered with large strategic maps and the idea was that I should first interview the general and that then he should get up and point out the eventual disposition of the forces under his command on the map. At last the door opened and a small cock sparrow of a man stepped into the room and stopped. There was great excitement among all the Germans present.

'Ach Herr General, wie gütig von Ihnen . . .' 'Wir sind geehrt . . .' And so on. The general stood where he was, looked arrogantly round the room and then barked:

'Also, ist alles schon fertig? Dann los! los! los! I had had far too many Germans say *los! los! los!* to me when I was a prisoner of war. It is a rude way of saying 'Get going!' or 'Get on with it!'

'No, *Herr General*,' I said, 'everything is not all ready. In a programme of this kind a good deal of explanation and preparation are necessary and if you are in too much of a hurry to agree to this, then we'll cancel the interview. It doesn't really matter.' To my disgust the general immediately smiled benignly and said:

'*Aber natürlich,* of course, you are the expert; you tell me what is to be done and I will do it.' I must say he took direction very well and the whole interview was a great success.

About the only German Tony de Lotbinière learnt during our three weeks in Germany was that word 'los!' To the astonishment of a number of Germans he used it constantly to correspond with the word: 'Action!' in film making in English.

We also wanted to find out how Berliners felt about the rearming of Germany – we had come across absolutely no enthusiasm in the Rhineland – *'Ich habe die Nasevoll von Krieg'* was the usual reply, which can be translated freely as 'I've had a bellyfull of war.' It was the same with the West Berliners. But we also wanted to see how the East Berliners felt. This was before the days of the Berlin Wall. Indeed on my many trips to Berlin after the war I had spent a great deal of my time in East Berlin. In those early days one could change West German marks into East German marks at the favourable rate of one to four. Armed with this money I would take the U-Bahn to the Alexanderplatz, go to the Soviet House of Culture, and buy wonderful gramophone records and books for a ridiculously small sum.

On this occasion we went to see the East German TV

authorities, who were enormously helpful. Who did we want to interview? Well, we would very much like to interview Otto John (who had just defected from the West). Ah, that might be difficult, but they would certainly get someone of similar standing. That evening we drove miles outside Berlin on the road to Frankfürt-an-der-Oder, to the East German TV studios. We had the full run of them for a couple of hours while I interviewed a university professor, an engineer, a factory worker and a housewife. Needless to say they were dead against the re-arming of Western Germany.

Later in 1955 Marjorie and I did a series of radio programmes which we called: 'I'll never forget the day', based on the idea that everyone says at one time or another: 'I'll never forget the day when—' something or other happened. We decided to get a number of celebrities to recall some special day that they would 'never forget' and tell it in the form of an interview, illustrated with music or any other appropriate sounds. One of the first people we recorded was Michael Flanders, who told, brilliantly, the terrible day he would never forget which was the day he contracted polio. His partner Donald Swann, composed a marvellous 'signature tune' for the series of programmes.

General Sir Brian Horrocks talked about the entry into Brussels in 1944. Ursula Bloom talked about her meeting with Ethel le Nève, Crippen's mistress. Norman Birkett about the Nuremberg trials. We went to Paris to get a story from Peter Ustinov and we got two, recorded ad-lib without a moment's thought and both, inevitably, quite brilliant. One was about his wait in the 'Fathers' Room' at a Los Angeles hospital when his daughter was born – all the expectant fathers were shattered to hear a woman screaming, when a young doctor came into the room:

'Don't worry fellers, those screams come from psychiatry, not maternity.' And the other about his army days when he had to get a story about some back-room boffins. While we were in Paris BBC Third Programme wanted a long interview with Alexandre Bénois, who had designed so many of the sets and costumes for the Diaghileff Ballet, notably those for Petrouchka. Alexandre Bénois was an old man of 89 at the time. He was Peter Ustinov's great uncle. Peter and I went together daily for nearly a week to talk to the charming old gentleman, firing a succession of questions at him which he dealt with brilliantly. Once, carelessly, I used the name 'Leningrad'. He pulled me up sharply.

'Monsieur Ward,' he said, *'vous me ferez le plaisir de dire Saint Petersbourg.'* Alexandre Bénois' flat in the Javel district of Paris was more crammed with books, magazines, papers, pictures, *objets d'art* and furniture than any I have ever seen. The living-room was very large but to get from one end to the other one had to circumvent countless obstacles. A samovar bubbled away all the time and our interviewing was constantly interrupted by people who drifted in like characters from a Chekhov play, talked inconsequentially for a few minutes, drank a cup of tea and drifted out again.

'I have been accused of being obsessed with the Eighteenth Century,' Alexandre Bénois said to me once. 'But really I feel in some ways that I can claim to belong to it. Few people can have such close links with such a distant past. Do you know that my grandfather was born in the reign of Louis XV – not Louis XVI, Louis the *Fifteenth*. He escaped the French Revolution and went to Russia. And finally I escaped the Russian Revolution and returned to France.' But Alexandre Bénois stayed in Russia for some ten years after the revolution as curator of the Hermitage Museum in Len – Saint Petersbourg.

'It was an exciting time to be curator of this great museum,' the old man said, 'because, of course, almost daily wonderful treasures kept arriving in truck loads. But you know one's joy at adding a masterpiece to the museum was tinged, often, by sad memories of where it had come from. How wonderful, I would think, to have that splendid Titian – but how sad to remember it so well in Prince so-and-so's dining-room where I had so often been a guest.'

In the end, sickened by Stalin's policy of selling treasures from the Hermitage and other Russian museums to American collectors in order to raise hard currency, Alexandre Bénois decided to leave the Soviet Union. The authorities allowed him to go but not to take many of his possessions with him. He went through hard times in the early days in Paris. Curiously enough although the Bénois family had been in Russia for three generations, Alexandre had not a drop of Russian blood in him. The following year, when Marjorie had a job to do in Paris and we had the children with us on our way to the South of France, I took Lalla and Nicky to see the old gentleman. He was enchantingly kind to them, giving them books and toys and sending out for special little cakes for their tea. He was ninety years old then and he died not long after. I feel very privileged to have met him.

Chapter Nineteen

In the summer of 1955 Ian Cox, whom I had known well when he was a Talks producer in the BBC and who was working for Shell asked me if I would go to Venezuela to make some programmes about the oil industry there, for broadcasting over radio systems in Asia and Africa. He also hoped the BBC would broadcast at least one programme as well. I told Ian that he knew as well as I did that the BBC would almost certainly take one programme about oil but that they wouldn't subsist on a solid diet of it. On the other hand surely it would be to Shell's advantage for other programmes to be broadcast about the country which was their most important source of crude oil. Ian agreed and the result was that in the three months I spent in Venezuela I probably saw more of the country than many people who had lived there for years.

After a week in Trinidad – oil and calypso, and I am no great amateur of calypso – I flew to Maiquetia, the airport of Caracas. I drove up the spectacular Autopista, a six-line double-track highway seventeen kilometres long that cost three million dollars a kilometre to build. But that was in the days of the Dictator Perez Jimenez, when the vast revenues from oil were squandered in grandiose projects like this. At that time Caracas looked as if it had suffered a severe bombing. Pleasant Spanish colonial-style houses had been torn down ruthlessly to build vast blocks of skyscraper flats.

I set off on my travels almost immediately and by the time I returned about six weeks later, the face of Caracas had changed.

The great blocks of flats on the hillside I had seen when I first arrived half finished, had mushroomed up another six storeys and more little houses were being bulldozed down. They built these enormous blocks of workers' flats at an almost unbelievable speed. A contractor told me that one, which was almost completed, had been started 45 days before.

'In another 25 days it will be completely finished and ready for occupation,' he said. 'All the painting and plumbing, the fitting of electric wiring, everything will be finished then.' One explanation of this astonishingly speedy building was that it was commissioned by a Government organization, who paid very high rates but inserted a penalty clause in the contract that really was penal. The contractors finished on time if they didn't want to be ruined.

This contractor was an Italian and Italians were pouring into Venezuela at that time at the rate of over 2,000 a week. It was amusing to go down to the port of La Guayra and watch the arrival of an immigrant ship. Italians, who had been in Venezuela for a year or two, drove down the Autopista in their American cars to meet their poor relations from the home country and showed off and patronized them. The Italians did and no doubt are still doing, a great deal for Venezuela. I found excellent restaurants in the remotest parts of the country. I found, too, that these Italian immigrants, like me, mixed up the two languages. They forgot a great deal of their own and never really learned Spanish or the curious slurred, lazy language that passes for Spanish in Venezuela. I got along very well in this hybrid tongue.

With all the building that was going on, land values soared to fantastic heights in Caracas. In the elegant new suburbs land that had been under coffee or maize or sugar cane not many years before was fetching no less than £150 a square metre. At least the people who had owned a small coffee hacienda and had become millionaires almost overnight had no notions of building neo-Roman palaces or small Alhambras. They wanted the most modern and the best. The result was that many first class architects from all over the world came to Caracas.

And there were several extremely good Venezuelan architects as well.

Shell organized a wonderful tour for me and my guide was a remarkable woman called Toby Green. I was somewhat astonished when she turned up at my hotel in a Caracas taxicab – admittedly a large and comfortable Dodge, because this seemed to me to be an extravagant way of covering, perhaps, well over a thousand miles of country. But Toby said that was the usual procedure and who was I to argue. The taxi driver, an amiable Andino called Maldonaro, would be invaluable in his homeland of the Andes, Toby assured me, and so, indeed, he was.

On our way to the Andes we stopped at the Guataparo Ranch near the town of Valencia. There were broad, green paddocks and shady trees; a patch of woodland here and there and in the distance hills, sloping up rather steeply. One might have been in one of the Yorkshire Dales. Cattle were grazing everywhere and Steve Abecassis, the ranch manager, pointed out the different breeds.

'Just plain Criollo. Those are Criollo crossed with Redpoll. There are some crossed with Zebu.' The Criollo are the native cattle brought over originally by the Spanish *conquistadores*. The word '*criollo*' has come to mean anything of real Venezuelan origin. Steve Abecassis explained that this was a 'finishing' ranch. The cattle had been brought from the plains of Apure in the south and they stayed at Guataparo for three months. But it was also a breeding ranch.

Down by the corrals cowboys were driving in a herd of beautiful, milky-white zebu cows, lovely animals with long, drooping ears and humps on their backs. They came from India originally but the forebears of these had been imported from Texas to improve the *criollo* breed. Then Steve showed me some of the prize Brahmin bulls, magnificent, great white beasts with a big hump and a dewlap hanging in a kind of frill reaching nearly to the ground.

'Watch out for those bulls,' Steve said, 'they can be wicked.' They were a far cry from the sleepy Brahmin bulls I had been used to seeing in India, which were as quiet as lambs. The fact that their diet was chiefly melon rinds and paper no doubt accounted for it. These animals had been imported originally to the southern parts of the United States and to South America because of their powers of resistance to tropical conditions and their ability to forage for food and travel long distances for water.

The Andes run like a great, jagged backbone down the whole length of South America from Venezuela and Colombia in the north, right down to the south of Chile. Standing on a spur of this mighty mountain range near the Colombian border an oilman said:

'If you kept walking south along this ridge, you'd end up in Chile, four thousand miles away.' Driving into the Andes for the first time will always for me be unforgettable. I wrote in my diary at the time:

'From open cattle ranches into thick, jungle country with palms and tall forest trees covered with parasite growths, orchids and lianas. Two brilliant, red, blue and yellow macaws fly over us just ahead. We reach the foothills of the Andes. Little thatched *ranchos* on the sides of the roads – the homes of peasants who keep a few head of cattle, grow bananas, a little maize, buy their groceries once a week and do casual work on nearby ranches and haciendas. We start to climb steeply, still through tropical rain forest. There are little farms on the mountainsides, with maize patches on the precipitous slopes. On through coffee country with guava trees shading the coffee bushes. The houses become much more prosperous looking. The villages are neat and clean with white and colour-washed houses. The people wear felt hats instead of straw ones. We stop at a restaurant seven thousand feet up kept by a Venetian. 'You ought to feel at home,' I tell him, 'Venezuela means "Little Venice".' 'Yes, signore, but it's too far from the sea up here!' He has his espresso coffee machine and his frigidaire and the inevitable juke box. The road gets steeper. We pass women carrying enormous bundles of firewood, with leather thongs strapped over their foreheads – just like the Kikuyu women in Kenya. Whole fields are now carpeted with wild purple lupins. More and more wild flowers – brilliant blue anchusa, scarlet lobelia and mauve mignonette. At least half the flowers in the average English garden must have come originally from the Andes.

'On up to ten thousand feet and the mountainsides crimson with heath. We climb up to the *paramo* as the high land of the Andes is called and the mountainsides change to grey and yellow with a plant called frailejon – yellow flowers and grey, furry leaves, a kind of outsize Andine edelweiss. From a little village with a mosaic of tiny fields divided by stone walls there is a stupendous view of the peaks of the Andes, towering up to over 15,000 feet. Two girls and a man in scarlet *ponchos*, standing by a shrine, make a wonderful foreground to a photograph. They are well aware of the fact and readily pocket the *bolivar* I give them. That's how they earn their living. On and up to the high pass of the Pica del Aguila, the Peak of the Eagle. And on the wall of the inn is painted the altitude: 4,118 metres, which is 13,400 feet. I run for a few yards along the road to get a photograph before a drifting cloud obscures the view and I pull up panting and gasping with exhaustion. It is far the highest I have ever been on the ground. It is very pleasant to be standing in front of a roaring fire in the inn.'

We drove down the other side of the pass and ended up in the charming old Spanish Colonial city of Mèrida, which was preparing for the Fiesta of San Miguel. It was very much like a fiesta in any little Spanish town with fireworks and a band playing paso dobles and a religious procession, of which the central point was the image of the city's patron, Saint Michael. And there were roundabouts and all the sideshows you see at any fair. That night I was invited to a party at the house of the Governor of the State of Mèrida. It was a gay, extremely smart party, the women dressed in the most expensive *haute couture* – Christian Dior had *two* shops in Caracas at that time, and the men elegant in their white jackets, fastened tight round the neck with gold buttons. During an interval in the dancing I persuaded the guitarist in the orchestra to play a typical Andino song and he sat down with his fellow guitarist and they played an enchanting serenade he had composed himself, of which I still have the recording I made.

The country between Mèrida and San Cristobal is a great stronghold of the Church and all the little towns we drove through had lovely old Spanish Colonial baroque churches. The Venezuelans have inherited the Spanish love of ironwork. The houses have exquisite wrought iron grilles outside the windows and the ironwork even extended to cars and buses whose luggage carriers were carried out in wonderful fancy scrolls and twists of wrought iron.

The little town of Lobatera, just outside San Cristobal, had been having a fiesta for a solid week and we arrived on the last day. To mark the close of the fiesta they held a bullfight in the main square, which had been barricaded off, with stands built behind the barriers. To make sure everyone knew when things had started, a man trailed a long rope with blobs about the size of a large egg at intervals of about a yard across the arena. Having done this he lit one end of the rope, which in fact was a fuse. Each time the burning rope reached an 'egg' – which was a small bomb – it exploded with deafening noise. There were about thirty of these little bombs and by the time they had gone off in succession the crowd was well awake and ready for the entertainment to follow.

It was a comic bullfight in which they didn't use a fighting bull but one of their mountain *criollo* animals, who was a lot more dangerous than a great many fighting bulls I have seen. He was also far too valuable to be killed and so a troupe of clowns 'played' him brilliantly and with great hazard to their lives.

I was very reluctant to leave the Andes. Life goes on in the old mountain towns and villages much as it has for centuries. Of course, for the Andinos, it is being made far easier with new hospitals and schools and splendid roads. But I believe, basically, they will hold on to their traditional way of living.

It was a shattering contrast to find oneself in the modern, highly commercialized town of Maracaibo, at the northern end of the great lake. Maracaibo used to have an appalling climate. It still does, but nobody with any money notices it. The well-to-do step from their air conditioned houses to their air conditioned cars and in turn into their air conditioned offices and they eat in air conditioned restaurants. They don't come into contact with the climate at all except for the few seconds they take to get in and out of a car. If they play any games or take any exercise they do so after dark playing tennis, for instance, under floodlights.

Maracaibo is the base of the Western oilfields of Venezuela. There are rich fields in the east of the country, but the most spectacular fields, which produce over half of Venezuela's vast output of oil are in and around the huge Lake Maracaibo.

I flew down one morning to Casigua, at the far end of the lake so see some of the earliest fields. We flew quite low in a small de Havilland Dove over the rain forest that covers the western shores of the lake. In a clearing I saw what looked like an enormous haystack.

'That's a Motilone Indian dwelling,' the pilot told me, and he circled it and flew lower. Men ran out of the hut, which must have been at least sixty feet long and perhaps twenty-five high, thickly thatched. The Indians waved at us. 'That's a nice change,' the pilot said, 'they're not a very friendly crowd usually.' In fact the Motilone Indians are a most belligerent tribe. They may have fallen for Western civilization since, but at that time they had no use for it beyond raiding outlying oilfields for things like axes and wire, and shooting with bows and arrows at anyone who ventured into their territory. It seemed extraordinary that almost nothing was known about these people who lived half an hour's flight away from Maracaibo. It was supposed that these large haystack-like dwellings were communal buildings like the Dyaks' 'long houses' in Borneo. But nobody knew what they were like inside. The Motilones were known to be tall for Indians and enormously strong physically.

It seemed curious to be sitting down to lunch in the oilfield manager's house at Casigua, in the jungle, to magnificent grilled soles, frozen in Holland and flown in from Maracaibo. They lived well in this remote part of Venezuela in spite of being shot at from time to time by the Motilone Indians. From Casigua I flew up to Lagunillas on the eastern shore of the lake. The sight of the forest of derricks stretching miles out into the water was fantastic. Near the shore they were very close together, some two hundred yards apart. Then there was a wide gap and they started again, far more widely spaced, twenty miles out into the lake. Later I had a wonderful bird's eye view of it all from a helicopter. We flew very low, at about 250 feet, just nicely clear of the tops of the derricks. At one moment the derricks looked all jumbled up and then, suddenly, they appeared in neat, straight lines, with here and there the collecting and separator plants standing up on their platforms like shining cake-tins. To the right the thickly crowded field of Tia Juana looked like hundreds of yachts lying at anchor. We flew over a crane barge from which they were setting down a derrick platform on iron legs over a hundred feet long. And then we came in to land on one of the drilling barges and settled on the landing deck on the helicopter's two long fat rubber floats that can be used on land or on water.

They are wonderful things these great drilling barges, about 150 feet long and half as wide. A barge is completely self-contained. Aboard it is the power to drive the drill; the tanks of special circulating 'mud' that is used to sluice out the drill hole and bring the rock chippings to the surface; and also to control oil and gas pressure eventually. There are stacks of drill pipe and well casing on the decks as well as spare bits and other supplies. They were hauling up a mile of drill pipe at this well to change a blunt bit, stacking ninety-foot lengths of pipe against the side of the tall derrick. It was a beautiful, calm day and everything was going smoothly. But you can get storms on Lake Maracaibo almost as bad as at sea. Then drilling has to stop and the barge is pulled away from the drilling platform until the weather calms down.

I flew 150 miles over the great pipeline that carries the oil from the Lake Maracaibo fields to the refinery at Cardon. Ten years before I was there the land on which the refinery stood was arid, scrubby desert. From a distance I saw the tall towers of the distilling plant standing up against the sky like a miniature

New York skyline. When they are lit up at night the local people call it '*el pequeño Manhattan*'.

From Cardon I flew to Valencia where I met Steve Abecassis and together we flew to San Fernando de Apure, the capital of the State of Apure and, indeed, of the Llanos, as the great cattle plains of the south, which stretch down to the Orinoco, are called. There we transferred to a small four seater plane flown by a young American called Tex Palmer, who knew the Apure country like a book because his job was to fly out from San Fernando to the different ranches, each of which had its own little airstrip.

The country was dead flat and quite thickly wooded at first. Then we flew over open savannah and the plain below was dotted with thousands of cattle and tens of thousands of little white egrets that fluttered and walked about among them. Then to the left I saw a muddy, winding river. Steve tapped me on the shoulder from behind.

'That's the Arauca,' he said. 'Now you're over the real plains – the Llanos. Ahead I saw a cluster of trees and some buildings. 'Matapalos,' Steve said. 'We'll land there.' Tex banked and circled and brought the plane down on a tiny airstrip just behind the ranch house.

Steve had some business to attend to at Matapalos and then we were in the air again, flying over thousands of head of cattle until once again there was a ranch house below and a line of coconut palms and this ranch was called Los Cocos.

The ground was wet and flooded when Don Gustavo Ferrer, the Venezuelan ranch manager, took me out on to the plains in a jeep. We drove straight across country through thick grass. From the bank of a creek an alligator slid into the water. The bird life was fabulous; lovely white herons and chocolate-coloured water rails which, when they took to the air, unfolded brilliant patches of yellow under their wings. We stopped to look at a pair of gigantic storks, standing nearly six feet high which in the Llanos are called soldier birds.

'You see those birds, Señor Ward?' Don Gustavo said. 'I started life cooking for a gang of cattlemen. There wasn't much money in the Llanos in those days and to save killing a steer they would go out and shoot one of those soldier birds. Many's the one I've cooked for them. They weren't bad eating either.' We drove on disturbing a pair of coro-coro, the lovely scarlet ibis, whose brilliant red plumage seems almost too good to be true. And then suddenly Don Gustavo stopped the jeep. 'Look, over there,' he said quietly, 'just by that pool. See the duck? Have a go and see what you can get' – and he handed me his twelve bore gun. I took the gun and began walking towards the ducks, thinking that when they rose with luck I might get a right and left. Don Gustavo had no such sporting instincts. He made it quite clear that I should make sure of things by shooting the birds on the ground. So I crept a bit nearer and then stopped and waited until three ducks were standing in line and then fired. I got all three of them. 'Estupendo!' shouted Don Gustavo, 'three birds with one shot!' I found out later that cartridges cost one *bolivar* each – two shillings, a strong deterrent to sporting instincts.

After picking up the ducks we drove on and then, away across the plain, I saw a herd of several hundred cattle. Three *peones* were driving them slowly across the pastureland towards us, singing in a strange, high-pitched minor key to keep the cattle quiet. The cowboys wore khaki shirts and trousers turned up at the knee so that they were almost shorts. They wore no boots and had spurs strapped on to their bare feet that rested in curious stirrups that tapered down into long points. They wore straw sombreros and carried knives in their belts in long, leather, tasselled scabbards and they had dark blue ponchos rolled up and slung in front of them across their high-peaked saddles. They were very fine-looking, dark skinned men, at least half Indian and magnificent horsemen. I saw them all again that evening in a very different setting.

A party had been organized. Long before it was due to begin they had built a long fire outside the *caney*, the large, barn-like shed which was the mess and common room of the peones and their women. They stuck long sticks into the ground along the length of the fire and fastened large pieces of meat to roast on them. They had just opened a few bottles of *caña*, a kind of powerful *grappa* distilled from the 'trash' from the sugar factories, when the orchestra arrived – a harpist, a guitarist and a maracas player. It wasn't long before the dance got under way. They played and danced *joropos* and *llanos* waltzes and *paso dobles*. The harpist was particularly brilliant, playing his instrument as if it were a guitar. And the cowboys really knew how to dance. They twirled their partners round stamping their feet to the rhythm of the primitive, Latin American music. One of the girls had long wavy hair down to her waist and it swirled out like a black catherine wheel as she spun round in a waltz.

'This, you know, is the real thing,' Steve Abecassis said to me. 'This is the real music of the plains. You've got to come down to the Llanos to hear it. Of course you can buy a lot of stuff in Caracas sung and played by professional musicians who've never been near the Llanos and don't know a horse from a cow. It's not the same thing at all. It's all fake.' I made some very good recordings and then at three in the morning, when the dancing was still going strong, we went to bed – at least I did; the others slept in hammocks, slung across the verandah.

After a wonderful breakfast of fresh ranch eggs we said goodbye to Don Gustavo and boarded the plane again. After a while Tex Palmer turned to me:

'Look! Down below. Wild horses.' He put the plane into a steep dive until it was less than a hundred feet from the ground. The herd of a couple of hundred horses stampeded madly. As we rose out of the dive I looked back and saw Steve in the back seat, looking very pale, holding his ten gallon hat in his hands, upside down in front of him.

'Don't for God's sake ever do that again, Tex,' he moaned. 'Not if you want to keep your contract with the company.'

I spent a wonderful few hours at the next ranch, called Turagua. We travelled several miles up a *caño* in a long dugout canoe with an outboard motor. During the short journey I saw a greater diversity of wild life than I would have thought possible in such a short time. Trees grew right down to the edge of the creek and the variety of birds nesting in them was extraordinary. There were herons and bitterns, big black and white storks and little white egrets; pale, rosy-pink spoonbills and rounding a bend of the creek the blue sky was flecked with scarlet as we disturbed a colony of over a hundred corocoro. Five-foot-long iguanas slithered into the water as we approached and alligators floated motionless like logs or basked on the muddy banks of the *caño*. Several times we came upon a little herd of chigüire – or copybara – looking like outsize guineapigs, as big as a large pig, which the local people permit themselves to eat during Lent because, since they spend so much of their time in the water, they count them as fish.

At one point we were approaching a clump of trees where some birds with the exotic name of hoatzins – or less romantically stink pheasants, were perching. They are the nearest surviving link to the prehistoric pterodactyl; their chicks are hatched with bat-like hooks on their wings. In order not to disturb them the man at the tiller switched off the engine and a *peon* began to pole the canoe along. It was while he was doing this that there was very nearly a disaster. The man got his pole stuck in the mud and almost accomplished the comic paper act of being left clinging to it while the boat continued on its way. In his frantic efforts to avoid this he very nearly upset the canoe. Everybody showed signs of the utmost alarm. There was something very like real panic aboard. I took it all quite calmly. The water was only about five feet deep; it was a very hot day; we were all wearing old clothes which would have dried quickly. All I was worried about was getting my cameras wet. The man finally fell back into the canoe without upsetting it and the relief on everybody's face was so obvious as to be ridiculous.

'What on earth was all the excitement about, Steve?' I asked. 'It wouldn't have done us all that harm to have had a soaking.'

'Just reduced us all to skeletons inside of a couple of minutes. That's all!'

'What on earth are you talking about?'

'D'you remember me telling you not to trail your hand in the water?' I did vaguely remember his saying something of the kind when we started off, but I'd paid no particular attention at the time. I hadn't trailed my hand in the water, though. 'Haven't you heard of caribes?' Steve went on. 'They're little fish not much bigger than your hand, but they've got teeth like razors and they hunt in packs. They'll bite every pick of flesh off your body in a couple of minutes. These *caños* are swarming with them. There's hardly an Indian around these parts who hasn't lost a finger or a toe or two.' A little further on Steve pointed out a large mound of earth and leaves on the bank like a big ant heap. 'That's an alligator's nest,' he said. We landed and Steve burrowed down among the hot, fermenting leaves and pulled out an egg about the size of a duck's egg. He broke it open and inside was a perfectly formed little alligator. He tossed it into the *caño*. At once there was a flurry in the water as a school of the savage little fish fought for the tiny prize. Steve looked at me.

'See what I mean?' he said.

We moved on down the creek. We saw terrapins on the banks; we saw ducks and geese and deer. If we had stayed long enough we would probably have seen tapir and possibly even jaguar – *tigre*, as they are called in the Llanos, where they are hated as savage and wanton killers of cattle, killing far more than they can possibly eat just for the fun of it. It was a wrench to fly back from this naturalist's paradise to the spurious civilization of Caracas.

I didn't stay long in the capital. I flew down to Puerto Ordaz on the Orinoco, where there is a large, green island in the middle of the great river. It is at least a mile from the port to the island and rather more to the far, densely forested bank. It was just about as far as Sir Walter Raleigh had penetrated up the Orinoco in his vain search for El Dorado.

The road to Cerro Bolivar, the Iron Mountain, led through dry, parched land dotted with chaparra bushes and desiccated scrub. After something over eighty miles I reached the Orinoco Mining Company's camp of Ciudad Pilar. The road twisted and turned up the 3,500-foot mountain. Half way up, its sides, and the road itself, were solid iron ore. By the top, on a wide ledge cut into the mountainside, a long train was pulled up and huge yellow trucks were feeding it with ore. They came up, each carrying a load of forty or fifty tons of iron ore, and tipped them with a flurry of dark red dust into the railway wagons. Underneath the grass of the whole mountainside was a thick layer of solid iron ore that contained over 60 per cent of iron. They reckoned there were somewhere around a thousand million tons of it and at the progress they were making then it would take them about forty years to clean the whole layer of ore off the mountain. After they have done that there are a number more mountains in the area that are equally rich.

Gigantic power shovels bit into the side of the mountain digging out the ore twenty tons at a bite. Two bites loaded a truck and that took a little under a minute. I was talking to an engineer as we watched these mighty machines working.

'Strange to think,' I said, 'that this very road we're standing on will be in Pennsylvania in a month or two.' The engineer scratched his head.

'You know I never thought of that, but you're quite right,' he said.

When the ore train reached Puerto Ordaz – with every conceivable safety device to stop over 100 cars laden with 12,000 tons of ore getting out of control descending a steep gradient, it stopped and they shunted the trucks one by one into a huge iron drum which clamped on to the truck, revolved, and sent the ore cascading into the crushers below. From the crushers the ore was either diverted to a small mountain below them – the stockpile – or sent straight to the 'loader' on the jetty and into the holds of a waiting ore ship along a fast moving belt.

I had seen them start to load a giant ore ship of 60,000 tons – although it was only possible to load her to half capacity because of the shallow water in the Orinoco Delta. I thought I would have plenty of time to go up the Iron Mountain, see what I wanted and be back to see the end of the loading of the ore ship. I was away nearly five hours and in that time they had poured 30,000 tons of ore into the ship's holds. I was just in time to see the last few hundred tons go aboard.

Back in Caracas I wanted to buy some presents to take home. Normally one buys something typical of the country one has been in. In Venezuela that was impossible. They make nothing in Venezuela. Everything seems to be imported. I bought a Navajo rug from Arizona; some amusing straw hats for the children that came from Ecuador; some key rings with baby alligators' heads attached from Colombia. At last I thought I had something for Marjorie that really was Venezuelan. It was a little gold orchid – the national flower of Venezuela – with a pearl set in it. It was made by a woman called Panchita, who was a superb craftsman. But it turned out that Panchita came from Trinidad.

Venezuela is frankly a *nouveau riche* country with very little cultural background. Even the Indians were backward and had had no kind of civilization. In the days of the Spanish Empire the country did not rate a viceroy. It was thought sufficient to make do with a Captain-General. It is ironic that as a result of the discovery of vast quantities of oil and other mineral wealth – as well as almost limitless iron there are enormous bauxite reserves – Venezuela has become far the richest country in South America.

The dictatorship of General Perez Jimenez ended not long after I was in Venezuela and the General decamped to Florida to be succeeded by more liberal leaders. In time it should be a wonderful country. The large influx of Italian and Spanish immigrants was already having a marked effect when I was there. But then the rich were still very rich and the poor very very poor.

Chapter Twenty

In the autumn of 1956 came the uprising in Hungary. Laurence Gilliam sent me out to report this tragic, epic event. With me came Colonel Jackson, who had joined the BBC and whom I had known in Paris, when he was a PRO for SHAPE. We arrived too late to get to Budapest, so we drove from Vienna to the Hungarian frontier, some six miles from the town of Sopron. The Austrian frontier guards would not allow us to drive our car into Hungary, so Jacko and I, together with an American called Bailey who I guessed worked for the CIA, walked across the hundred yards of No Man's Land to the Hungarian post. It was manned, needless to say, by members of the resistance. While we were waiting to hitch-hike into Sopron in some kind of a vehicle, I noticed a number of pamphlets, written in cyrillic script. They had been produced by the American authorities and they told Soviet troops that they had been hoodwinked into fighting a freedom-loving people and urged them to disregard the orders of their officers. From the Soviet point of view they were highly subversive documents. Thinking that the Russian section of the BBC might be interested, I put a few of these leaflets into my pocket. Then a truck turned up and we jumped aboard and headed for Sopron. As we reached the top of a rise overlooking the town, we could see the Red Army moving in from the other direction, only a few miles away.

'Well, I don't know, Ed,' Bailey said, 'but unless you're set on interviewing the Red Army commander, I think we'd better get the hell out of here. I've seen all I want to of those boys to last me a while. I was driving along a road, couple of days ago, when rounding a bend I found myself right up behind a Soviet tank. A minute later there was a terrible noise behind me and there was another tank coming up towards me. I drove on slowly between the two for about a quarter of an hour, wondering when the fancy would take them to shoot me or for the tank behind me to run me down. At last there was a small turning to the right and you should have seen the speed I made getting down it. I was followed by roars of laughter from the tank crews.'

It was easy enough to get transport going towards Sopron, but quite another matter heading for the Austrian frontier. Everybody wanted to do that. We had to walk four of the six miles, expecting to be overtaken by the Red Army at any moment. At last a bus crammed with people stopped in a small village. We managed to cling on to the outside and get back to Austria. It wasn't until that evening when I was taking things out of my pockets that I found the leaflets urging Soviet soldiers to disregard their officers' orders. That, I thought, would have been a fine thing to have been caught with if the Red Army had overtaken us!

It was that very day when the news of Suez came through and the Hungarian story took second place in the newspapers of the West. On the Hungarian frontier I was ashamed of my nationality.

Later that same year I went, with Jacko again, to Poland. After the Poznan riots earlier in the year, a short-lived period of liberalism began and it was still at its height when we arrived in Warsaw in December.

During their period of new-found freedom Poles were allowed to travel abroad. The first thing they did was to write to friends or relations in Britain or America asking them to send them – anything. A large tin of Nescafé, for example, fetched the equivalent of £30 on the black market at the official rate of exchange. And Poles were able to buy air and rail tickets in zloty at the official rate of exchange. A dozen large tins of Nescafé, or better still a few suit lengths of good English worsted, would buy a ticket by air to South America. Poles were buying return tickets to Buenos Aires. Then, when they reached London or Paris or wherever they *really* wanted to go, they claimed a refund on the return London or Paris – Buenos Aires, and lived very comfortably for a month or so on the proceeds.

When we were in Warsaw in the winter of 1956–7 there was the saying that an unemployed Pole was a Pole with only one job. Taxis were very scarce; but any car – even a Post Office van – would stop if you hailed it and the driver would take you at least near to your destination.

There was a wonderful feeling of freedom at Christmas that year. A Pole I had come to know well came up to me the day before and said in an ecstatic tone of voice:

'I never thought I should live to see this! Last night at a night club an UBO looked over my shoulder at the bill the waiter had just brought me. I turned round, took him by the collar and the seat of his pants and threw him into the street! I never thought I should live to see the day when I could do that to a member of the secret police! They always used to snoop about looking at bills and if it was an unduly large one you'd be hauled off for questioning about how you came to have so much money. I suppose this one couldn't get out of the habit.'

Christmas was a long series of parties and soon after Jacko and I left on our trip to the south. In Kattowice – which had just reverted to its old name after having been called Stalinograd ever since the war – I was collecting some material about coal mining and our guide offered to drive us to Krakow. He had to go there anyway, he said. Was there anything we would like to do on the way? We both said we should like to see Auschwitz.

'Oh, you don't want to go there,' the Pole said. We said we really did want to. Obviously very unwillingly he agreed. It was getting on for five o'clock and pitch dark when we arrived at the infamous concentration camp. The Germans blew up nearly all the gas chambers and crematoria just before Auschwitz was over-run by the Red Army but there was a frightening atmosphere about the evil place. As I trudged through the snow towards a large hut that the Poles have turned into a horror museum, I felt that if ever a place could be haunted, Auschwitz was that place. Inside the hut were hideously realistic models of crowded gas chambers. But what was far more horrifying were show cases which ran all the length of the wall of a large room. They were glass fronted and perhaps eight or ten feet high by twenty long and four or five feet deep. One was entirely filled with human hair that had been cut off the corpses after they had been taken out of the gas chambers. It was later sent back to Germany, where it was used for various purposes like stuffing mattresses. Another show case was filled with suitcases, mostly with Jewish names on them; another with boots and shoes. The most poignantly pathetic of all was the case packed with children's toys. We were taken down into some cellars where there were cells for special punishment where a man could neither lie down nor stand up. When at last we left this fearful place and were walking back to the car, our Polish guide said:

'I feel very grateful indeed to you two gentlemen for having insisted upon visiting Auschwitz. You must have noticed that I was not at all willing to go. But now I am very glad I have seen it and got an impression of what it must have been like there. You see, my father died at Auschwitz.' Neither of us knew what to say. We felt very embarrassed. But we need not have been. He was genuinely grateful to us for having dragged him there.

Back in Warsaw we went to the ballet, organized by an ex-ballet dancer whom I remembered well in the old pre-war days of the Diaghileff Ballet, Woizikowski. It was not a brilliant production of *Swan Lake* but there were some dancers with great promise and I was thrilled to be able to persuade Woizikowski to come round the next day to our hotel for a drink. He was so delighted to be able to talk to people who remembered his performances in the old pre-war ballets. I remembered in particular his dancing the Three Cornered Hat and that gave him great pleasure because it was one of his favourite roles.

And then we met the famous Polish Air Force 'ace' Skvalski, who had a galaxy of British medals – DSO, DFC and bar and so on and so on apart from rows of Polish medals. What pleased him particularly was that he was now able to wear his RAF 'wings' and medals on one side of his uniform and his Polish insignia on the other. We sat in our room in the Bristol Hotel and drank whisky and talked over old times and Poland seemed a very agreeable country to be in at the time. Of course this free and easy atmosphere didn't last long.

After my sponsored journey to Venezuela I seemed to be becoming more and more involved in the oil industry. The next thing was that Shell commissioned me to write a book about the men who work in oil – a real, human interest account of the industry. 'Commissioned' is perhaps not quite the right word because what, in fact, Shell did do for me was to pay all my travelling expenses to Nigeria, the Sahara and one or two journeys to Holland. This I welcomed at the time and I enjoyed the trips very much, but the resultant book was not at all a commercial success in view of the long time I had taken to collect the material for it. I began by travelling to Cornwall, where a former Shell executive was living in retirement. He was a most colourful personality and told me some marvellous stories, most of which I couldn't use at the time. But I remember one, in which he played a leading part in negotiations with a ruler on the Persian Gulf over an oil concession. They had reached the point when a very substantial 'signature' fee was due to be paid by the oil company. It ran into several million rupees. The oilman, whom I shall call Dick, went to see the Arab ruler's British adviser.

'Right,' he said, 'that's fixed. Four million rupees. I'll arrange for a cheque—'

'Oh, I'm afraid he doesn't like cheques,' the adviser broke in, 'no, it'll have to be cash, I'm afraid. Rupee notes will do.'

'But how on earth can I get all that money in notes by tomorrow?' Dick asked.

'Well, my dear chap, that's your affair, I'm afraid. Anyway

you may consider yourself lucky that he'll accept notes. Usually he insists on gold.' With the utmost trouble Dick managed to get his agent in Bahrein to scour the bazaars and collect the necessary amount of rupee notes. An aeroplane was chartered which brought several trunks and suitcases packed with filthy currency. Dick and his assistants sat up for hours counting the money. It was right. He called in the adviser.

'Well, let's get this taken round to the palace at once.'

'Oh, dear me no. He wouldn't like that. Wouldn't like his relatives to know about it all. No, my dear fellow, you must keep it at your place. Then bring it round in the morning so that you can hand it over personally immediately after the signature.' Dick's 'place' was not much better than a mud hut. Anybody could have broken through the walls with a good kick. He put the highly valuable suitcases in the 'cellar' and sealed the door with some scotch tape – for what good that did. However nobody did break in and he was able to take the money over for the signature ceremony the following morning. When that was done he thought his job was finished. A few days later he was summoned to the ruler's presence.

'I am sure you will agree, Sir,' the ruler said, 'that the happy conclusion these negotiations have reached might have been much delayed – might even not have been reached at all – had it not been for the excellent work done by my chief minister—'

'I do indeed, sir.'

'I am glad you agree. So that in the circumstances I do feel that some slight token of appreciation on the part of your company might be in order?'

'Oh, indeed Sir. Might I ask what you would suggest?' The ruler leaned back, thought for a moment, scratched his beard.

'Oh, I don't know, perhaps a Cadillac?'

'Of course, Sir.' A few days later the ruler's Chief Minister called on Dick.

'I am sure you will agree,' he opened, 'that had it not been for the most co-operative attitude of our ruler these negotiations which have reached so happy a conclusion, might well have been much delayed, indeed might not have been reached at all.' –

Dick waited for it and wondered 'how much?' 'In view of this,' the Chief Minister continued, 'I do feel that some slight token of appreciation on the part of your company would not come amiss—'

'Indeed not,' Dick replied. 'What do you think he would most appreciate?'

'Well,' replied the Chief Minister, 'he is shortly paying an important state visit and I feel that the status of his retinue would be enhanced by the addition of – shall we say – three Cadillacs?' Dick agreed. What else could he do?

I talked to many old oilmen about their past experiences and adventures. One had been in Mexico in the days when civil war had almost come to be accepted as in the natural order of things. The oilmen, naturally, had to keep on good terms with the warring generals and one, in particular, always made a point of having a reasonable amount of money in his safe to hand over if necessary. He hid his main payroll money elsewhere. On one occasion a general he didn't know had defeated a rival who for long had held the part of the country where these particular oil installations were. The new general rode his horse up the steps of the administrative building and roared:

'Who is in command here?' The oilman stepped out of his office, walked up the general, bowed and said:

'You are, my general!'

I flew to Nigeria early in 1958, and after a few days in Lagos, flew on to Port Harcourt. From there I continued my journey by road to the small township of Owerri, at that time the headquarters of the Shell-B.P. oil venture in Nigeria. It was a distance of about eighty miles and the excellent road led through thick bush. We passed dozens of decrepit, ancient lorries that had been converted into buses known as 'mammy-wagons' and which travelled precariously to the peril of their packed loads of passengers. They all had slogans painted on their sides, mostly religious exhortations or invocations to the Almighty. One which seemed somewhat disrespectful to the Deity was written on a mammy wagon that lay, overturned, in a ditch at the side of the road. 'GOD IS RESPONSIBLE' the legend read.

Shell had established an extremely comfortable, so-called 'oil camp' at Owerri. I had been to many such camps in Venezuela, so I was not surprised to find it consisted, not of tents, but of comfortable bungalows, an excellent club and a swimming pool as well, of course, as offices, technical installations, stores and so on. I spent a little over a week at Owerri picking up background information, and while I was there I met the chief, a splendid old character called Njemanzi. Peter Hollis one of the Shell men took me to see the old man.

'We'd better take a bottle or two of whisky along,' he said, 'the old boy likes his nip and he'll open up better. His father was a notorious slaver, around the turn of the century and, indeed for a good many years into this one. It got so bad that travellers used to make wide detours to avoid going through Owerri and almost certain enslavement. Ironically enough,' Peter went on, 'the present chief joined the police in Port Harcourt when his father was at the height of his slaving activities. He must have found himself in a very difficult position. Anyway you'll see a tremendous marble statue of the old man in Njemanzi's garden. As an act of filial piety he had it sculpted in Port Harcourt and lugged all the way here. It must weigh a good many tons.'

Chief Njemanzi was a stocky man in his sixties, with grey frizzled hair and a huge mouth, which was always smiling – except when it was being used for drinking. He thanked Peter for the bottle of whisky, immediately opened it – it was before nine in the morning – poured a few drops on the ground as a libation to some earth spirit, fetched three glasses, poured generous tots and we started drinking and talking. I asked him about his father. The chief laughed.

'Oh yes, you know it was embarrassing to me sometimes in Port Harcourt. It still is. Even today some middle aged man will come up to me and say: "Hey you there, Chief Njemanzi, your father sold me as a slave when I was a young man and I reckon you should pay me some compensation." But I say I am not responsible for what my father did.' Peter asked him about cannibalism, which still goes on in the 'bush'.

'Oh well,' the chief said, 'there have been a few cases of wires being stretched across a road and people getting caught like that. But it's not so much. And the order about meat in the "bush" markets is being enforced.' Peter explained that by law, and for obvious reasons, all meat sold in 'bush' markets has to have its skin attached!

I had always supposed that cannibalism had some esoteric mysticism connected with it; that in tribal wars if you ate the flesh of your enemy, you absorbed, in some way, his courage and other desirable qualities. There was nothing so romantic about it. In the old tribal wars if you killed a few of the enemy you ate them because it was a wicked waste of good meat not to – and besides it saved killing cattle for food.

My stay in Owerri included two Sundays and I spent them studying Juju. My guide and instructor was Albert Anonyi, also an employee of Shell. Albert didn't believe in juju but he knew a great deal about it. After a while I thought there was a lot to be said for it. One day we saw a pile of curiously shaped melons piled up at the side of the road. They were oval shaped and had fluted skins and looked like fifty-pound bombs. Albert told the driver to stop the car and pick up one of the melons to show me. The driver was sorry, he didn't dare touch the melons. There was a juju on them.

'You see,' Albert said, 'anything can be left lying about and it's quite safe. All the yam barns have a juju put on them and nobody will touch them. A man can go away and leave his house door open with all his valuables in the house and nobody will dare go into it if he has had a juju put on it. Of course,' he added, 'you have to pay the juju priest quite a bit sometimes to fix the juju.'

'It's like a kind of insurance,' I said.

'Exactly,' Albert replied. 'That's just what it is and it works very well.'

It seems that it works very well even at high level. The story was that when the oil companies started operations in Nigeria the time came when they wanted to drill some exploration wells. The local people got it into their heads that the oilmen were somehow going to drain the oil away from the palm trees – palm oil was the only oil they had heard of and it was one of their main sources of livelihood. The land was all marked out for drilling when a priest put a juju on it. Nobody would go near it, let alone work on it. The powerful oil company was in a fix. They offered higher wages, all kinds of inducements. Against the fear of the juju they were meaningless. Then one of the oilmen had a brainwave. He found another and more influential juju priest and paid him a large sum of money to put a counter-juju on the plot of land. This stated that, on the contrary, it was a most auspicious place to work; that anyone who did would have great good fortune; his wives would bear more children; his goats would have more kids; his hens lay more eggs; his yam plots produce bigger and better yams. Men flocked to work.

One Sunday Albert and I drove along small dirt roads deep into the bush. At one village, where the community was Methodist, we heard them singing hymns in their wooden church. At the next Albert took me to a sacred grove in the forest, where a group of men squatted in a circle while juju priests made their incantations over the 'ofus' – the sacred fetishes that looked like bundles of leaves, twigs and feathers. They knew Albert and so we were allowed to stay and watch – and I even to record on tape – the strange, primeval rites.

In the bush villages Albert took me to several 'M'beri' houses, kind of rural museums with strangely sophisticated clay figures depicting every aspect of village life from procreation to burial – with some very comical three dimensional portraits of British officials.

On the second Sunday we began the day badly by drinking whisky with Chief Njemanzi. In the first village we visited we drank large quantities of palm wine, a brew made by tapping the sap of a palm tree, which should be treated with more respect than at first one might suppose. Later we drank some liqueur smuggled in from the island of Fernando Po; and finally we were entertained in yet another village with glasses of tepid Guinness. The Guinness advertising campaign in West Africa has been enormously successful. Using the theme of 'Guinness is Good for You', there are enormous posters everywhere in West Africa of great, powerful Africans, with bulging muscles, holding a glass of Guinness with the slogan: 'Guinness Makes you Strong!' There may even be some truth in this but in any case the Africans believe it implicitly and drink large quantities of this beverage, which I would have thought to be anything but suitable for the hot, damp climate.

Just outside this village was a large board, nailed to a tree, which said that the chief, a powerful doctor and soothsayer, could be consulted on any matter ranging from a prospective marriage to the purchase of a piece of land. When we entered the village, a cluster of huts with the chief's house, an imposing building in comparison, in the middle, I saw two taxis parked outside a low hut. I realized they must have come from Port Harcourt – a long taxi ride – and I remarked on this to Albert.

'Oh people come from much farther away to consult this man,' he said. They even come from Lagos. His charges run rather high. It costs you about £20 to get his advice.' We walked straight into the hut. Albert never worried about anything like that. Inside the hut the chief, wearing nothing but a loin cloth, was squatting on the floor in the semi darkness, shaking two tortoiseshells filled with pebbles. A small group of men wearing European clothes sat on a bench, watching the proceedings intently. It was all something to do with buying some land. The consultation lasted for a quarter of an hour or so and then a lot of money changed hands and the chief got up and greeted us. He took us back to his house and that was where the session drinking warm Guinness began. Over the drinks the chief turned to Peter Hollis, who had come with us on this Sunday.

'Now it is my turn to ask for advice,' he said. 'I have a son who is studying law in England and I want to send him some money.'

'That should be quite easy,' Peter said, 'I'll arrange a draft for you through the bank. How much had you in mind?'

'Oh, I don't know,' the chief said, 'somewhere around £500 or £600, I thought.'

I could imagine the law student son in London telling his friends:

'Of course my father is an important chief back at home. What's more he's a very famous doctor. People come to consult him from all over the country.' So, of course, they do and what's more his fees would put a Harley Street specialist to shame.

I flew from Port Harcourt to see some of the oilfields. Things were still in their early stages then. The oil companies had sunk the best part of £100 million into the venture and they still weren't sure how it was all going to turn out. (A few years were to show that their gamble had been a shrewd one.) We flew in a helicopter over tropical rain forest, the monotonous green here and there broken by the brilliant scarlet of a tall flamboyant tree. Then on over swampland where the trees, white-trunked, stood in milk-chocolate-coloured water. On to the first drilling rig which stood on an island in the middle of a swamp where the mangroves sprawled like huge, obscene white spiders over the black mud where sinister mud hoppers, lizards with only two front feet, looking like little monsters out of an Hieronymus Bosch painting, skipped over the surface with jerky movements. The island on which the rig stood had been man-made almost entirely. Gangs of Africans in long canoes had brought up bucketfuls of mud from the bottom of the Niger Delta and these had been dumped one on top of another until a large island had been built. It would have been hard to imagine a more back of beyond place in which to work but life had been made more tolerable by bringing in air conditioned caravans and houseboats in which the oil crews could at least have comfortable nights.

I drove back to Lagos, crossing the mighty Niger River by the ferry at Onitsha and leaving the country of the Ibos later to be called Biafra. Owerri, where I had spent such a pleasant time, was, nine years later, one of the worst famine areas. The oilmen had long since left there to set up their headquarters in the outskirts of Port Harcourt and Chief Njemanzi's days of glory had been only too short. I wonder if he survived to cope with the terrible problem of starvation.

I spent a couple of days in Benin. It was as short a time ago as the turn of the century that a British force was sent to this part of Nigeria to put a stop to the orgiastic cruelties of the then Oba of Benin. The country had been converted to Christianity in the sixteenth century by the Portuguese and the only thing they really seemed to have appreciated about the Christian faith – certainly retained from it – was crucifixion. When the British force arrived in Benin they found the Oba's palace swimming in blood from human sacrifices and numbers of unfortunate men spreadeagled and nailed alive to the large, spreading tree outside the main entrance.

The present Oba of Benin was a tall, thin man, who wore tight white trousers and a high necked, long skirted tunic coat. He looked very much like a black Mr Nehru. I was accompanied by a young Nigerian from Shell's Benin office. We were ushered into a large reception room, the chief room of the palace, a fort-like building with walls (appropriately) the colour of dried blood. I shivered as I entered the room and remembered that it had been the scene of such hideous cruelties. But my mood changed to one of suppressed laughter when I saw, occupying the place of honour, as it were, an immense, white refrigerator with 'OBA OF BENIN' stencilled on it in large capital letters. The Oba came in, begged me to sit down, and sat opposite me. His major domo, who wore a khaki jacket with sergeant's chevrons on it, opened the refrigerator, took out a bottle of Vat 69 whisky and a siphon of soda water and poured me out a large drink. It was eight o'clock in the morning. The Oba and I talked generalities. He said he was convinced that oil would be found in his territory. He wanted to know the purpose of the tall structure just outside Benin City, which was lit up so prettily at night. I said it was the derrick of an exploration well and explained in simple terms how it worked. It came to be time to go. When I had said my goodbyes the young Nigerian who had accompanied me said:

'Excuse me, Your Highness, but we are very anxious to

install a new filling station at the corner of the main road, almost opposite the entrance of the palace.' The Oba looked benevolently amused.

'Certainly, young man,' he said. 'My personal secretary will arrange an appointment for you to come and see me about it.' As we walked away from the palace I said:

'You don't miss your chances do you?' He looked pleased.

'Well, it would be good for me if I could fix that filling station,' he said. 'It seemed a good opportunity when I was with the Oba. I've never seen him before, you know. It was a lucky thing for me to come with you this morning.'

Chapter Twenty-One

No sooner was I back in London, than I had a telephone call from Julius Edwardes, the Public Relations Officer of the Iraq Petroleum Company. He wanted Marjorie and me to go out to Baghdad and make a report on the possibilities of the IPC helping to produce programmes for Iraq Television. The origin of Iraq TV was curious. About a year before there had been a Trade Fair in Baghdad and a British manufacturer of television and radio equipment had set up a complete TV transmitter with studios and a limited number of receiving sets. When the fair ended the Iraq Government bought the whole affair lock, stock and barrel for about £100,000. Having got it they didn't really know what to do with it. They imported a few more receiving sets and these were installed in cafés; and for programmes they relied at first entirely on old serials which had originally been shown on the BBC. They were immensely popular and the cafés with TV sets were crowded out and people were looking over each other's shoulders at the screen from out in the street.

Easily the most popular of these serials was 'Robin Hood'. None of the viewers understood a word that was said but the action more or less spoke for itself. So much so that a local burglar called himself 'The Robin Hood of Baghdad'. He would break into a rich man's house, roll up all his Persian carpets and put his other valuables in a sack and before leaving with his loot would deliver a lecture. It was quite wrong, he would say, for anyone to possess such riches and it was only right that they should be taken from him, sold and distributed among the poor. 'The poor,' of course, meant himself.

By the time Marjorie and I reached Baghdad they had been enterprising enough to start some 'live' shows in their studio. These were of the most ludicrous 'village hall' quality and we began to see that Iraq TV might well benefit by contributions from IPC. The first thing we had to do was to convince the right authorities that this was desirable. First we had to win over the Minister of Guidance and Propaganda, a brigadier (retired) who was responsible for all radio and TV in the country. After a great deal of persuasion he agreed in principle that Iraq TV would benefit, provided that the head of radio and TV thought so too. The latter was a most enlightened and forward thinking man and he welcomed any outside contributions provided that he had a say in the selection of them. We then began to write our report and recommendations. We thought the IPC should do a series of serious factual programmes showing how the country was benefiting from the oil revenues. Then we suggested other types of programmes of a purely entertainment nature, to be done, of course, in Arabic so that everyone would understand. We worked out in some detail a kind of Arab Mrs Dale's Diary, to centre round a lower middle class Iraqi family. Marjorie had plenty of experience of this kind of thing because for several years during the war she had produced a weekly serial called 'Front Line Family'. We wrote a very long, detailed report and we both almost came to believe that our ideas really might work. Unfortunately while the IPC were studying it, the bloody revolution broke out in Iraq, in which the little King, his uncle and the Premier, Nuri Said were butchered, and the TV was used for the more sinister purpose of reporting political trials and the delivering of death sentences. These included several of the officials we had so assiduously wooed round to the idea of accepting help from the IPC. Many other Iraqis whom we had come to know well were either executed or given long terms of imprisonment.

Back in London again, Shell agreed to a request of mine

to travel to the Sahara to get more material for my book about the oilmen. I flew to Algiers and a few days later was in the oasis of El Goléa, on the edge of the Great Western Erg, one of the two great dunelands of the Sahara, where Shell were carrying out a seismic exploration, creating a series of little earthquakes by exploding charges of gelignite on the surface of the desert. The explosions send shock waves thousands of feet down into the earth, which rise again and are picked up by instruments called seismometers or geophones. These instruments are connected with a truck, which records and photographs them. The result is a long strip of paper with a series of zigzag lines on it, rather like the paper on a barograph, which records the weather. From this a seismologist can build up an accurate picture of the underground rock formations and can forecast if there are any rock structures where oil might lie. But he never can guarantee that there is oil there – he can only say that there might be – or that the formation of the rock even points to the likelihood of there being oil there.

El Goléa (well named the 'Pearl of the Desert') was an enchanting oasis. At the French 'Annexe', or headquarters, there was a beautiful park-sized garden, with powerful artesian wells: a marvellous example of what water can do with the desert. Wandering through the gardens one could scarcely believe one was deep into the Sahara with the barren dunes of the Great Western Erg only a few miles away. Under the date palms were little avenues of rose trees, growing in luxuriant profusion. Fruit trees of all kinds flourished in El Goléa, peaches, apricots, citrus fruits, pomegranates and almonds and every vegetable that is found in Europe. There was a deliciously cool swimming pool and little streams wound their way between the flowerbeds.

There is an enormous underground water reservoir known as *'La Nappe Albienne'*, a concentration of 'fossil' water, which has accumulated over the ages by infiltration. Much of it comes originally from the Atlas Mountains and from there it has flowed through underground channels to feed this immense natural reserve. A remarkable calculation shows that four oases, including El Goléa, receive through this underground supply route the fantastic amount of ten thousand million cubic metres of water a year. In fact they are, together, drawing it at the rate of just over half a million cubic metres a year. The comparison of the two figures gives an idea of the possibilities; so does the lush fertility of the oasis of El Goléa compared with the surrounding Sahara. But the '*Nappe Albienne*' can lie as deep as 3,500 feet and it costs a great deal of money to drill an artesian well to such a depth. Nevertheless before the French left Algeria a start had been made, and several artificial oases had been created.

I flew from El Goléa to the camp which was the headquarters of the group who were carrying out a seismic survey in the desert near the Great Western Erg. I had stayed in a good many so-called oil camps but here, in the heart of the Sahara, a thousand miles from anywhere and about as far away from civilization as you could well get, I expected conditions to be on the rugged side. True the place had a pioneering air; we lived in tents, but I was astonished to sit down on my first evening in this barren wasteland, to a dinner which began with fresh asparagus and was followed by roast duck. Fresh food was flown in to the camps once a week and was kept in outsize '*frigos*'. Of course it was very expensive to bring such good things to these lonely parts of the Sahara. It cost the equivalent of about thirty shillings a head a day to feed each man there.

They were trying out what was then a new method of seismic survey at this camp. Instead of causing shock waves by making explosions, they used an enormous truck which had a three ton weight at the back. This was dropped by a special release mechanism. It hit the ground with a tremendous thump and started off shock waves in the same way that exploding dynamite did. Stretching away behind the weight dropper was a long 'spoor' of large, oblong depressions, where the three-ton weight had fallen. They looked like the tracks of some monstrous prehistoric animal, far larger than the dinosaurs that once roamed the Sahara and whose bones are still found there.

I returned to El Goléa to find the place in a state of alarm. The oasis with its 200,000 date palms and its gardens was threatened by a large swarm of locusts, that had hatched about ten miles out in the desert, where were many patches of scrubby vegetation, each several acres in extent. I drove out with a French army officer. With us were a gang of Arabs and in the truck two machines worked by small petrol motors which sprayed insecticide in the form of a fine white powder.

When we reached the first of the patches of little shrubs and bushes it was still only just after sunrise and from a distance they looked surprisingly green. When we got near I found that they were absolutely covered with young, green 'hoppers'. Then the work of destruction began. The machines were mounted on a kind of platform with four handles, so that each could be carried by four men. Insecticide powder was poured into them from sacks and with one man directing the nozzle they went systematically over the area, puffing a cloud of fine dust at the insects. As the sun rose the young locusts climbed off the bushes, where they had gathered during the night and began marching over the sand, advancing in little hops of a few inches at a time. We worked on until midday when it became too hot to continue. I developed a vicious hatred for these insects and stamped on them until I was tired. I must personally have killed many thousands. With the machines we probably killed literally millions.

'We've got a week to finish them off in,' the French officer said to me. 'After then they'll be starting to fly and then it'll be a devil of a job to get them. But I think we'll just about manage it. It was about thirty years ago that El Goléa was last seriously attacked and we didn't have good insecticides then. The locusts completely destroyed every green thing in the oasis. They even ate all the leaves off the date palms. None of the fruit trees bore fruit for four years and the date harvest was negligible for several years. I found out later that our efforts had been successful. The swarm of locusts was almost entirely destroyed before it could fly and the lovely oasis was spared.

On the day I left El Goléa there were rumours of strange things happening in Algiers and when my plane landed at

Maison Blanche airport I found myself in the middle of the generals' revolt. It was impossible to leave Algiers – not that I wanted to. The '*paras*' wearing berets and camouflage uniform, tall, blond Germans many of them, patrolled the streets, armed to the teeth and lolled arrogantly round the steps of the huge *Gouvernement Générale* building. The half acre open space in front of it was crowded with an excited crowd, including many *colons*, who had left their farms to join in the celebrations. Squads of hand-picked Arabs marched by carrying banners proclaiming: '*Nous sommes Français!*' Cars hooted incessantly 'Ta-ta-ta TA TA' which stood for '*Algérie Fran-çaise!*' There were impassioned speeches from the balcony of the *Gouvernement Générale*. Roars of cheering when General Salan or the fire-eating *para* General Massu appeared to speak. De Gaulle was the idol of the day – but certainly not of the year! Jacques Soustelle who had been Governor General was expected any day.

The St George Hotel was crowded with foreign correspondents. Wild rumours changed hourly. After a week, during which I telegraphed reports to the BBC, I felt it was time for me to get back to England and make arrangements for an immediate return properly equipped for television coverage. But it was impossible to get transport of any kind. Algiers was shut off from the world. Then late one evening in the hotel bar a French correspondent came up to me in a very cloak-and-dagger manner and whispered:

'If you want to get out, be in the lounge at 3 a.m.' I obeyed these instructions and found myself in company with the French correspondent and a French general who was returning in a clandestine way to make a personal report to General de Gaulle.

'It's all a bit tricky,' the French journalist told me. 'We daren't fly over France because we might be forced down – or even shot down by French fighters. We tried to get permission to fly over Italy but they refused. So anyway, we're going to fly over Italy – at about 40,000 feet – and we'll land at Geneva.'

We had a large Air Algérie plane to ourselves. We flew very high over Italy and landed safely at Geneva.

'If you want to get back,' the pilot said to me as we said

goodbye, 'I'll be here for three days and you're welcome to a lift.'

Back in London I did a piece for Panorama and BBC TV agreed to my return to Algeria. Of course nothing was ready within three days so I missed my Geneva connection and went to Paris with a producer, but no cameraman. The Canadian Broadcasting Corporation would lend us one, I was told. Things had eased a little since I had left and with great trouble we succeeded in getting seats on a plane flying to Algiers.

Things were just as hectic. Soustelle had arrived and General de Gaulle was expected before long. The whole Canadian Broadcasting team had gone to Corsica, where de Gaulle was expected to be calling on his way to Algiers and it was only by the greatest piece of luck that I ran into an American cameraman whom I had met on the Hungarian border two years before. He helped us out but by the time I had arranged an interview with Jacques Soustelle, through valuable 'contacts' I had made on my earlier visit, his camera had developed a fault and was out of action. In desperation I found two freelance American cameramen and they promised to film my interview provided they could follow on with one of their own.

'That's going to be very difficult,' I said, 'but as long as you agree to ask exactly the same questions as I do I think it might be managed.' They agreed readily to this. They wouldn't have had a hope on their own of getting an interview at all.

Soustelle, who spoke perfect English, gave me a very good interview. When it was finished I threw myself on his mercy. I explained that my camera was out of action and that these American colleagues of mine had kindly agreed to film the interview for me. Naturally they would like an interview themselves; but they would ask exactly the same questions. The camera and the lights were already set up and the whole thing would only take about three minutes. To my relief he agreed.

In the summer of 1959, Associated British Pathé, for whom I had done a good deal of work from time to time asked me if I would write the script of a film they were going to make about the Queen's proposed visit to Ghana later in the year. Terry Bishop was to be the director and we flew out to Accra together. Terry was an admirable companion and fortunately we both had more or less the same idea of what form the film should take. As far as possible we wanted Ghanaians to tell the story of their own country rather than have one overall narrator – such as myself.

We spent about a week in Accra which at that time, like the whole country, was dominated by Kwame Nkrumah, whose statues and portraits were everywhere. We were looked after by Jimmy Moxon, an enormous man – largely as a result of the excellent table that he kept in his big, comfortable house. Jimmy had originally been in the Colonial Service and had been a District Officer in different parts of what had then been the Gold Coast, so he knew the country and its people well. He was now head of the British Information Office that acted in liaison with the Ghana Government. (When Ghana later became fully a republic, Jimmy took on Ghanaian citizenship and was made a paramount chief, with his own village.)

The head of the Ghana film unit at that time was an old friend of mine, George Noble, whom I had known in wartime days. He was enormously popular in Ghana and didn't care what he said to Ghanaians. When we began our drive to the Ashanti he would shout at a driver:

'You stupid black bastard what the hell do you think you're doing?' The man just laughed. If I had spoken to a Ghanaian like that I'd have been deported within twenty-four hours. George rose to his greatest heights when we visited the sports stadium at Kumasi, the capital of the Ashanti. It was to be opened by Prince Philip and wasn't quite finished yet. We were being shown round by the mayor of Kumasi and several other local dignitaries. We stood right at the top of the stadium and looked down at the imposing arena. There was a moment of silence and then George Noble's voice broke it.

'Well, all you need,' he said in a loud voice, 'is f——ing Africans one end, f——ing lions the other and a squad of machine gunners to keep the natives in order!' There was dead silence for a moment and I thought this time George had overdone it. Then there was a great guffaw of laughter from all the Africans.

'Ha ha ha! Very very funny Mr Noble,' the mayor of Kumasi laughed, 'we must indeed adopt your idea one day.'

We spent an interesting hour at the offices of the *Ashanti Pioneer*, the local newspaper, which published courageously frank articles, attacking the Nkrumah régime, under which, they said, the Ashanti were getting a very raw deal. Behind closed doors the editor of the paper and some of his staff enlarged bitterly on the iniquities of Nkrumah and wondered how long it would be before their paper was forcibly closed down.

We drove on northwards towards Tamale, capital of the Northern Territory. George continued to curse the drivers but when it came to the end of a day the first thing he did was to insist that Terry and I subscribe a few shillings each for the drivers' 'chop', and he would never dream of eating or even having a drink himself until he was satisfied they were being well looked after.

Everywhere we went we asked local notables what their plans were for the royal visit. At Tamale they were to hold a great durbar and hundreds of horsemen from the far north would come down. It would all be a very splendid affair. We also looked out for people who could narrate a section of the film and had chosen provisionally several excellent 'possibles'.

One morning I walked into the office of the secretary of the Provincial Governor, a Scotsman.

'Have you heard the news?' he greeted me.

'Oh we're far too busy on this film to be concerned with news,' I said.

'You'll be concerned with this news,' he said and handed me a strip of tape. It said baldly that on account of the fact that she was expecting a baby the Queen regretted deeply that she must put off her visit to Ghana. Terry Bishop and I looked at each other.

'We'd better get on to Jimmy Moxon in Accra,' I said. We managed to get through quite quickly on the telephone.

'Just carry on regardless,' Jimmy said blithely.

'What do you mean regardless?' I said, 'it's one thing to ask a paramount chief how many horsemen he is sending to a durbar when the Queen comes in three months' time. It's quite another to say: "If the Queen should come in a year's time how many horsemen might you send to a durbar if it is decided to hold a durbar?" No, Jimmy, it's impossible.' Terry picked up the telephone and said he felt the same. Nevertheless our orders were to carry on. We drove southwards to talk to the people whose land was about to be flooded by the Volta Dam. We returned to Accra and from there drove along the coast and saw the great battlemented castles Cape Coast and Elmina from where a century and a half ago the slaves were shipped to the Americas. The barracoons and markets are still there. We watched them cutting down the huge African mahogany trees, powerful Africans swinging axes from platforms fifteen feet from the ground, built round the splayed trunks of the trees. We returned to Accra and wrote a long report full of suggestions, which we both felt sure would never be used because there would never be a royal visit to Ghana. We were right.

Chapter Twenty-Two

Early in 1960 I went to Holland with John Drummond of Shell, who had helped me with the editing of my book about the men in oil. As we were driving along the broad, flat Dutch roads one day he said to me:

'Eddy, you know quite a bit about the oil industry by now, I've got a suggestion to make to you.'

'You're not suggesting I work for Shell?' John laughed.

'No. But there's a job going begging. Have you heard of the Petroleum Information Bureau in London?' I nodded. 'Well the head of it is just about to retire. Why don't you apply for the job? It's a cinch you'll get it.'

'Oh, I don't know, John. A nine to five job after all my years as a freelance. Anyway I'll think about it.' I did. I thought to myself that jobs in radio were wearing very thin and that any fame I might have achieved in sound radio was anything but a recommendation for a job in TV. So I decided to apply for the PIB job and got it, at a reasonably good salary. But it wasn't to be for nearly a year.

That Easter Marjorie and I and the children drove to Italy. Our friends Alan and Lucy Moorehead had settled near Porto Ercole, on the Monte Argentario peninsula near Grossetto. They had built a new house on the hillside overlooking the little port and when we got there it was barely finished. We stayed in a *pensione* down by the water's edge. In those days there were no hotels in Porto Ercole. We found it one of the most beautiful places we had ever seen and decided that we must try and buy a house there. The thing to do, we were told, was to get Beppo, the taxi driver from Orbetello, who knew about everything that might be for sale. First of all we walked all round the place and picked houses we liked the look of. Then we told Beppo what we had selected and he went to investigate. After an hour he came back saying that unfortunately none of the places we had chosen were for sale at any price, but that he had found three large rooms, all opening on to a common balcony, right down by the water's edge. We went to see them and we thought they had great possibilities. The only thing was that all the rooms were occupied. We went to see the owner. He guaranteed that by the time we returned in the summer all three rooms would be empty and ready for occupation by us. We bought the property for the equivalent of about £800.

We could hardly wait to return in July. We were enchanted by Porto Ercole. Dining one evening at a restuarant high above the harbour we had watched the fishing fleet setting out, all the boats lit up. Away in the distance stretched the purple hills of the mainland. It was indescribably beautiful.

We arrived back in July with beds and a kitchen sink and various other pieces of furniture, all ready to move in to at least one of our three large rooms. Only one room was vacant – and that because its former occupant had died. The other two were very much occupied by enormous families. The Mooreheads couldn't put us up. We stayed at another *pensione*. The climate was like Africa. There had been an invasion of English – rich stockbroker types, who thronged all the good restaurants and talked across the room to each other in loud Kensington voices. Geoffrey Keating came to stay with the Mooreheads and we took him to see our three rooms – we had had a certain amount of work done on the vacant one. He thought they were wonderful.

'If you ever decide to sell,' he said, 'give me first refusal.'

We stayed on for another fortnight. There was no progress as far as evicting the other tenants of the rooms was concerned. In the end, disillusioned with Porto Ercole, by the summer heat, the English visitors, the appalling noise of the Italian juke boxes, we decided that we greatly preferred France to Italy and told

Geoffrey Keating we were prepared to sell. He was delighted to buy. We made a reasonable profit; he got a bargain and so everybody was happy. Since then Porto Ercole has become a very fashionable resort and we wish we could have held on to our little piece of property.

Early in 1960 a publisher had asked me to do a book about the Sahara. I approached my friend Jean Duroc Danner of the Compagnie Française des Pétroles in London and he said he thought his company, who operated a large part of the oilfield of Hassi Messaoud, would help. And help they certainly did. With Charles Lagus, the BBC cameraman-director, I flew out to Algiers. From there we flew to Hassi Messaoud. I had thought that all oil camps were pretty luxurious but one must go to a French one to know how really well one can live miles from normal civilization.

Just by the entrance to 'Maison Verte' as the Hassi Messaoud camp is appropriately named, there is a sign post saying that Paris (Porte d'Italie) was Kms. 2,567.400 distant. I stayed in the VIP guest house, air conditioned and deliciously cool. I had a delightful bedroom and my own bathroom. It was like staying in a first class hotel. I went to lunch at the senior mess, a beautifully furnished, comfortable, air-conditioned room and this was the menu:

Hors-d'Oeuvres Variés
Rognons Sautés, Sauce Madère
Entrecôte Mirabeau
Haricots Verts Isigny
Salade Verte
Patisserie
Café

There were also two kinds of wine. The general mess, where the 'roustabouts' and 'roughnecks' from the drilling rigs ate, had exactly the same menu. The oil companies believed in feeding their employees well as some compensation for planting them in the middle of the desert, hundreds of miles from anywhere.

Late that same afternoon I had a swim in the lovely tiled swimming pool that is one of the delights of Maison Verte. It sounds an extravagant luxury to have a swimming pool in the middle of the desert even if there is a large water supply. But to men working like these desert oilmen it is more of a necessity than a luxury. Working in the heat of the sun a man sweats a litre an hour and he has to put that moisture back otherwise he will become completely dehydrated and die. Indeed, if a man takes any kind of exercise – even walking – and doesn't drink he will be dead within twelve hours. So it wasn't surprising that these oilmen drink, on an average, 20 litres – or over four gallons – of water a day – apart from the beer, wine and *apéritifs* that they drink after their shifts. I didn't take any strenuous exercise and I drank at least half that amount. But one needs, if possible, to absorb water through the pores of the skin as well and the swimming pool is the answer to that. I heard a horrific story of a man who was found in the desert almost dead from thirst and dehydration. He had lost many pounds in weight in a very short time. One of the first things his rescuers did was to throw large quantities of water over him and to their fascinated horror his skin absorbed it all, like a sponge.

Drilling for oil is much the same whether it is in the jungle, the desert or even under the sea. We watched work on a couple of rigs at Hassi Messaoud. Their chief difference was that of expense. On an average it cost about £400,000 to drill a well in the Sahara, because all the heavy equipment and material has to be hauled to the spot from several hundred miles away and the cost of transport is very high. Fortunately they drilled hardly any 'dry holes' at Hassi Messaoud.

From Hassi Messaoud we drove through the oasis of Ouargla to one of the most beautiful oases in the Sahara, Ghardaia, the chief of the five towns of the M'zab, that a Berber sect called the Abadhites built with great labour between the eleventh and fourteenth centuries, digging deep wells by hand to water their date palms and gardens. This barren valley, as it was when they found it, was the last refuge of the fanatical, puritanical followers of Abadhism, a sect that had broken away from orthodox Islam soon after the death of Mahomet. They were persecuted by the successive waves of Arab invaders until at last they were left in peace in their final inaccessible refuge.

It is a wonderful experience to approach Ghardaia after driving for miles across forbidding desert and suddenly to see the green of hundreds of thousands of date palms. From the market place of Ghardaia there is a breathtaking view of the little city, which is built up the slopes of a steep hill in the form of a pyramid of little box-like houses, painted in pale colours, blue and mauve, pink and yellow and dominated by the towering minaret of the mosque. From the flat roof of a house, which overlooked the colonnaded market place, I watched the lines of camels grunting in protest as buyers examined them carefully. There were flocks of sheep and goats, and donkeys loaded with firewood – tamarisk wood brought in from the desert and sold at enormously high prices. There were fruit and vegetable stalls in the centre of the market and under the arcades shops selling carpets and brass-ware, shoes and clothing. A great many of these shops were owned by Jewish merchants, of whom there was a large colony in Ghardaia.

The most lovely of the towns of the M'zab is the holy city of Beni Isghen, a small walled city that looks exactly as it did when it was built in 1347. No foreigner is allowed to spend the night there – and a foreigner means anybody who is not a Mozabite as the Abadhites are known today. The city gate is closed at sundown. In Beni Isghen Abadhism is still practised in all its puritanism. There is not even a café.

In spite of their piety, the Mozabites are extremely good businessmen. You may see a merchant riding to Ghardaia market on the back of a humble donkey, but that does not mean to say that he is not, very likely, a rich man. They have extended their business activities well beyond the M'zab Valley. They have almost cornered the grocery trade all over Algeria and you see Mozabite shops everywhere in Algiers and in all the big cities and oases. The young men emigrate from the M'zab to make their fortunes and only return for short visits until they are old men when they come back to spend their last years and to die there. Their womenfolk, on the other hand, scarcely ever leave the M'zab and their babies are always born there. On account of the long absences of the fathers and their rare appearances in Ghardaia and the other Mozabite cities, a woman is conveniently reckoned to take two years to bear a child, which solves what might otherwise be an embarrassing problem.

All the expatriate Mozabite merchants send money back home and that is why the oasis is so beautiful, with lovely, cool gardens and fine plantations of date palms. Without the subsidies that come in from the grocery shops of Algeria, none of this horticulture would be economic because the cost of watering this sterile land is so high. But the Mozabites look upon it as a point of honour to keep up the plantations and gardens which their ancestors created with such hard labour.

Having read a great deal about the hardships and privations suffered by the early explorers of the Sahara, I felt almost ashamed to be flying in great comfort to Tamanrasset in the Hoggar Mountains, in a small, luxurious six-seater plane called the 'President' because it is the same type that Eisenhower used to fly about the United States in when he was President. On the way south, just as we were approaching the oasis of El Goléa, the pilot leaned back and said:

'If you feel like a drink you'll find quite a selection in the ice box under the back seat.' I found some quarter bottles of chilled champagne and, thinking of poor Henri Duveyrier, a century before, being chased out of El Goléa and forced to eat lizards to stave off his hunger, I shamefacedly drank to his memory.

Tamanrasset, which at the beginning of the century was a village of 'twenty fires', as a great Saharan figure, Père de Foucauld described it when he first settled there, is now quite an imposing little town, its houses built of red ochre-coloured mud, their sides ridged in curious lines made by the masons running their fingers down the mud while it was still wet. There was an excellent hotel admirably run by the former master-cook of the French battleship *Richelieu.*

Tamanrasset lies right at the edge of the Hoggar Mountains and there is a passably good road that runs some sixty miles into the middle of these fabulous peaks. The little town itself stands four thousand feet up. It is always cool at night and although it is about a thousand miles from Algiers it was at that time developing into a popular tourist resort. There was a weekly plane service and people came down at one week-end, stayed the following week, made the journey in the mountains to the Assekrem plateau, where Père de Foucauld lived in his hermitage during the summer months, visited the *bordj*, where he was murdered, made a pilgrimage to his tomb and to that of his friend General Lapérrine, another great name in the history of the Sahara, which lie side by side, gazed at the fantastically beautiful sunsets and, before taking the next plane back, hoped to see some Touareg. To gratify this wish of the tourists a little group of very scruffy and by no means aristocratic Touareg remained permanently encamped at the convenient distance of about two miles from Tamanrasset and at a piratical price, that rose steadily, they permitted themselves to be photographed. Somehow I think that hard times will have fallen upon these desert opportunists. I doubt if there is much if any tourist traffic from Algiers to Tamanrasset these days. The tourists were French or at any rate European and I cannot see the Arabs making pilgrimages to a remote mountain town, associated primarily with the French conquest of the Sahara.

However, in 1960 the French were still in charge. A man called Guarinos, a former *colon* of Spanish origin, who had become our guide advised us to go and see the *adjudant de gendarmerie* if we wanted to see Touareg because he knew all about the movements of these nomads in the Hoggar area.

'You're in luck,' the *adjudant* said. 'You couldn't have come at a better time. There is a wedding tomorrow evening about forty kilometres from here and after the wedding there will be an *ahal*.' Before explaining what an *ahal* was, the *adjudant* gave me a short history of the Touareg. Almost certainly of Berber origin the immediately striking thing about them is that the *litham*, or veil is worn by the men and not by the women. They seem to have been veiled for about a thousand years but precisely why they wear the *litham* nobody seems to know. Probably it is a combination of plain utility – it keeps the sand and dust away from a man's face – and the deliberate creation of an air of mystery and romanticism. Because the Touareg sword hilts and camel pommels are in the form of a cross a fantastic legend grew up that they were descended from crusaders who escaped from the Saracens. In fact just after the Arab invasion of North Africa they were converted to Islam and have been lukewarm Mohammedans ever since, not bothering overmuch about praying five times a day or observing fasts.

The most remarkable thing about the Touareg is the status of their women. An Arab woman, in the desert at any rate, is generally nothing much better than a beast of burden. The Touareg woman, the *Targuia*, on the contrary is far more independent than most European women and is greatly looked up to. The Touareg women are the poets and musicians; they do no work, apart from the lightest household tasks. For that matter neither do the men. The aristocratic tribes of the Hoggar call themselves *Ihaggeren*, which means 'nobles'. They still live like medieval noblemen, ready, until fairly recently, to soil their hands with the blood of their enemies but certainly not with anything else. They will go so far as to drove their herds of camels, sheep and goats; they will organize caravans; but they will do no manual work such as cultivating the land. This is all done by a Negro people called Harratin, or by the descendants of the Negro slaves their grandfathers brought up from the south. Even today these Negroes are still more or less slaves. They are clothed and fed; they are treated as members of the family; but they are not paid and they have no freedom to go away.

The Touareg society is not strictly a matriarchy but it very nearly is. They follow a matrilinear system. The chief of a tribe is not succeeded by his own son but by his sister's son. This of course is a logical and practical way of ensuring that the family blood runs pure from one generation to another. A man may not, after all, be certain who his father is but at least he has no doubt about his mother. A *Targui* has no say whatever in his daughter's marriage. She chooses her own husband often in a curious ceremony called an *ahal*. People who believe that the Touareg are descended from the crusaders point to the similarity between the *ahal* and the *courts of love* of the Middle Ages in Europe. The main difference is that the women play the part of the troubadors. This in a way is a logical arrangement. Among the Touareg a man can improve his children's social position by 'marrying above himself'. A woman can marry whom she pleases because her children will inherit her rank not her husband's.

The *ahal* is becoming a fairly rare ceremony these days and I was very lucky to have seen one. The film Charles Lagus made of it is, as far as I know, unique. I was greatly surprised that we were allowed to film at all.

The *caïd* of the tribe was in his garden when we arrived. There was a little cultivation round an almost dry *oued* and small patches of green stood out against the tawny-coloured desert. The *adjudant* went to meet him and a few minutes later returned hand in hand with a dignified looking old man. The *caïd* was very pleased with the gift of sugar loaves and tea that the *adjudant* had advised us to bring with us. He said we could take as many pictures as we liked.

There was no ceremony about the wedding at all. All that happens at a Touareg marriage is that the bridegroom sits alone in his tent. The women of his family go and fetch the bride whom they deliver to the tent and that is that. But the women of the tribe took advantage of the occasion to hold an *ahal*. Sometimes this is the affair of one young, unmarried woman. She lets it be known that she is holding the ceremony at a certain time and place and, depending upon her beauty and accomplishments, young men of her own tribe will assemble and men from other tribes will ride in on their camels from as far as a hundred miles or more away. As dusk falls the girl sits with her *amzad*, a primitive Touareg violin, and her suitors squat on the ground in a semi-circle a little way away while she sings old legends from the far distant past or songs of battle like the lament over the Battle of Tit, where the French finally crushed the power of the Touareg but had the good sense to treat them generously afterwards; or poems of successful *razzias* when the tribe was enriched by the pillage of a wealthy caravan; or love songs, sometimes extremely beautiful like this one translated by Père de Foucauld from the *Tamabaq,* (the Touareg Language) which I have turned into English.

> 'Shall I compare him with a white racing camel, with a shield of Tarmai?
> With a herd of antelopes of Kita?
> With the fringes of a crimson belt of Jerba?
> With a grape just ripened
> In a valley where beside it ripens the date?
> Amoumen is the cord around which the pearls of my necklace cluster;
> He is the string on which hang the talismans on my breast;
> His is my life.'

or this poignant 'declaration':

> 'A certain thing, of which there is no doubt;
> That if the agony of love could kill
> By God I would not live until this night,
> The sun would rise no more for me to see.
> Gegge, thy love is cruel to my heart,
> It has dissolved the marrow in my bones;
> Has drunk my blood, devoured up my flesh,
> I know not what has now become of them.
> Only my whitened bones remain to me
> Which hold together how I cannot know;
> Slowly and silently beneath them gasps
> My breath. Oh tell me was there e'er a soul
> In which there dwells a veritable hive
> Of torments and which yet remains alive?
> Go to the lovers' meeting places, go;
> Hark to the violins and play and laugh.'

Sometimes, however, they are of a crudity that would have shocked Rabelais. All through the hours that the girl has been singing and reciting poems she has been glancing at the young men, carefully making up her mind about which one she will choose eventually. At last at the end of her recital, she will throw her violin bow at the feet of the lucky man and go off with him into the night. The others take their defeat philosophically, mount their camels and set off on their long journey home.

That is one kind of *ahal*. The one I saw was a much more free for all kind of affair. All the young unmarried women and widows of the tribe were holding a joint 'court of love', to which all the young unmarried men of the tribe were to come as well as a number of men from a neighbouring one fifty miles away, who rode over on their camels. It was a kind of desert 'love-in'.

We arrived long before things began to get under way, while the sun was still high. The Touareg slaves had nearly finished putting up a low tent covered with red tanned goatskin, in front of which they laid brightly coloured rugs for the notables (including us) to sit on. A few young men had already ridden in on their camels and some of the men of the tribe were saddling theirs, tightening girths and fixing the single rein decorated with coloured beads, to the accompaniment of grunts of protest from the camels. I watched a Touareg *méhariste*, a camel cavalryman from the *Compagnie Saharienne* at Tamanrasset, who had come with the group of French officers and men and ourselves, changing into ceremonial robes. Yard after yard of fine, indigo-dyed cotton material was wound over the top of his head, down under his chin, over and under, over and under until at last only the man's eyes could be seen through a narrow opening.

At last the women decided the time had come to start the *ahal*. A party of forty or fifty of them trooped across the sandy ground to a point about a hundred yards from the 'grand-stand' tent. They squatted on the ground and five of them grouped themselves round a drum. They started beating it in a slow, monotonous rhythm, that gradually increased in tempo, chanting a curious melody at the same time. As a kind of chorus some of the women burst into loud ululations, their mouths wide open and their tongues oscillating rapidly.

The women wore great quantities of barbaric silver jewellery; their chests were covered with immense silver breastplates; long necklaces were twined round their necks and their earrings were so big and so heavy that they were pinned to their hair for extra support. Their fingers were almost hidden by rings. They wore lovely, sari-like robes with hoods over the top of their heads; but they were completely unveiled and not in the smallest degree shy when I came close to take photographs. Some of them wore beautiful indigo-dyed shawls, which stained their hands and faces a pale indigo colour – which they consider very attractive; others wore shimmering robes of a metallic cloth which is very expensive. After the monotonous black of Arab women's clothes, the Touareg women made a marvellous splash of colour. Some wore dark red robes, some bright green, others indigo blue. Their silver ornaments flashed in the sinking sun as they sang and drummed and uttered their piercing cries, clapping their hands noisily to the rhythm of the music. Some of them were very beautiful.

And then the men entered the scene, tall, lean men in flowing robes and tightly-bound *lithams*, which even from a short distance away looked remarkably like medieval knights' vizors. They came in pairs, riding their splendid white and pale cream racing camels, riding very slowly and sedately, their camels' heads drawn proudly back, their magnificent saddle cloths and trappings and fine, decorated saddles adding to the pageantry of the scene. Slowly the men strutted in pairs past the seated women, who appeared not to take the smallest interest in them; but one could detect an occasional quick glance as a woman assessed the points of one of the competitors, comparing him with others who had already ridden past, wondering if a better one might come later.

The slow procession in pairs continued for a long time and then, abruptly, all the *méharistes* joined together in a single group and began circling round the women, increasing their speed as they went until they were moving at a gallop. By this time it was almost dark and it was becoming extremely hazardous for the onlookers. A young French lieutenant turned to me:

'This is artistic anarchy,' he said, laughing, 'you never know when something is going to start or when it's going to finish but just the same it's very fine. It brings to mind a little Dufy's paintings of the races at Longchamps.' I agreed with him, thinking as I did so that I could scarcely imagine an average English lieutenant making such a remark.

The parade was over. The men dismounted from their camels, handed them over to slaves and then, by mutual consent, they paired off with the women and all sat down in the desert in a large cluster. The drumming started again and the women resumed their chanting and later food was brought and then they began dancing. By now it was pitch dark and it was impossible to see what was happening.

'The Touareg like doing all this in the dark,' the lieutenant said. 'Naturally enough, I suppose, though personally I would be worried about picking the wrong sex! They'll go on dancing until at least four in the morning and then off they'll go together into the *oued*. The Touareg have absolutely no morals at all, which personally I find rather refreshing. Do you know that when de Foucauld was compiling his dictionary he discovered that they have no word for virginity!'

We were all invited to supper by the *caïd* at the big tent. It had been so hot and there had been so much dust from the galloping camels that for some time I had been calling at one of the French trucks to quench my raging thirst by taking long draughts of rather evil-tasting water from a goatskin *guerba* which was slung alongside it. Supper began with some little lumps of what looked like pre-masticated meat. Then came huge bowls of couscous, liberally mixed with sand and dust, followed by a *mechouei*, hunks of leathery mutton hacked off a sheep of venerable age that had been roasted – a long time before – on a stake over an open fire. This revolting meal was washed down with cups of intolerably sweet mint tea. I was glad to discover that the American authority on the Sahara, Cabot Briggs, shares my low opinion of Touareg food.

'Duveyrier considered it "delicious",' he writes, 'but he was a romantic soul. Even such hardened old Saharans as Maurice Reygasse, not to mention my tenderfooted self, have found it all too often revolting in the extreme.'

But if, gastronomically, the meal cannot be said to have been a success, as an expression of cordiality and generosity on the part of our Touareg hosts it was a fine gesture. I was filled with admiration for the French officers who were guests. As each dreadful dish arrived, they praised it to their hosts and even contrived to eat large quantities – I surreptitiously buried most of mine in the sand. These Frenchmen's easy relationship with the Touareg was quite remarkable. They all seemed to be on a completely equal footing.

These men of the *Compagnies Sahariennes* were most carefully selected for their qualities of tolerance and understanding. They were absolutely dedicated men of a very fine type. They loved the Sahara. They read about almost nothing else. They were steeped in its history; they were almost all fascinated by its pre-history – and what a pre-history the Sahara has, going back to the times when it was covered with lush rain forest and lakes, with all the animals you find in Central Africa today. They spent much of their spare time collecting pre-historic weapons and utensils which they searched for themselves in the desert and encouraged nomads to look out for on their behalf. And – they really did seem to know how to get along with the people of the Sahara. They looked upon it as their country. Algiers was a long way away; it was a place from which they expected to receive frustrating orders. Paris was even more remote. All French Saharans believed – generally quite rightly – that Paris did not understand their problems. It is sad – even tragic – to think that there is no further employment for these truly dedicated men. I am convinced that the Sahara will miss them, will be far worse off without them. I am sure the Arabs of Algiers will never have the fanatical love for the desert and its strange peoples. They will look upon it – aside from those parts of the desert that produce oil – as a liability, as not worth expending much time and trouble on. There will be no more *blédards* – the graphic French term for a man who is really a part of the *bléd*, or desert. And if I find this sad, what must those Frenchmen feel who gave their lives to service in the Sahara and who so strongly identified themselves with the desert?

I sat on the rugs in front of the tent on this wonderful cool – almost chilly – summer night, with the stars a glory above me, and I turned to the young lieutenant I had spoken to before. I asked him how he liked being stationed at Tamanrasset.

'I love it,' he said. 'I don't know where in the world I'd rather be. I hope they keep me here a long time.' Perhaps, without knowing it, he could have looked forward to another couple of years.

It was one o'clock in the morning when we got up to say goodbye to our Touareg hosts. They had been very kind, very hospitable. I wished I could have talked their language or even Arabic which they understood. I found it hard to believe that these people with whom we had spent such a pleasant evening, had been until so recently, such implacable enemies of the French. The *caïd* of this tribe must have been a boy of at least ten years old when the Battle of Tit had been fought with such fury. Some of the old men must have been infants when their fathers and grandfathers savagely annihilated the Flatters Mission. There used to be plenty of criticism of French colonial administration, but in the Sahara, at any rate, I found nothing but admiration for it.

It seems sad, too, to think that the Touareg, these aristocratic warriors of the Sahara, are inevitably doomed. Their gradual eclipse began when their chief occupations, pillage and extortion, were taken away from them. They no longer fulfil their one-time more or less legal purpose of controlling caravan traffic across the desert, often by questionable means. They struggle on, fighting a losing battle but refusing to change what is left to them of a traditional way of life, still, anachronistically, refusing to consider doing any kind of manual work. Against the dazzling competition of the oilmen, the mineral seekers with their planes and helicopters and the spendid trans-desert highways that follow in their wake, the Touareg, the Blue Men of the Sahara, seem already to be a people of the past. Under French rule they might have survived longer.

I particularly wanted to meet Frère Jean-Marie, who lived up in the Hoggar Mountains in the summer like his predecessor, de Foucauld, carrying on his work of compiling a French-*Tamahaq* dictionary. Frère Jean-Marie had been an officer in the French Navy who, distracted by the death of his wife just after the war, joined the order of *Les Petits Frères de Jésus* which was formed after de Foucauld's death and carried on the great man's work. De Foucauld's hermitage on the Assekrem had been turned into a chapel and Frère Jean-Marie had built a retreat of his own a few hundred yards away largely to escape the numbers of tourists who at that time were making the journey up to the high plateau.

Our guide Guarinos took us in his car and we invited the pilot and navigator of our little plane to come with us. It was a fortunate thing that we did. Although it was extremely cold when we started, the ancient car started boiling after we had only covered fifteen miles, and long before we had started climbing seriously. We had a series of breakdowns every few miles and in the end we had to give up all hopes of meeting Frère Jean-Marie and turn back. We shouldn't have got nearly as far as we did had it not been for the navigator who turned out to be a first class mechanic with a great gift for improvisation. But we did see a great deal of the Hoggar Mountains.

Countless extinct volcanoes erupt from the ground in fantastic domes and cones, some with fluted, basalt sides, thrusting upwards like monstrous phallic emblems. These 'chimneys' were the cones of the volcanoes and spread widely around some of them are piles of huge, round, granite 'cannon-balls' which must have been sent hurtling into the air like brobdignagian shrapnel. When all these volcanoes were active, the Hoggar must have been an inferno so titanic as to be unimaginable. Huge chunks of what looks like colossal masonry, like pieces of giant Ionic columns, as if some vast Grecian temple had been shattered by an earthquake, lie scattered round depressions in the ground. It is an outrageously fantastic landscape.

In 1933 a Lieutenant Brenans, a *méhariste* officer, was leading his troop of camel cavalrymen on a police patrol. They entered a deep gorge in the Tassili Mountains which, as it happened, had never been traversed before by a European. Suddenly Brenans noticed strange figures engraved on the steep rocky sides of the gorge. He dismounted to observe them more closely and to his astonishment he saw, engraved deeply into the sandstone, pictures of elephants trumpeting, of hippopotami emerging from a swamp, of rhinoceros, giraffe – an entire zoological collection portrayed with great skill. Brenans marched on half a dozen miles until he found the gorge blocked by a fall of rocks. All along the way he found these remarkable rock carvings and in the caverns scooped under the walls of the gorge, which had evidently been used as dwellings by bygone hunters, he found wonderful paintings. This was something entirely new. Rock carvings had been discovered earlier in the Hoggar and elsewhere in the Sahara, but the paintings were a sensational find and several experts, including Henri Lhote who, between the wars, had made an exhaustive study of the pre-history of the Sahara, hurried to the spot. Brenans had already made some copies of the paintings and Lhote copied many of them too. But it was not until 1956 that he returned to the Tassili with a team of artists and a photographer and did a really full scale job of copying these pre-historic works of art. Long before this, in 1938, when Brenans had become *Chef de l'Annexe* of the oasis of Djanet, in the foothills of the Tassili, he, Brenans, discovered the most dramatic paintings on a little massif of sandstone called Jabbaren. Lhote took his team there and was astounded at what he saw. Jabbaren in the Touareg language means 'the giants' and here were immense paintings of monstrous men with round heads, looking like Martians. There were curious paintings of little horned demons, of elongated dancers, of bird-headed men and women, which Lhote attributes to Egyptian influence. It was at Jabbaren, too, that Lhote discovered the splendid painting of extraordinary sophistication that he calls *Antinéa*, the goddess of ancient Libya, and the lovely, delicately drawn pair of negro girls that are considerable works of art by any standards.

Before leaving for the Sahara I had seen the magnificent collection of copies of the Tassili paintings at the *Musée de l'Homme* in Paris that Lhote and his team brought back after sixteen months of gruelling work. As a result of these paintings by neolithic men, far more is known of life in pre-historic Sahara than of the period of from about 1,000 AD until a little over a century ago. We know that they had horse-drawn chariots. We know that at first the country was tropical with all kinds of tropical animals; that later it began to dry up and become a kind of savannah land, where the human inhabitants had flocks of sheep and herds of cattle. We know how they hunted and how they lived. They left behind them a remarkable pictorial record.

I travelled on from the Hoggar to Djanet with the main purpose of seeing as much as I could of these Neolithic rock carvings and paintings. But I discovered that to see the best examples, at Jabbaren, meant at least a two-day journey by camel, a stay of a day or two on the spot and two-day journey back. As our special plane could only wait a limited time I had to content myself by seeing what I could in the neighbourhood of the oasis. There were some quite fine rock carvings nearby and without really looking seriously I picked up a number of flint arrowheads and pieces of neolithic pottery.

Driving along the *oued* leading into the oasis, my companion, a French officer, pointed out a *zeriba* on a ledge, perched high up on the precipitous cliff that lines one side.

'When Brenans was *Chef de l'Annexe,*' he said, 'that is where he and his Touareg wife used to go when he had his annual leave. Nothing would persuade him ever to go back to France. He was a real blédard.' So was Capitaine Rossi, a Corsican, who had succeeded Brenans and who had also married a *Targuia.* Just over thirty years ago, he told me, he had been a private soldier serving in the oasis of Ouargla, six hundred miles to the north of Djanet as the crow flies. One day his commanding officer sent for him.

'Rossi, they're a man short in the *Compagnie* at Djanet. I want you to report there for duty as soon as possible. Make your own arrangements.'

'Very good, *mon commandant.*' Rossi got hold of two camels one to ride and the other to carry his baggage and provisions. He set off alone across an appalling stretch of desert. It took him forty-five days to complete the journey. That was in 1930 and he had never left Djanet since, not even when he was asked to return to France for his daughter's wedding. She and her fiancé had to come to Djanet and be married there.

I talked to Rossi about the neolithic paintings.

'It must seem to you sometimes that you have been here since pre-historic times yourself,' I said in the course of our conversation. Capitaine Rossi's beady eyes twinkled.

'Oh, I assure you it does. You know one of these days that fellow Lhote is going to discover my portrait painted on a rock up on the plateau. He'll copy it and the next thing'll be that I'll be on exhibition in Paris!'

Flying north from Djanet, over the plateau of the Tassili n'Ajjer, great dry canyons hundreds of feet deep cut their way across the extraordinary, almost lunar landscape, where erosion has left curious pinnacles, towers and chimneys so that the landscape looks like a sandstone forest. These dry canyons were obviously once great rivers and I saw vast depressions that evidently were once the beds of great lakes. It was like looking at a skeleton and picturing it as it once was, covered with flesh.

The more I read about the history of the Sahara and the unbelievably brave explorers who first tried – and sometimes succeeded – in crossing it the more I began to understand its fascination. Of course, today all the risk and excitement has gone. One can drive across the great desert in any ordinary car, partly on good roads and partly on quite passable *pistes.* In Tamanrasset we met a party of Rhodesians who were on their way from Salisbury to Algiers. They had had some minor trouble and I was able to help them, because they couldn't talk French. But they didn't think they were doing anything out of the ordinary. As for flying, today the Sahara is on many main airline routes and a bare thirty years ago General Lapérrine died from exposure and hunger after his plane crashed in the desert.

Chapter Twenty-Three

It was after I had been Director of the Petroleum Information Bureau for a couple of years that Marjorie and I bought a shop in the Portobello Road. We had for many years been addicts of the shops and markets there and this was one of the main reasons for the sad state of our bank balances. One day a friend of ours down there said there was a shop for sale.

'You're always complaining about spending so much money in the Portobello Road,' he said, 'why don't you buy the shop and make some instead?' This struck us as a good idea. We got on to the agents; we saw the bank; we arranged a mortgage and within a couple of days the shop was ours. It needed a good deal doing to it and from unhappy past experience we decided for once to employ a large firm and get everything done properly and quickly. One of the largest contractors in London had done some work at my offices at the Petroleum Information Bureau and so I approached them, admitting that the job was not on the scale they were accustomed to. They said they would be delighted to take it on.

A certain amount of the ground floor needed gutting right out and certain alterations had to be made elsewhere. For weeks two venerable and very pleasant old men occupied themselves making bonfires out of pieces of wood that had been torn out of the structure of the building and brewing innumerable cups of tea. We were naturally desperate to open the shop as soon as possible because we had been piling up stock, which we had bought largely in the Bermondsey Market, where we had gone before dawn every Friday morning, and from many other sources. At last in despair, with the ground floor still a mass of dust and rubble and without even the electric light working, we opened shop one Saturday, with candles providing the only illumination. To our delight and astonishment we took in about £150, and from then on the shop has never really looked back.

After a lot of deliberation Marjorie hit on the name of 'TRAD', because, on the whole we deal in more or less traditional things and during the years we have come to specialize in four or five main things – in all of which we are personally interested. Firstly, anything to do with fairgrounds. We have in a very short time made a remarkable collection of merry-go-round animals and birds – I'm certain we have the only zebra and possibly the only two small 'juvenile' goats. Apart from the more ordinary horses we have bears, peacocks, donkeys, a lion, cats, bulls, cockerels, ostriches, turkeys. Our latest acquisition is a giraffe, and we hope to add some more to this fairly comprehensive list. We have sold (and kept) some remarkable fairground carvings and we have even bought such large objects as a gipsy caravan, and Marjorie is now planning to open a museum of the fairground.

Secondly we sell anything to do with pubs. We always have some splendid pub mirrors. We stock pub signs and beer handles and engines. Our third main 'line' is anything manageable to do with ships – lamps, binnacles, compasses, logs, naval architects' half-models, large shipping company models, portholes, rum measures and pumps – everything and anything that has been part of the 'furniture' of a ship or yacht.

We deal, too, in anything to do with shops; shop signs; shop fittings, if they are of a certain age, and attractiveness, things such as 'drug runs' from chemists' shops, apothecaries' jars, decorated tea canisters from grocers; large coffee grinders; scales from butchers or grocers; tobacco and snuff jars from tobacconists; milk churns, ladles and so on. Our last main 'line' is country furniture; heavy oak and pine chairs from Wales and the West Country; Welsh dressers and farmhouse tables. And then a certain amount of general things, lamps, small agricultural implements, old carpenters' tools and so on.

We have become pretty well known as dealers in these rather off-beat things and among our clients are some of the biggest dealers in the United States. And I will say straight away that our American clients are by far the nicest to deal with. They know what they want; they don't haggle and argue in the way many others do and we have made many good friends among them.

In the early years of TRAD, I was still running the Petroleum Information and films Bureaux. I lived a strangely schizophrenic life in those days. On a Friday evening I would be dressed in a tail coat, sitting at the top table with all the tycoons at some oil industry function at Grosvenor House or the Dorchester; the following morning I would be down in the Portobello Road in old clothes, nosing round the stalls and coming back to the shop up the hill laden with curious purchases – wheeling an old Victorian perambulator, perhaps, or a penny-farthing bicycle. Occasionally one or two of the big names in the oil industry would come down to the Portobello Road to pass the time on a Saturday morning and we would run into one another. I think they looked upon it as a harmless eccentricity on my part. Then I would be paddling round in the rain and mud of Bermondsey Market at six and seven in the morning, picking up stock and a couple of hours later, having hastily changed, I would be in my elegant office in Brook Street.

In the end, for various reasons, I decided to give up my job in oil. The big oil companies and I had quite different ideas about the function of the Petroleum Information Bureau, so there was little point in my continuing to try to run it. I was sorry at first. I had enjoyed trying to build this little organization up into something that could have been useful. But before long I began to feel a sense of relief and to enjoy the freedom of working for myself. I am devoting a good deal of my time to TRAD and on the whole am working harder than ever.

Over the last few years Marjorie has built up what is probably the best collection of fairground animals in the country – over twenty varieties. She also has some splendid examples of fairground carvings. Her museum of fairground art, which is something that does not exist in this country should open almost any time now. This, of course, will tie us more than ever to London and our original plans to spend a great deal more time in the South of France do not look so likely to come about now.

Our daughter Lalla has some time to go still in the Central School of Speech and Drama into which she passed, the youngest entrant, one of twenty out of a total of two thousand contestants. She has a passion to become an actress and we have great hopes for her. Our son Nicky, who is at Westminster, is developing intellectually at such a rate that in comparison with him I feel extremely ill-educated – which in an academic sense is no more than the truth. After making an excellent start at my preparatory school, I forgot most of what I had learnt, largely through laziness, at Harrow. And the Army Class that I was obliged to join there, owing to my father's wish for me to follow in his footsteps and join the Regular Army, completed the sorry story. On the whole I educated myself through travelling all over Europe just before World War II, working for the BBC and during my years as a prisoner of war.

I suppose, in a way, that I have been a victim – although I prefer not to look upon it in that way – of the social revolution that has brought about so many changes in our country. All through my life I had passively taken it for granted that I would succeed not only to the title but to a considerable degree of financial security when I inherited Castle Ward and the life tenancy of the Bangor estate. If I had worked hard towards this end, of course, I could have achieved this at least to a certain extent. But the idea of living more or less penuriously in a large house never appealed to me. I had known what it was like to live in a reasonably grand manner at Castle Ward and I preferred to live in my own way in a small house that was really my own than to 'picnic' in a vast mansion that didn't even belong to me but to the National Trust.

I know myself well enough to realize that all this is not much more than an excuse for having side-stepped responsibilities and indulged my love of travel and adventure. The result of this choice is that I have saved no money; I have always spent everything I have earned and usually a good deal more. I have no pension to look forward to. I haven't had much from the wreckage of the Bangor Estate. But at least we have some tangible assets. We have our house in London; we have our house in the South of France; and we have TRAD, which we own. I really have no regrets – except for a few things I didn't do when I had the chance. If I had concentrated on my Irish inheritance; had studied agriculture and estate management, I suppose I would have ended up as a country gentleman, farming, shooting, sitting on a lot of local committees and, of course being Lord Bangor of Castle Ward. I suppose, too, that if I had worked diligently in the Liverpool shipping office back in my early twenties, I might have ended up as a respected director, possibly even as a director of Cunard, the parent company. And that would have meant spending the better part of my life in Liverpool – anyway in offices. I might, too, have ended reasonably high up in the administration of Reuters, if I had stayed the course; or for that matter, of the BBC, if I hadn't always been far more interested in putting together programmes. But selfishly, I suppose – oh yes, of course, selfishly – I wouldn't have had things much different from what they have been. I've had a wonderful life. I don't live in a castle, but I've lived like a lord!

Index